30 DAYS TO A

WELL-MANNERED

DOG

ALSO BY TAMAR GELLER

The Loved Dog:
The Playful, Nonaggressive Way to Teach Your Dog Good Behavior

30 DAYS TO A WELL-MANNERED DOG

THE LOVED DOG METHOD

TAMAR GELLER

WITH JONATHAN GROTENSTEIN

G

GALLERY BOOKS

New York   London   Toronto   Sydney   New Delhi

Gallery Books
A Division of Simon & Schuster, Inc.
1230 Avenue of the Americas
New York, NY 10020

First Gallery Books trade paperback edition August 2011

GALLERY BOOKS and colophon are trademarks of Simon & Schuster, Inc.

For information about special discounts for bulk purchases, please contact Simon
& Schuster Special Sales at 1-866-506-1949 or business@simonandschuster.com.

The Simon & Schuster Speakers Bureau can bring authors to your live event. For
more information or to book an event contact the Simon & Schuster Speakers
Bureau at 1-866-248-3049 or visit our website at www.simonspeakers.com.

Designed by Davina Mock-Maniscalco

Manufactured in the United States of America

10   9   8   7   6   5   4   3   2   1

The Library of Congress has cataloged the hardcover edition as follows:
Geller, Tamar.
    30 days to a well-mannered dog : the Loved Dog Method / Tamar Geller.
    p.   cm.
    1. Dogs—Training. 2. Dogs—Behavior. I. Title.
SF431.G383 2010
636.7'0835—dc22   2010016596

ISBN 978-1-4391-7670-2
ISBN 978-1-4391-7770-9 (pbk)
ISBN 978-1-4391-7769-3 (ebook)

To my two "sons" Clyde and Duke—
For your love, gratitude, and devotion to me,
for your trust and courage to go beyond your fears in the name of love,
for your undying playfulness and joy, for being great leaders—
forever I'll be thankful and grateful for having you in my life
even if it's just for such a short time.
I LOVE you!!!

CONTENTS

30 DAYS TO A WELL-MANNERED DOG

INTRODUCTION

"Frog farmers?!"

I was listening to a lecture by Alison Armstrong, an absolutely brilliant thinker when it comes to describing the reasons men and women are so often out of sync. She was speaking about the classic fairy-tale fantasy, the one where a woman kisses a frog who magically turns into a prince. Only, Alison's version had a twist: After twenty years of studying relationships, she'd reached the conclusion that many women, without knowing it, were actually turning princes into frogs. These women were "frog farmers"!

A flashbulb immediately went off in my head: How many dog owners were doing exactly the same thing to their dogs, taking fantastic dogs and unwittingly turning them into badly behaved "frogs"? Instead of understanding and celebrating their dogs' animal natures, marveling at their desire to connect, or giving them the tools and coaching they needed to grow, these owners were focusing on all the ways that their particular pet wasn't a natural-born Lassie.

Well, let me tell you something: Not even "Lassie" was Lassie. It took five different dogs to play the perfect pet.

What makes it so difficult for people to have perfect, well-mannered, and loving dogs? They have been given bad information. They've been taught, for example, that any sign of aggression in a dog means a "bad" animal, or that a dog who isn't obeying is acting "dominant." They've learned that the best dog is a submissive dog, and that it's up to them to play the role of the "alpha dog." I've met a lot of people who think that saying "No!" while they shove their dog's nose into a pile of excrement is the best way to teach housebreaking. Later, these owners will wonder what's wrong with their dog, who doesn't come running happily toward them when they call his name!

These owners don't understand how dogs think or how nature has made them, concepts that for me began twenty-four years ago, when I had the opportunity to spend a few months observing wild wolves in the Israeli desert. It didn't take me long to realize that they weren't, as I first thought, a nipping pack of savage beasts, but a family-oriented group with complex rules, a social order, and a very strong need for affection and mutual reassurance. I was particularly struck by the importance of play. The games the wolves engaged in—chasing, wrestling, tug-of-war—weren't just entertainment, but the way the pack formed its social hierarchy and the wolf cubs learned critical survival skills from their parents. These "games" literally meant the difference between life and death. I began tailoring a method of dog training based on similar principles of teaching through play, the way a coach might teach an athlete, empowering him or her to succeed instead of yelling orders and doling out punishments for failure.

Since then, to my delight, more and more people have begun to question the ideas behind conventional dog training. One major development has been a rethinking of dogs and their place in society. Science has confirmed that dogs' emotional and intellectual capacities are similar to a human toddler. Your average eighteen-month-old toddler is much more like a dog than, as was earlier believed, a chimpanzee. Like toddlers, dogs are often driven by their instincts and emotions, but have the ability to think and make conscious choices. They even understand that those choices have consequences.

Another change has occurred in the field of child psychology. Experts in childhood development have redefined their thinking about how to best raise children. The basic idea is that using positive reinforcement to associate good behavior with pleasure creates happier and more resourceful children than using punishment in an attempt to scare them into not making mistakes. A new philosophy of education has grown around the concept of teaching through play—which is exactly what I saw the wolves doing in the wild!

Finally, there has been a growing awareness that humanity in general might benefit from living in harmony with nature rather than always trying to dominate it. Like us, dogs have basic needs, not just for food and shelter, but for companionship and emotional support. Many so-called problem behaviors—aggression, barking, jumping, stealing—arise when these needs aren't being met. In other words, rather than simply punishing our dogs for "being bad," it's up to us as owners to examine our own behavior—are we doing our part to make sure that our dogs are getting what they need? Are we ignoring those needs and imposing our power, hoping our dogs will submit to our will, or are we sharing our power to nourish our friends, creating a more harmonious relationship along the way? Are we being good coaches, showing our dogs how best to have their needs met without relying solely on their instincts?

Dog "parents" have tried for years to do the best with what they've been given. But they haven't been given much, and much of what they've been given has been bogus information. It's like telling someone to climb Mount Everest while giving them the equipment for a weekend hike in the hills. When that climb doesn't succeed—when a dog fails to get with the program—many trainers blame the dog, reminding the owners that it's not easy to get up Mount Everest.

Well, guess what? Dogs aren't Mount Everest, not when you're equipped with knowledge.

The Loved Dog™ Method offers new and exciting tools and options for interacting with our dogs. But more important, it's about creating a major shift in the context we use to understand them. Dogs who misbehave aren't adversaries who need to be conquered—this is a caveman's mentality. The Loved Dog Method is about seeing dogs as a different species that is at the same time both similar to and different from us. It's about reminding ourselves that there's more joy in teamwork than in conquest, and that we're really on the same team. Dogs want desperately to please us—their instincts tell them that their very survival depends on it!

So why do so many dogs misbehave? That's a little like asking why a car has stopped working. We can freak out because we've got a lemon, or we can look for a logical explanation, working through a checklist of possible causes. Is the key in the ignition? Is there fuel in the tank? Is the battery working?

Fortunately for us, dogs are easier to understand than cars. The vast majority of "problem" behaviors are actually rooted in three things.

The first is miscommunication. We often look at our dogs as if they are just like us. We expect them to know the answers instinctively, as if our human notion of good behavior was built into their DNA. It's the same way some women expect the men in their lives to do or say "the right thing" without giving them any clues. When they enter our homes, dogs are strangers in a strange world who rely on a connection—to us, their owners—in order to help them learn their way around. It's up to us to guide them away from operating by their natural, wolflike instincts and into making humanlike choices. Dogs don't need to be "trained" as much as they need to be "coached."

The second is when one (or more) of a dog's basic needs aren't being met. In this regard, dogs are a lot like us. We might get grumpy when we're hungry, or snappy when we're feeling insecure. We also tend to give other human beings a lot more credit than we do dogs. If your child or significant other "growled" at you, you'd probably look first for an underlying problem, instead of searching—as many trainers do with dogs—for a way to eliminate the growling, or worse, simply writing them off as "bad" people and shipping them off to the local shelter.

Finally, a dog may *choose* not to listen to you. Wanting your dog to listen to you *because you say so* is like a kid (or a teenager, or many adults) wanting to buy things without having the money to pay for them. You need to save before you can withdraw, and for dogs, that currency is trust. And trust is rooted in pain and pleasure. If your dog trusts you as a source of pleasure, he'll do anything to please you. But if he learns to associate listening to you with pain, you're going to have a difficult time convincing him to behave the way that you want him to.

This book is meant to be an operating manual, helping you to better understand the reasons your dog acts the way that he or she does, while giving you the tools to help you get your dog to behave by using humanlike choices instead of wolf instincts. For the next thirty days, I'll give you solutions that I've been testing and using successfully for more than twenty-two years. But you'll notice throughout that I prefer the term "coaching" to "training." Training is often associated with repetition and regimentation. Coaching, on the other hand, requires creativity, compassion, and having fun! As a coach, you need to be able to manage your expectations. You'll have to be flexible in your approach, encouraging success while maintaining your patience through the failures. Instead of looking for ways to squash your dog's most vital instincts, I'll encourage you to work *with* those instincts, helping your dog to be the best that he or she can be.

I don't want you to read this book only looking for "right" answers—it's my profound hope that, in reading it, you will be empowered to become a better coach. Along the way, you may discover that your dog is the best teacher of all, if you just pay attention to what he or she has to tell you. Sometimes you will be the student.

The term "man's best friend" gets thrown around so often that it's easy to forget what it means. We all long for love and connection. Dogs, more than any other (nonhuman) creature on earth, can give us that. In fact, they want nothing more than to give it to us. All we have to do is take the time to understand them and love them back. Why can't we be dogs' best friends as well?

But I'm not talking about the word "love" in the way an infatuated teenager might use it. Love is not a condition. It's a verb. It requires active engagement with your dog, a constant give-and-take. That engagement is the key to this style of coaching. You're not always going to have the right answers. But if you're willing to engage, to put aside your preconceptions and anxieties and really live *in the moment* with your dog, you'll be amazed by how often the right answers begin to present themselves.

Like any relationship, your experience with your dog will be a living, ongoing process that needs to be tended like a garden. But in thirty days, you can build an unbelievable foundation with any dog, regardless of his breed, age, or previous training. You can create an environment where your dog will look to you as the primary source of pleasure in his life, where he's addicted to learning, where he displays proper manners—not because he's scared, but because he feels great when he does.

Finally, I hope you'll discover that the techniques I've laid out don't just work with dogs. We can use them to improve our relationships with girlfriends and boyfriends, our spouses, our children, our friends and coworkers. We can give everyone in our personal realm the tools and the room they need to succeed, to best express themselves as the individuals they are. That's where the juice of life is. That's when we feel our hearts move. And along the way, in doing so, we discover that our own needs have been met, way beyond our wildest dreams, while making the world a better place for people and animals!

ABOUT ME

Where I grew up, in Israel, you weren't considered cool just because you were pretty or had the latest Louis Vuitton bag—for us, it was all about melding with nature. My weekends were usually spent on long hikes through the wilderness, along the flowing creeks of the Golan Heights, over the rocky peaks of the Galilee, and across the majestic desert in the south.

We named every plant and tree we encountered, learning which ones were good for healing or nourishment and which were poisonous and to be avoided. We studied the patterns left by snakes in the desert, reconstructing the dramas of hunter and prey that had taken place the night before. In the springtime, we could hike to the wild fig trees around Jerusalem, spending hours stuffing ourselves with the juiciest figs imaginable, courtesy of Mother Earth.

These joyous experiences existed in stark contrast to the

dramas that I lived through at home. My mom and dad, bless their hearts, were a horribly mismatched pair. Divorce was uncommon in those days, so they fought constantly and cheated on each other. The only thing that brought them together was the arrival of a common enemy, their firstborn child: me. Having a child made them feel even more stuck than they had before.

So you can imagine why nature provided such an important refuge for me. After I'd spent time in the Israeli Army—an intense stint as an intelligence officer working with Special Forces—I was thrilled to have the opportunity to return to the desert, this time as an assistant to a research team studying the behavior of wild animals. In nature, I felt most connected to myself, my heart, and my soul. In nature, I found my peace.

While studying a desert bird called the *zanvanim,* I met a man who was researching wild wolves. He showed me how to drop a dead animal in a wolf "feeding station" to get a front-row seat for one of the desert's most amazing shows. I immediately became hooked, spending hours sitting in the deafening silence of the dry desert floor, until the wolves arrived. From my vantage point, I watched them play out their grooming and bonding rituals, social hierarchies, and the reinforcement of their hunting skills.

By "play out," I mean exactly that: Most of what they did was play. Real aggression was rare and short-lived, ending quickly when one wolf submitted to another, rolling over onto his back and writhing like a worm. The "victor" might respond with a few menacing growls, but always accepted the "loser's" apologies, allowing him to lick his ears or lie down beside him.

I came to see the natural genius in this ritual. It wasn't harsh, painful, or scary, and had little to do with our often flawed conception of a dominant alpha. It was more like a dance, one that quickly restored peace within a family while staying true to the love that bound them.

I had a couple of unruly dogs at home and decided to see if I could incorporate some of the same ideas into my relationship with them. Those ideas eventually evolved into the Loved Dog Center, a cage-free boarding facility in Los Angeles, California, and The Loved Dog coaching philosophy that I've used successfully to create amazing bonds and inspire fantastic behavior from all kinds of "unmanageable" dogs and their loving owners.

I also incorporated what I learned into my nonprofit program Operation Heroes & Hounds, where we ask returning GIs to coach orphan dogs (shelter dogs) in The Loved Dog Method. The wolf pack camaraderie, loyalty, and sense of purpose are not that different from what GIs experience while fighting for our country, and there's a real sense of loss upon their return to civilian life. Coaching grateful dogs provides an opportunity for miracles to happen. In a short period of time we see real joy in these war veterans' eyes, as well as improved sleep patterns and reduction of prescription drug intake. Thank God for that time I got to spend with the wolves.

HOW TO USE THIS BOOK

I believe that everything in this book is important, and I have tried to structure the information in a way that makes sense. You've got to know what drives a dog before you coach him, which is why we'll begin with the "triad" for understanding his behavior. Trying to teach your dog fancy tricks before he's mastered the basics—"sit," "come," and "leave it"—is like trying to teach a child how to be polite without teaching him "please" and "thank you."

But building a relationship isn't like building a house, where you place one brick at a time. It's free-flowing and everything is interconnected. I've incorporated a lot of my ideas about coaching, for example, in Week 3, but they're ideas that are just as important in Weeks 1 and 2. If your dog is jumping on your houseguests, there's no reason to wait until Day 12 to address his behavior. And you don't have to wait until Day 23 to cook your dog a meal.

So while I recommend that you follow these steps in order, I encourage you to at least leaf through the entire book *before* you bring your new dog home, to familiarize yourself with the important concepts.

I have worked with Oprah Winfrey in the past, coaching her beloved golden retrievers. And I was thrilled to get a call to coach her two new rescue springer spaniel girls—Lauren and Sunny—and help them integrate into the lives of her other three dogs. But there was one hitch. Due to a tight schedule, Oprah asked me to do it all in two weeks, and she would film our progress for her program.

I was in the midst of writing this book on how to coach one dog in thirty days, and I loved the challenge of coaching two dogs (littermates, no less) in half that time. Throughout this book, when it's applicable, I mention my great experience with Lauren and Sunny and their incredible journey to becoming well mannered.

THE TRIAD

People get dogs for all kinds of reasons. Their kids beg them for one. They want to feel protected. But the most common reason—and the most profound—is to experience a sense of connection to a living creature who is never affected by the stock market or how much weight you've gained or lost, but is simply happy to see YOU.

Dogs never say, "Go away, I'm busy now." When you develop a relationship with them, they are always ready to engage with you for as long as you want. They are the same creatures they've been for 300,000 years: loyal, loving, and steady companions. No matter what the world looks like a hundred years from now, a dog will still be a dog.

Dogs come in many shapes and sizes, and there are differences among breeds. But for the most part, those differences are like flavors of ice cream—at their core, they're all the same. Every dog, purebred to mutt, has essentially the same "operating manual" written into his or her DNA!

Most of us, at least unconsciously, tend to view dogs as slightly different versions of human beings, ones with four legs and a fur coat. The relationship expert Alison Armstrong likes to point out that men and women do the same thing to each other all the time—women look at men and see hairy women, while men look at women and see men who are, to paraphrase Jack Nicholson's character in *As Good As It Gets,* devoid of reason and accountability. In truth, Alison believes, the real differences between men and women are built into their DNA. In order for the human species to survive, men evolved as single-focus hunters—if they don't want to talk, it's because they're busy stalking a deer; women evolved as gatherers, able to take in all the details of a meadow without startling any animals, and speaking often to share what they'd learned. When you look at men and women in this way, you start to see why they have trouble communicating, as neither side can understand the other's different motivations and perspectives. Instead of trying to reconcile these "factory-built-in" differences, we often refuse to validate the other's behavior, wondering what's wrong with them, what keeps them from seeing the world like *we* do.

When we see a dog behaving "badly"—stealing food, barking incessantly, or going potty where he's not supposed to—we have a tendency to believe that he's being intentionally difficult, stubborn, or disrespectful. Some dog trainers have made a career of perpetuating this way of thinking, claiming that you've got to become the leader of the pack, the dominant alpha, resolving behavioral issues by keeping your dog submissive, respectful, and fearful of stepping out of line.

This kind of thinking fails to consider the possibility that dogs often have very good reasons for doing the things they do. If we can understand their operating manual, if we can start to see things from their point of view, not only can we begin to make sense of their behavior in a profoundly different way, but we'll be blown away by the awe-inspiring recognition of the incredible effort our dogs will make to share our lives and love us so fully. When our perspective shifts this way, it allows us to see that there's nothing wrong with our "misbehaving" dogs. They're not damaged, disrespectful, or crazy; they're just expressing their wants and needs in the way that nature intended. By understanding and validating them—by truly *seeing* our dogs, instead of agonizing over why they're not more like us—we can begin to influence their behavior in a way that's loving, fun, and effective.

Understanding their "operating manual" is the first and most important step. Fortunately, it's not a long or complicated manual: Nearly every part of a dog's behavior can be described by employing three concepts I call the triad: instinct versus choice, the seven basic needs, and pain versus pleasure.

INSTINCT VERSUS CHOICE

Human infants are very much driven by instinct. They behave like little Neanderthals, just following their urges, peeing or pooping wherever they happen to be, and crying when they want something (until they learn how to grab it!). But as they grow into toddlers, children begin to show the ability and desire to learn "adult" manners for the first time. They know when they've done something right . . . and when they've done something wrong. They rely on parents to guide and coach them from instinctive behavior toward manners based on making conscious choices, a process we call *socialization*.

The same thinking applies to dogs. They begin life nipping and biting, clawing and digging, going potty whenever and wherever is most convenient. These wolflike instincts, written into their DNA, work very well in a wolf society. They just don't happen to work so well in our human society.

Like infants who are coached by their parents to behave based on conscious choices instead of baby instincts, dogs can be coached into socialization. If left to their own devices, dogs will behave like wolves, but they are capable of logical reasoning and understanding the difference between right and wrong. It's our job to help them expand their identities. We can teach our rules and values, enabling them to grow beyond their instincts into creatures that make choices that work better in their home environments and our human society. All they need are good parents to help coach and guide them.

When we look at behavior through the filter of instinct and conscious choice, the world begins to make sense in an interesting way. In humans, we can start to distinguish between actions that are based on survival instincts and those that come from conscious choices. The ability to see this difference makes it a whole lot easier to feel compassion. In the case of my boyfriend, for example, I know that when he gets home from work, he needs time to decompress, get some food into his belly, and transition from his role at work to his role as my loving man. It has nothing to do with how much he loves me or wants to connect with me—his caveman instincts are telling him that he will die if he doesn't get a chance to eat and some alone time to collect his thoughts. Understanding that this mentality is a built-in "factory spec" helps me to empathize and make room for his needs.

With dogs, the distinction is even more obvious. It's usually very easy to see when a dog is tapping into his wolf instincts as opposed to his ability to make humanlike, conscious choices. As we get better at identifying this difference, we gain a better sense of where our dogs are coming from. We feel more compassionate and often gain a clearer idea of what we can do to help them meet their needs, while guiding them away from their instincts and into good choices.

THE SEVEN BASIC NEEDS

Dogs are adaptable to all kinds of environments. So adaptable, in fact, that we sometimes forget they have needs of their own. I'm not just talking about food, water, and the occasional walk. Imagine if parenting children were reduced to food, shelter, and letting the kids go outside to pee. Would it really be surprising if they grew up to be adults with serious emotional or behavioral issues?

Human needs can be complicated. But a dog's needs are

much easier to understand. Whether it's an expensive pure-bred pampered in a Park Avenue apartment or a mutt scavenging for food in an African village, all dogs have the same seven basic needs.

By "needs," I mean the things our dogs have to have in order to function at a basic level. When these needs aren't being met, it's nearly impossible for dogs to focus on anything other than finding a way to fulfill them, the same way a starving or exhausted person thinks about food or sleep. Dogs whose needs go unfulfilled quickly become confused, frightened, even depressed, while their efforts to meet those needs often appear to us as "problem behaviors."

On the flip side, when our dogs' basic needs are fulfilled, we're going to have happy, dedicated companions. As loving owners, it's important that we recognize our dogs' needs and do our best to help fulfill them on a daily basis. Here are the seven basic needs that every dog owner must consider:

1. SENSE OF SECURITY

It's impossible to be at your best when you feel like you have to fight for your survival. Think of the fear and uncertainty you would feel if you lost your job or found out that your child or spouse had to be retested for cancer. People living in war zones don't have the luxury of "normal" days. In order for us to enjoy our lives, we need to feel some sense of security. Certainty allows us to catch our breath. Without it, we're anxious and maybe snappier than we'd like to be. It is as if time stops and we can't resume our normal lives until the issue that is plaguing us is resolved and our need for security and certainty is fulfilled.

Dogs have the same need for security and certainty. We can help them by establishing some semblance of a routine. I'm not saying that breakfast every morning needs to take place at seven A.M. sharp, or that your dog is going to lose his mind if work keeps you late. But he does have to know that he's going to get a consistent supply of food, water, and shelter.

In addition to physical security, dogs need the emotional security that comes from a loving owner. It's one of the main reasons I'm so opposed to trainers who teach owners to use fear when interacting with their dogs. Our dogs count on us as their primary source of security and connection. They need to know that they can rely on us, that we'll behave consistently, that we won't go crazy on them, correcting them for a behavior today that was okay yesterday. They need to know that we're there to interact with them, even after they've grown out of the cute-puppy stage, and that when they hear us speak their names, we'll be there, looking at and talking to them. They need us to be predictable and consistent.

2. COMPANIONSHIP

Although they've been domesticated for centuries, dogs are still wolves at heart. And wolves are family oriented, having learned that survival is easier through cooperation than by going it alone. They live in groups with complicated social rules—hunting and playing together, constantly engaging in physical contact, even sleeping on top of one another at night.

Yes, our dogs have this same instinctive need for companionship. It's the reason they greet us at the door when we return home, prefer to nestle in whatever room we happen to be using, or squeeze into a small space next to us instead of lounging on their own in a big, fancy backyard. We can help fulfill this need by giving our dogs active feedback throughout the day. Whether it's a simple smile or a strenuous game of tug-of-war, our dog needs to know that he's a valued part of our "pack."

I'm talking about active companionship. Allowing your dog to lie nearby while you work from home isn't enough, any more than a husband or wife's mere physical presence is enough to feed a marriage. You have to be there emotionally, engaging and playing with your dog.

In a study that was very painful to watch, researchers discovered that monkeys given the choice between companionship and food will decide to starve. For social creatures, companionship is that important. Prisoners will tell you that being in isolation is the worst punishment anyone can get. A dog who lives alone in a yard, even if that yard is the gardens of Versailles, is being severely deprived of one of his basic needs

3. UNDERSTANDING THE HIERARCHY

Social hierarchy is an important part of the pack mentality. Wolf packs have very defined pecking orders, and every member knows his or her place in the pack. A lot of conventional trainers confuse this hierarchy with some kind of military structure, imagining alpha dogs barking orders at submissive grunts. This metaphor completely ignores the fact that these wolves are all related to one another. Wolf packs are families! And they may have rules and boundaries that are more similar to human families and different from what is customarily described in the dog world.

In your home, for your dog, you are the leader of the family. Your role is much more like a parent or a coach than a tyrant or a general. Your dog needs you to provide clear guidance, feedback, and boundaries. Without that direction, he'll rely on what he's got—his "factory-built-in" wolf instincts—to help him make decisions. And he may come up with answers that are perfectly appropriate—for living in a society of wolves. Unfortunately, a lot of wolf behaviors don't translate very well into human society.

What kind of boundaries should you set? One example is mealtime: In the wolf pack, the alpha dog always eats first. I can't tell you how many households I've seen where this dynamic has been reversed: The dog is fed before his owner scarfs down a quick breakfast. You should, at least at the beginning of your relationship, let your dog see you eating before you feed him, even if it's just having your morning coffee! This is particularly important when kids are involved.

The leader also sleeps in a higher place than the rest of the pack. It's not about ego, but survival: The other dogs need to know that their protector is watching over them while they sleep. This doesn't mean that you can't let your dog sleep in your bed, just that it needs to be clear that it's *your* bed—your dog needs to know that he's been *invited* to join you. And the same rules apply to the couch.

The alpha dog is also—usually—the winner of every game. He'll often join a game between two other dogs just to challenge the winner. We'll get into this a little more later on in the book, when we discuss which games are appropriate (and which are inappropriate) to play with your dog.

The important thing is to remember that being the alpha dog is about guidance and boundaries, not some aloof or macho tyranny. Real power isn't imposed, it's shared. We'll come back to this idea on Day 15.

4. EXCITEMENT AND SURPRISES

Think about your favorite food. Now think about eating it at every meal, every day of your life, with no other options. How long do you think it would take before your "favorite" food became the one you were most sick of eating?

No matter how great a dog parent or owner you are, dogs need surprises and variations to their routines. Before giving up all hope and settling into a life of depression, bored dogs look for ways to entertain themselves, usually with their favorite "wolf" games: chewing, barking, digging, stealing, and running away. Most behavioral problems—and a lot of physical problems, as well—arise when a dog lacks enough mental stimulation, when he doesn't have anything to look forward to.

A good rule of thumb is to try and surprise your dog at least once a day with an activity or an outing. It keeps their minds engaged and their mental batteries charged. Some dogs—especially highly intelligent breeds like border collies and Australian shepherds—require far more stimulation and many surprises.

5. PHYSICAL STIMULATION

Most of us look at exercise as a chore (I sure do!). But from your dog's point of view, exercise is a reward. What could be more fun than running around outside, chasing down a Frisbee or sprinting after other dogs?

When dogs don't get the opportunity to expend some of their energy exercising, they're going to find some other place to direct that energy. For us owners, that usually means "behavioral problems." I won't even begin to address coaching a specific dog unless I know he's getting real exercise each day.

Most dogs—especially young dogs—need more than a walk around the block, even if it's three times a day. They need to have some exercise that connects them to their wolf instincts. They need to play with other dogs on a regular basis, to feel the wind in their ears, and to smell the fresh scent of nature, off the leash if they're ready. There's nothing better than a good hike or run along the beach.

So even if you don't work out every day, it's important to make sure your dog does. In fact, it's one of the ways my dogs have helped me the most, encouraging me to take a hike or walk along the beach on a daily basis. I know that I'll never be as active as they are, so I bring along a tennis ball for them to fetch, allowing them to run back and forth, covering way more ground than I do. Play dates with other dogs, visits to the dog park, and a few hours at doggy day care are all great opportunities for exercise.

6. MENTAL STIMULATION

For most people to feel great about themselves, they need to feel like they're being mentally challenged. We're exhilarated by the feeling of growth—learning new things, mastering skills that we thought were beyond us. Dogs feel the same way. If your dog seems to find new ways to run away from home or new items to destroy, or if he is yawning all of the time, he may not be tired—he might be bored!

I've found that the best way to tickle a dog's brain is to teach him new behaviors. Dogs, just like toddlers, love to please their "parents"—they feel great when they can show off after learning a new trick. You don't even have to stop what you're doing to foster this love of learning—just naming aloud the objects your dog comes into contact with or narrating the behaviors he's performing can keep him feeling mentally fulfilled. Just don't forget to throw in the occasional game of treasure hunt (see Day 11).

It's also important to be patient with your dog's own efforts to stimulate his mind. For example, during a walk, when your dog seems to want to read his "p-mail"—sniffing what seems like every square inch of ground—remember that he's just trying to process the wide range of sights, sounds, and smells that are being thrown his way. Let him have a few minutes at the beginning of every hike or walk—even old dogs like to learn new things and smell the latest happenings in their neighborhood! They get so much information and pleasure from this activity.

7. LOVE AND CONNECTION

Recent studies confirm that most dogs have a mental capacity similar to that of an eighteen-month-old toddler. So it shouldn't be surprising that they also have a similar set of emotional needs.

Child psychologists like to talk about "attachment theory": when a child feels loved by and connected to his parents, the relationship creates an invisible connection—a "secure attachment"—that nourishes the child even when the parents aren't around. Your dog doesn't need you to be there every single moment of the day (although he'd be happy to have you!). As long as you strive to fill your time together with love, bonding, and mental stimulation, the connection will endure even when you're apart. You can help the process by learning to speak to your dog in a deep, slow, and sincere tone (Day 2) and by providing the right kind of physical contact (Day 26).

PAIN VERSUS PLEASURE

The most basic instinct of all living creatures is to move toward things that bring pleasure and away from things that bring pain. So if we want a person or a dog to behave a certain way, we have the highest chance for success if we can get them to associate that behavior with pleasure; if we want somebody to stop a certain behavior, we're most successful when we get them to associate it with pain.

When I talk about pain, I don't mean something physical, but mental: a sense of loss, whether it's affection, fun, or something that we normally associate with pleasure. Many people associate pain with loss: having a falling-out with a friend, being fired, breaking up with a boyfriend or a girlfriend, or cutting sugar out of their diet. So many people are afraid of the pain of failure that they don't even try to take the first step toward making their dreams come true in their work or love lives. Pleasure, on the other hand, feels good. It's usually very easy to convince someone to do something that they associate with pleasure.

When it comes to raising kids, many child psychologists have come to the realization that the old ideas, made popular by Dr. Spock, may need adjusting. The children with the best chances of leading happy, well-adjusted lives are those who have a strong emotional bond (the "secure attachment" mentioned earlier) to their parents or caregivers. Coaching that is rooted in pleasure—positive reinforcement, praise, and consistent nurturing—builds trust and makes the emotional bond stronger. Inconsistent or negative reinforcement, like criticism, angry threats, physical punishment—pain—might scare kids into behaving a certain way, but ultimately weakens the attachment between child and adult, as well as the child's self-esteem.

This isn't to say that parents shouldn't set rules or boundaries, which are a must to make kids (and dogs) feel safe and secure. (Remember that security is a basic need!) It's the reason I sometimes hear people say that you have to be your

THE TRIAD

child's parent, not her friend, only I've never understood why there has to be a contradiction between the two! A good coach, like the Lakers' Phil Jackson, can play the roles of parent and friend at the same time. Just because you're in charge and set the rules doesn't mean you have to act like a tyrant. You can be a parent who is trusted, the nourishing source of so much good in a child's life, while still maintaining clear guidelines, boundaries, and consistent goals.

The same ideas apply to dog coaching. According to the old methods, or what I call the Dark Ages of training, dogs need a tough leader. Give a dog power and he'll just use it against you. Better to keep him in line with a tough approach, choke chains and prong collars, or techniques like "alpha rollovers" to show him that you're the real leader of the pack. God forbid that a dog shows some sign of independent thinking!

But what kind of dog will these methods produce? A dog who "behaves" not because he wants to, but out of fear. A dog who is anxious, is not resourceful, and is afraid to make any mistakes, and therefore not eager to learn new things. A dog who is distrustful, maybe even aggressive toward its owner and the rest of the world. Follow this protocol with your dog—or your child or the other people you love—and you'll find that you're a world-class "frog farmer."

When dogs (and most people) encounter a new situation in life, they always try to assess whether it's going to cause them pain or pleasure. The Loved Dog Method is built around teaching a dog that the behaviors we ask of him—as well as the process of learning itself—will bring immense pleasure. At times, we'll also associate pain with a behavior that we want to eliminate, but it's emotional, never physical: a sense of loss when we take a toy away from a lunging dog or turn our backs on a dog who greets us with an Olympic-level jump. But mostly it's about the pleasure that we bring to our dogs—the games, toys, food, treats, walks, hugs, and kisses they will associate with us. Your dog is going to learn good manners not because he's afraid of punishment, but because he trusts you and wants more than anything else in the world to please you. Your love is his ultimate pleasure.

How great is that?

DAY 0

SHOULD I GET A DOG? AND CHOOSING A DOG

SHOULD I GET A DOG?

I have a friend who recently relocated his family from Los Angeles to New York City for a new, high-pressure job. The move was particularly traumatic for his seven-year-old daughter, who had to say good-bye to all of her friends. So he called me to say that he was going to get her a dog to help ease the sting, and asked if I had any recommendations.

"Yes," I replied. "Are you sure this is the best time to get a dog?" Moving across the country was difficult enough, I explained. They were going to need some time to adjust to their new lives. My friend was going to be busy with the new job and helping his three young kids to assimilate into their new life in the big city. Who would be the dog's coach? It wasn't realistic to expect his seven-year-old to take on that kind of responsibility. I thought there'd be a very good chance that he, his daughter, and the dog would all wind up miserable. And who was going to pay the ultimate price for their misery? The dog, who would probably end up in a shelter.

Maybe I was wrong and the dog would have been just fine. Maybe I've just spent too much time around animal shelters, full of dogs whose only crime was starting life as a pet "for the kids." Without the love and attention of an adult coach, many of these dogs wind up being placed on a virtual shelf—or unvirtual backyard or basement—until the kids are ready to interact. By then, a dog may have so much bottled-up energy that she's too much for the kids to handle!

Have you ever heard the comedian Jeff Foxworthy do his routine about "rednecks"? "If you've ever taken beer to a job interview, you just might be a redneck"? Or "If you had to remove a toothpick for your wedding picture, you just might be a redneck"? I've got a similar routine (although not anywhere near as funny) for potential new dog owners. If you're getting a dog because your two-year-old thought it would be a good idea, you might be acting irresponsibly! If you work 24/7 and think the housekeeper is going to take care of the dog, you might be acting irresponsibly! If you are getting a divorce and decide to bribe your kids with a puppy, you just might be acting irresponsibly!

A dog is not a Roomba! You can't just plug him into a family and let him roam around the house, expecting that he'll know the right way to behave. When you introduce a dog into your home, you are starting a relationship with a living creature who is going to need your guidance, attention, consistent feedback, and love.

I want everyone to enjoy the pleasures of having a dog. But I can't tell you how much heartbreak could be avoided—for people and dogs—if every *potential* dog owner would just make a simple vow:

I vow to meet my dog's seven basic needs to the best of my ability.
I vow to respect my dog's wolf instincts, while doing my best
to unlock his potential to make humanlike, conscious choices.
I vow to become a source of pleasure for my dog,
not a source of pain.

I'm not trying to discourage anyone from adding a dog to the family. I just want you to consider the dog's needs and how they will impact your life before you run out and get one.

One of my clients, whose kids constantly begged her for a dog, finally agreed—on the condition that the kids first sign a contract committing them to taking care of it. If they didn't live up to their end of the bargain, they'd lose some of their privileges as well as their allowance. It took her kids five years before they felt like they were ready to sign the contract, and now they have an incredibly well-behaved dog that they rescued from a local shelter.

But not all kids are ready for that kind of responsibility. Another client of mine had a truly perfect and patient dog—and a jealous four-year-old daughter. Under the guise of hugging the dog, the little girl would squeeze the air out of his lungs. Soon the dog was growling whenever he saw the little girl in the vicinity.

CHOOSING A DOG

Before discussing specific breeds and ages to help you determine what kind of dog is right for you, please let me dispel one myth: You do not need a yard in order to have a dog! Most dogs prefer to be with their parent/owner and not by themselves in a yard. The yard is a good potty place and playground only if you're there too.

Puppy Love

Everybody loves puppies. They're cute, fuzzy, and have that fresh, new-puppy smell. But over the years I've come to realize that if they weren't so damn cute, no one would ever put up with them! Puppies are narcissistic. It's not their fault—it's how nature built them—but they're programmed to act as if the whole world revolves around their needs. They will completely disregard your personal space, your kids' personal space, and other dogs' personal space (don't scold them for growling at the puppy), both physically and emotionally. They are going to disrupt your life in untold ways. They may require near-constant care and supervision, at least if you want to keep your shoe collection or living room furniture intact. And let's not even get into the endless bathroom breaks and sleepless nights.

It's easy to say (particularly for children), "I want a puppy."

But is it as easy to say, "I want a dog that is going to require an incredible amount of my patience, time, attention, and money"?

My friend's mom, a woman in her eighties, recently adopted a boxer puppy, as she'd always had boxers. They're having trouble getting along, not because there's anything wrong with the puppy or the owner, but because their needs just don't align at this particular point in their lives.

Imagine a man who isn't particularly driven or ambitious when it comes to his career, but is superenthusiastic about his outdoor sports. He's married to a woman who values a sense of financial security. She wants him to work harder and play less golf; he wants her to chill out and let him do what he loves to do. Neither of them is wrong—they're just not a good match for each other, regardless of whatever chemistry brought them together.

The same goes for the boxer puppy—who wants to play, play, play—and the elderly owner, who has earned the right to enjoy a more relaxed, contemplative life. The woman, who had owned many boxers during her lifetime, may have fallen in love with the way the puppy looked, but they are just not a good match. I wish she'd adopted a six- or eight- or ten-year-old dog!

Some people tell me that they want a puppy because they don't want a "problem dog." If getting a puppy is the solution to avoiding behavioral problems, then how come the majority of the calls I get are to help coach misbehaving puppies? I get far fewer requests to help misbehaving adults, even if they're rescued from shelters. It's no coincidence that most of the dogs who end up in shelters are younger than one year, usually abandoned right around the time that their cute puppy features stop seeming so cute.

The biggest (and maybe only) advantage to getting a puppy is the chance to socialize him yourself (a concept we'll come back to often), as most of a dog's socialization to strangers, children, other dogs, etc., takes place during the first sixteen weeks of his life. But if the puppy has been with a breeder, who may have kept the dog away from strangers, household sounds, or children for the first eight weeks, you've already missed the most crucial part of that window.

My "son" Clyde is a Doberman mix. I adopted him after someone threw him out of a moving car on the 405 freeway in Los Angeles. He was about eight months old, and he was just done with that cute puppy look. A Good Samaritan picked him up and took him to a vet, who called to tell me that there was a dog who really needed me. You can imagine the pit that I get in my stomach when I hear those words.

Clyde was certainly a handful, a bundle of wolf instincts. I have to admit that it took me a few months to fall in love with him. I thought he was obnoxious! Now he's thirteen years old, a wise old man very much connected to the conscious choice-making side of his personality. Despite his age, when it comes to chasing a tennis ball, no one can keep up with his endurance and stamina. They say that forty is the new thirty. Well, I'm saying that for many dogs, thirteen is the new six.

Age does not mean what it used to, especially if our dogs come from a big gene pool (in other words, mutts), we feed them well (we'll talk about diet on Day 23), and tend to their seven basic needs. Dogs, like people, are living longer lives and remaining far more active into their quote-unquote golden years. Youth is overrated!

When you adopt an older dog, you get a creature who is far from narcissistic, one who is absolutely grateful to you, has been around the block, and knows what really matters in life. Ask almost anybody who has rescued an older dog and you're likely to hear things like "It's the best thing I've ever done," and "I'm so grateful to have this dog in my life." There's no feeling like opening your heart and sharing your life with an older dog.

THE CASE FOR RESCUING DOGS

A friend of mine, someone I'd describe as down-to-earth—a hippie, in all the good ways—recently told me that she'd finally gotten a dog. "Great!" I said. "Where did you rescue him?"

"From a pet store!" she replied.

I stared at her for a moment, incredulous: "You gave money to an industry that habitually and systematically tortures dogs?" (If you're interested in hearing the longer version, I've included "Puppy Factories" in the appendix section of this book.)

People have so many preconceptions about rescuing a dog from a shelter, the main one being that the dog is there because of some kind of problem. Of course he is! The problem is that the dog was in a relationship that didn't work out, but not necessarily because of him. That's all! We've all had relationships that didn't work out. Does it mean that there's something wrong with us, and that we should be euthanized? Maybe we married the right person at the wrong time in our lives, or a great person who just wasn't a good fit for us. Imagine if divorce meant that we'd be "put down," as 50 to 60 percent of all shelter dogs are! Crazy, right?

Here are the main reasons that dogs end up in shelters:

- No time for dog (or children lost interest)
- Divorce
- Moving or landlord issues
- Cost of maintenance
- Too many animals
- Behavioral problems: hyperactivity, housebreaking accidents, barking, chewing.
- Dog is old or ill

Would parents dump six million kids into shelters for the above reasons? No, of course not, that would be crazy. And yet we drop off six million healthy and sweet dogs at shelters every year in the U.S.

I've also heard people worry that getting a dog from a shelter means bringing the "unknown" into your home. Are you bringing the "known" home when you get a puppy? In one litter, seven puppies have seven different personalities. What do you really know about the particular puppy that you selected? You're not going to get the real scoop from the owner of the pet store. Even if you go directly to a so-called breeder that you found on the Internet, there's no guarantee that he or she is going to be honest about the health and personality of the puppy you've chosen.

I don't mean to say that rescuing a dog won't have its challenges. But they're nowhere near the number of challenges you'll encounter with a new puppy. The most common challenges, like anxiety or aggression, are fear-based and almost always the result of a previous relationship where his or her needs weren't being met. (We'll come back to "nervous aggression" throughout the book, especially on Day 18.) By meeting those needs and providing loving coaching for your dog, those challenges will, 99 percent of the time, decrease until they completely melt away. These days, most shelters and rescue groups put a lot of time into training dogs, improving their manners and making it easier to find them "forever homes." The dogs are tested to make sure that they're good with kids and to determine their personalities, how much exercise they need, and their favorite activities. Even if you're dead set on a puppy, there are plenty of good ones at shelters. And any dog you choose comes with the amazing feeling of knowing that you saved a life!

However a small number of rescue dogs have serious behavioral issues—particularly aggression toward people, dogs, or other animals—and "love" won't be enough to help them. It's impossible to get a good read on a dog who's locked up in a cage. But if you take him out for a run around the yard and spend some good, quality time with him, and he doesn't "shake it off," you may want to think twice about adopting that particular dog. I believe the techniques in this book can be used to help a dog with serious behavioral problems, but only if you're ready to spend most of your free time working with them for months, even years.

That being said, I have found that most shelter dogs are absolutely fantastic and are simply the victims of circumstances that were beyond their control. There are so many amazing rewards that come with rescuing a dog from a shelter. If you happen to believe, like I do, in karma points, you'll be earning a small fortune!

CHOOSING A BREED

Earlier I said that at their core, all dogs are the same—breeds are like flavors of ice cream. There are some differences, however, that you might want to consider before you choose one.

For example, a lot has been written about border collies, who are generally recognized as the "smartest" breed. And it's true—the average dog can learn 150 words, while some border collies can learn twice that number. Just keep in mind that the smarter the dog, the greater his or her need for mental stimulation. When you're not ready or available to provide it, a smart dog is capable of concocting all kinds of destructive schemes in an attempt to meet his basic needs. Whenever someone tells me they have "a really smart dog," I sigh for them.

Dog "breeds" aren't distinctions that arose from nature, but are the result of centuries of selective breeding, by human owners, to enhance certain traits. Hounds and retrievers were bred for chasing prey, so they'll keep you on your toes if there are small animals nearby. Terriers were selected for their ability to find and kill rats and will often "reward" their owners with their handiwork. The "northern" breeds, like huskies and malamutes, still have a lot of their original wolf characteristics, so be prepared for a lot of exercise and a strong prey drive. Beagles think with their noses. I often hear that Labradors make good family pets, and they do, but only after two to three years, when they outgrow their puppy phase—and if their tails are not at the same height as a child's face, as they wag a lot!

Many people like to choose a dog to fit a "look" or an image, which is never a good idea (whether it's a dog or a human partner!). I recently filmed a segment for the TV show *Extra,* where I was supposed to help Mario Lopez choose a dog. I asked him a trick question: "What are you looking for?" In order to find the best dog for him, I needed to know about his lifestyle, like his favorite outdoor activities, how much time he could realistically spend with a dog, and if he wanted a dog who would travel with him. But I didn't tell him any of that, allowing him to respond, without hesitation, "I want a bulldog."

That's like answering "a blonde with blue eyes" when you're asked what you're looking for in a mate, which, I guess, a lot of people do. But the greatest relationships are based on a connection that goes beyond looks, often with people who, at the beginning, didn't seem to be each other's "type."

Back to gorgeous Mario . . . I told him that I needed more information, asking him why he wanted a bulldog. "I'm a tough guy," he said. "I want a dog who's tough like me." It was a cute answer, but it was time to get him thinking about life with a dog in a different way.

"Are you a light sleeper?" I asked him. "Because bulldogs snore loudly." Mario hadn't considered that.

Mario happens to be in great shape, a true workout fiend. "I know you love to go running and hiking," I said to him. "You know that bulldogs have smushed noses, right? It makes it hard for them to breathe when they overexert themselves. A bulldog won't be able to join you on your outdoor excursions."

He hadn't considered that either. "And you travel quite a bit," I continued. "Have you thought about how you're going to travel with such a big dog who doesn't fit under an airplane seat?" When I suggested a smaller dog, he resisted, worried that a small dog wouldn't fit his image—a common response for many men. So I told him about Laird Hamilton, the Adonis pro surfer, who proudly walks two Chihuahua mixes—both rescued from shelters—on the beach in Malibu every time he's in town. I thought Mario might do best with a Jack Russell terrier mix, a dog who would have a big, often tough-guy personality in a small, athletic body, could travel with him and keep up easily with his workouts.

The other big mistake I see people make—specifically previous dog owners—is to find a dog who reminds them of their old dog. "In our mind there was no other option," one client told me. "All boxers will be like Rudy: the prince." They're already setting up their new dog to fail. The dog knows he's an individual. You have to know the same. I'm not telling you that you *can't* get a dog who's the same breed, but make sure that you can make an emotional distinction between your old dog and the new, giving the new dog the chance to be all that he or she can be.

Beyond breeds, it's important to remember that every dog is unique. Yes, most Labradors like water. But I've met plenty of Labradors who absolutely hate the water, and I can't count the number of Chihuahuas and dachshunds I've seen on the beach happily fetching balls from the waves.

Even within a litter, each dog is unique. I often ask my clients if their brothers and sisters or children have the same personalities they do. They'll inevitably chuckle and say no. I recently worked with Oprah's two new rescued springer spaniel littermates, Lauren and Sunny, and discovered that I had to come up with different games for each of them: Lauren was interested in connecting with people; Sunny couldn't care less. It took me twice as long to convince Sunny that coming to me when I called could be more fun than chasing birds, but it was smooth sailing from there—as long as I remembered that she was much more of a tomboy than her girlie sister.

In the end, it's not going to be about your dog's breed or looks, or the number of compliments and prizes his ancestors won at the beauty show. It's going to be about the quality of the relationship you develop with your dog. The best advice might come from the dating world: Choose a partner you want to hang out with, can communicate with, and who likes to do the same things that you like to do.

SHOULD I GET MORE THAN ONE?

People ask me if they should get two dogs at the same time, as they can keep each other entertained. I'll almost always tell them that it's a bad idea (particularly two puppies from the same litter)!

1. Yes, the dogs might be happier—as they reinforce each other's hard-wired wolf instincts, like jumping, nipping, and barking—making your life a living hell and making it that much harder to coach them to make conscious choices instead of acting on instinct.

2. You won't be the primary source of pleasure in their lives; you're just the person who fills the food and water bowls, a beloved butler. And you do it for free— they won't feel like they have to earn your praise and affection through good manners or good behavior.

3. Two dogs will constantly increase each other's state of arousal as they compete to see who eats the fastest, runs the farthest, jumps the highest, and pees on the most sofas and beds.

The best path, in my experience, is to take it one dog at a time, allowing yourself the one-on-one time your dog needs to build a strong attachment and appreciation for you as her coach and trusted source of pleasure. When I worked with Sunny and Lauren Winfrey, I separated them so that I could develop a strong relationship with each dog. They enjoyed playing together, but because I made sure that bonding with me was the most pleasurable experience, when they had to choose who to follow, they chose me. Only after we'd achieved that were they allowed to be together at all times.

PREPARING FOR THE ARRIVAL

Preparing for your dog's arrival is a little like getting ready to bring a baby home from the hospital, only you're probably going to get a lot more sleep! Here are a few tips to make the transition an easy one:

Dog- and puppy-proof your home. It's going to take a while for your dog—especially if he's a puppy—to learn the rules of the house. You can save yourself a lot of stress by covering or removing your expensive furniture and rugs. Make sure your treasured personal items are stored out of reach, especially books and magazines on low shelves or coffee tables. Get into the habit of closing the door to any rooms that are going to be off-limits to your dog, using baby gates if you need them.

Establish the rules before your dog comes home. Will your dog be allowed to hang out in every room in your house? At every time of day? Are couches or beds off-limits? Who will be responsible for feeding the dog? Walking the dog? When will the dog be fed, walked, or hiked? Is someone going to be the primary coach? If not, is everyone on the same page? The easiest time to answer these questions is before the dog arrives home, so everyone in your household will be prepared.

Have a plan for your other pets. If you already have a dog (or more than one), make sure that she's prepared for the new arrival: Test her willingness to share her life by dog-sitting for a few other dogs, over a period of time, before you commit to bringing a new dog home. Fostering a dog before adopting can eliminate any uncertainty. As for your new dog, be prepared to begin socializing him right away to your other pets (see Day 10 for more details).

Plan your schedule. There aren't too many employers who will give you "maternity leave" to care for a new dog, but you may want to take some time off from work to help your dog adjust, even if it's just lunchtime visits. If you can't take time off, seriously consider hiring a professional pet-sitter to come in the middle of the day until you're sure that you know your dog can handle staying home alone.

ABOUT SECOND (OR THIRD, OR FOURTH, ETC.) DOGS

New dogs—like new siblings—mean a huge adjustment for the dog or dogs that you already have. This is especially true with puppies, who enter the world without any sense of others' personal space or boundaries.

It's important to be sensitive to your previous dogs' needs upon a new dog's arrival. Introduce them to one another in a neutral area, like someone else's backyard. Bring yummy treats that you can give them to encourage them to make pleasurable associations with one another, as well as a spray bottle in case you need to distract one of them from getting too rough or serious with the other. Make sure that there are clearly defined, separate spaces for sleeping, as well as separate toys and treats. Don't forget to remind your first dog that she's special, greeting and feeding her (at least at the beginning) before the new dog. But you're also going to have to help her to associate the newcomer with pleasure, not pain, a technique I'll describe on Day 10.

When choosing a new dog, try to pick one that will be compatible with your current dog—if you know she doesn't like puppies, for example, then don't get a puppy. If you do get a puppy, don't let him completely disrupt your first dog's life—make sure she is still getting sleep, exercise, and time engaging in her favorite activities with you by herself, as she's used to doing. And make sure the puppy has plenty of room to blow off steam—chances are he's going to have a lot more energy (and many more needs) than your current dog.

Finally, unless things seem to be escalating toward violence, give your dogs a chance to work things out on their own. Like wolves, dogs settle into natural pecking orders as long as we don't get in the way. A lot of people feel it's unfair to treat their dogs differently, inadvertently creating even more tension among them as they work to establish their hierarchy. If one dog is clearly the leader—even if it's the new dog—respect her position by greeting, feeding, and walking her first. (For dogs, hierarchy is not necessarily determined by seniority. But if your older dog corrects the puppy, let her do your work for you—she's helping by socializing the puppy and teaching him to be well mannered and respectful toward other dogs.) If there's only one bone to chew on, that bone goes to the leader. It's not always easy for us, as owners, to behave this way, but doing so will help your dogs feel more secure and bring peace to your home. As my friend Lona pointed out to me, her four dogs stopped fighting when she stopped trying to treat them as equals, ignoring who "got there first" or who she felt sorriest for.

SHOPPING LIST

Here are a few things to get before you bring the dog home.

- Crate (see the sidebar opposite)
- Sleeping pad (preferably white; see sidebar opposite)
- Baby gates (to keep your dog out of certain areas)
- Current dog food (whatever your dog is being fed at the shelter, store, etc.)
- New (higher-quality) dog food (that you can transition into your dog's diet over a period of ten to twelve days—see Day 23 for more details on diet)
- Odor and stain remover
- Four-foot leash
- Nylon collar (that can be expanded if your dog is still growing)
- Treats
- Tags with your address, two phone numbers, and your dog's name. I strongly urge you to consider microchipping your dog as well—see Day 22 for more details.

PREPARING FOR CRATE TRAINING

Crates can be confusing for many new dog parents. "They make me feel like I'm putting my dog in a jail!" my clients often tell me. "It seems too cruel to lock them up in there."

Despite how it might seem, dogs don't hate going into a crate. What they really hate is not being able to come and go as they please, the freedom to roam and destroy everything that's in their path. Even if you don't believe me (although I promise you, it's true), then consider a crate for the thousands of dollars it will save you in damaged goods and—should your dog get into a box of toothpicks, as one of my clients' dogs did—enormous bills from the veterinarian.

Misusing a crate can be cruel. The crate should never be a punishment for bad behavior, or a place to keep your dog locked up as you trot off to work for the day. Never keep a dog crated for more than two to three hours at a stretch during the day, or six to eight hours at night while everyone is sleeping. Use a crate correctly, and he will see it as a treasured personal space, an instinctual reminder of the dark, underground dens where wolf cubs are born. They also make traveling a whole lot easier, giving your dog a portable home and a sense of security when you're on the move. If you can associate the crate with pleasure, your dog will have a much easier time if she's got to stay at the vet's overnight. In the aftermath of Hurricane Katrina, the laws regarding evacuation shelters were amended to allow pets who were housed in crates, as many people were refusing to leave their homes without their beloved animals.

Most important, crate training is the fastest and most effective way to teach housebreaking and to prevent your dog from chewing on the wrong things. We'll get into the details on Day 1, but it's a good idea to have the crate set up before your new dog first arrives home.

Crates come in many different colors and styles to suit your preference. But the most important quality to consider is the size: It should be big enough for your dog to stand up, turn around, and lie down, but no bigger—you don't want it to be so big that your dog can "do her business" on one side, while staying dry and comfortable on the other. If you're starting with a puppy, you can buy a crate that will fit your dog when he's fully grown and use a metal divider (often sold separately by the manufacturer) or stack a few cardboard boxes to shrink the space to the right size. I recommend a wire crate that has a removable tray at the bottom, as it's easier to clean than the big plastic crates.

The crate should be a comfortable, cozy place where your dog will want to hang out. You can make it super cozy by lining the bottom of the crate with a soft pad or blanket—just make sure it's a light color, like white, so you can see when he's peed on it. Cover the top and two of the sides with a towel to make it seem more like a cave. Finally, place the crate in an area where you and your family spend the most time, like the kitchen or the family room.

WEEK 1

Do what is right. Be pure. At the end of the way is freedom. 'Til then, patience.

—*the Buddha*

I would fain ask such stupid people whether by beating a boy they would teach him to read without showing him the alphabet.

—*the Duke of Newcastle*

DAY 1

BRINGING
THE DOG HOME

The first day! Today we're going to cover one of the most stressful (and easy to remedy) issues that every dog and puppy owner has to contend with: housebreaking.

NEW HOME, NEW RULES

I was once invited to the *Today* show to demonstrate a few Loved Dog techniques for bringing a new dog into the home. We had just finished a practice run, having set up the stage and rehearsed the segment the day before I was going to film it live. The stagehands were working their butts off to clean everything up, and I happily joined in—until one of them asked me to stop.

I felt surprised and confused—I was just trying to help, to show them my gratitude for all of their hard work. Why on earth would they ask me to stop? What I didn't know was that there was a set of regulations, established by the unions and the insurance companies, that assigned specific tasks to specific people. Even something as small as moving a salad bowl from one table to another represented a violation of the rules.

It felt unnatural not to be able to help, but as I was learning, the TV world had its own rules that I had to obey. Thank God the stagehands were patient enough to understand that I didn't know those rules, explaining them to me instead of smacking me with a rolled-up newspaper, spraying Binaca in my face, or choking me with a chain, telling me that they were the alpha leaders and that I shouldn't misbehave or act so dominant.

When dogs enter our homes, they're in unfamiliar territory. They don't speak the same language that we do. Their wolf instincts don't naturally mesh with the rules and customs of our homes, our society, or what we would consider to be good manners. Even if we could provide our dogs with great coaching every minute of the day, they'd still make mistakes, at least at the beginning. Is it right to blame the dogs for being ignorant? Of course not! It's up to us to communicate the rules in a way that our dogs can understand. It's our job to teach them to make good choices, remaining patient and consistent while our doggies are doing all that they can to understand us.

It's like that kids' game where you hide something and tell them whether they're getting "warmer" or "colder." Dogs are never going to learn what's expected of them if you only tell them when they're cold—or if you're only going to say, "No!"

Nothing is going to happen in a day. Your dog will need time to absorb and implement your lessons. Building trust and rapport takes time. So will learning the skills you're going to need to be a successful dog coach.

HOUSEBREAKING

One of the first unwanted behaviors you'll probably face is the inevitable accident. Housebreaking a puppy or dog who has not yet mastered the skill will require a crate. However, if you adopt an older dog, you may not need the crate—just a few repetitions of going out and celebrating a successful pee or poo will do the trick. When your new dog soils your favorite rug, you may feel the urge to yell, smack her with a newspaper, or rub her nose in the mess. Your instincts may tell you that you've got to let her know she's done something *wrong*.

But what has she done that's so wrong? Think about it from her perspective: In wolf society, it's appropriate to poop or pee whenever the urge strikes, wherever happens to be convenient, without having to ask for help or permission; the same is true of toddlers. To live in your home, your dog is going to have to learn (from you, her coach and teacher) an entirely new set of skills and rules:

1. She has to learn how to "hold it."
2. She has to learn the appropriate places to go.
3. She has to learn how to get to those places, or how to ask you to take her to one of those places.

That's a lot for your dog to digest, although not that much for you to teach. It isn't brain surgery, but it will take a large chunk of your time and will probably test your patience in direct proportion to the value of the rugs, books, and curtains your dog is soiling. (Again, it's a good idea to move your most treasured possessions to a safe place until your dog has better control over her bladder.)

Housebreaking is nowhere near as hard as it sounds. It does, however, take time. The average dog takes four weeks to learn all the housebreaking rules. She might not seem to get it at all, until one day it clicks and you realize that it's been a week since the last mistake.

Let's start with number one: The fastest way to teach her how to hold it is to use a crate, which you've hopefully set up as described on Day 0.

As I said earlier, the crate should always be associated with pleasure, not pain. Toss a few small treats into the crate to get her inside. You can feed your dog in the crate during mealtime—you want your dog to associate the crate with the things that are good in her life—but you should remove any food and water once mealtime is over and take her outside immediately to relieve herself. Also, teach your dog that she gets her toys only when she goes into her crate. She can come out right after, but she will learn to associate walking into the crate with pleasure.

Remember, we're trying to teach her to hold it, hopefully for a couple of hours at a time. There's a direct connection between drinking water and peeing. If you let your dog drink randomly, she's going to pee randomly—you're setting her up to fail.

For your first few weeks together—until you're fairly sure your dog knows the appropriate places to do her business—the schedule should go something like this.

1. **Two hours in the crate, then let her out.** Some of my clients ask me what they should do if their dog is sleeping. Let her sleep! Puppies grow during their sleep, which is why they sleep so much.

2. **Immediately offer her some water.** When you take her out, rush her to the water bowl. I call this "loading up." While you don't want her to drink inside the crate, you want to make sure that she's getting plenty of water—dehydration can damage your dog's kidneys. If you make sure she gets all the water she'd like with every meal, plus every two hours when you let her out of the crate, she should be getting plenty.

Designate a specific area for the water bowl so you can monitor your dog's intake. It's best to keep the water by the door that leads to the housebreaking area, or even outside, so as to limit any opportunities for accidents along the way. If your puppy can't make it to the water bowl without peeing, take her outside first. After she's done, let her drink some water, and take her out to pee again in five or ten minutes.

3. **Take her outside.** Lead her to the place where you'd like her to poop or pee. If you've got an unvaccinated puppy, she won't be ready for the outside world, so designate a toilet area in the corner of your yard (preferably behind bushes, someplace where children are unlikely to play), on a patch of grass, or on a balcony where you can lay down a "pee pad."

It's crucial for you to accompany your dog—she may find other things to keep her busy outside and wait to come back inside before doing her business. Accompany your dog to the area you've chosen and wait for it to happen. As she's going potty, give the behavior a name, something that you won't use in any context other than this one—I like to use the phrase "hurry up." (It can also be something fun—Oprah uses the word "poodie" with her two dogs.) Repeat it in a calm voice, for as long as your dog is going, like a lullaby. Try not to look at her—if she sees you staring at her, she may quit too early and rush over to be with you.

When she's finished, show your dog how happy you are. Smile and clap your hands. Enthusiastically repeat "Hurry up!" or whatever you called it, using the specific phrase as opposed to a generic "Good dog!" or "Good boy!" (More on this later.) Reward your dog with a special "gold" treat, like a few tiny pieces of steak (about the size of a raisin), or chicken, and occasionally a little bit of hot dog or cheese—we'll go more deeply into treats on Day 2. You want your dog to know that, right now, this is the biggest deal in the world, and you want her to have the biggest and most amazing treat as a reward.

I call this process "making a party"—clap your hands, smile, and give your dog a jackpot of treats. When you do it, you'll be creating positive associations with whatever behavior you're trying to teach—in this case, relieving herself in the designated area. Try to start the party as soon as she's finished. Soon she'll start to look forward to it, speeding up the process and saving you from spending a lot of time waiting for her to go.

One common mistake is to reward your dog *after* she's back in the house—instead of giving her a fantastic association with the outside bathroom area, you'll have a dog who would rather linger next to the refrigerator or treat jar. Make sure you have the treats with you in the place where you want your dog to go to the bathroom. I recommend having a small glass jar with special treats outside and a plastic bag in the fridge with precut super gold treats that you can grab on the go.

THE LINGERING DOG

Some dogs take a long time, once they're outside, to do their business. Usually it's a sign that they love the outdoors and are afraid that as soon as they "go," the excursion will be over. You can solve the problem by reversing the sequence, waiting until after she's gone to the bathroom to begin the walk. Your dog will learn that going faster doesn't shorten her time outside (which she associates with pain), but will allow her to get to the fun part faster (creating an association with pleasure).

---

4. Treat your dog to a half hour of free time. Once you're back in the house, give your dog thirty minutes to play freely. When you're sure she can go a half hour without peeing, you can start to extend this free time, first to forty-five minutes, then to an hour, etc.

When free time is over, you have a few options—you can take her out again, put her on a leash and tie her to your belt or the chair you're sitting on, or put her back in the crate.

Some dogs may protest for fifteen minutes or a half hour when you first put them back in the crate, but if you can ignore them with consistency, they'll quickly learn the routine.

If you're following this routine and your dog still pees in the crate, chances are that you're probably not spending enough time outside focusing on the task at hand. But there's always the possibility of a bladder infection, so take your dog to see her vet.

WHY "GOOD BOY," "GOOD GIRL," AND "GOOD DOG" AREN'T GOOD ENOUGH

See things from your dog's point of view: She sits and you say, "Good girl!" You call her and she comes to you, and you say, "Good girl!" She goes potty and you say, "Good girl!" How is your dog going to learn which behaviors you're praising if everything is "Good girl!" and you're not going to help her distinguish which one is which? The more specific you are with your praise, the clearer your coaching and the faster your dog will learn to speak your language. Giving each behavior a name allows your dog to know what she's supposed to repeat the next time you make the request.

When your dog does "hurry up," say, "Good hurry up!" or just, "Hurry up," in a singsong voice. If she comes when you call, say, "Good come!" and when she moves away from something, say, "Good leave it!" Say "Drink" when she's drinking and "Be a goat" when she's eating grass. Be creative and have fun with it!

As your dog begins to learn English, her reactions will help you know what she wants to do. When I ask my dog Clyde if he wants to eat, he'll lick his lips if the answer is yes. I can also give him options—"Do you want to go see Maddy, play with Shadow, or go to Malibu?"—and gauge his reaction to each to understand his real preferences. You probably have friends who have to spell things around their dogs, who are quick to learn the meaning of words like "walk," "treat," and "ball." If you put in the time talking to your dog and paying close attention to her responses, people will be blown away by just how smart a dog you have!

If your dog is going to spend the night in the crate—a good idea until she's learned how to hold it—be sure not to give her any food or water for three hours before bedtime. However, if your dog constantly soils the white pad or towel, do remove them and let your dog sleep on the barren floor. If she does have an accident while in the crate and this time it isn't absorbed by the towel, she'll realize, "Yuck, I'd better hold it from now on!" It won't take more than three of these experiences to drive the lesson home. But give your dog the best chance possible to succeed by making sure she's "empty" before putting her in the crate for the night. She'll be okay—even a seven-week-old puppy can be expected to hold it for six hours of sleep.

By the way, if you bought your dog at a pet store, you may want to consider an alternative to crate training. These dogs are forced to eliminate in their crates and have already learned how NOT to hold it while they're in a crate. Use a crate when you can't watch them, but otherwise you're going to have to tether her to you on a four-foot leash and take her out frequently. Yet one more reason why I don't recommend buying a dog from a pet store!

WHEN PEEING ISN'T A HOUSEBREAKING ISSUE

Not all "accidents" are related to housebreaking. Some dogs, for example, will let out a squirt or a few drops from the excitement of greeting you. The best solution is to ABSOLUTELY ignore the dog when you first come home or guests arrive. Act as if you don't even have a dog, allowing her a few minutes to collect herself emotionally. After about five minutes, you can greet your dog in a super-calm manner.

Some dogs pee from fear—usually they'll be cowering or lying on their backs. The worst thing that you can do is to correct her, which will only increase her fear. These sorts of situations should become less common as you socialize your dog and build her confidence by using the principles in this book.

WHEN DOGS HAVE TO "GO"

When they're puppies, they have to "go" more frequently than adult dogs, especially:

- After eating and drinking
- After napping or sleeping
- After chewing
- After playing

DEALING WITH ACCIDENTS

No matter how smart your dog is, he's going to make mistakes. How you handle those mistakes depends on whether or not you catch him in the act.

When you catch the mistake as it's happening . . .

Congratulations—this is a teachable moment! Celebrate the fact that you can show your dog the bull's eye. Make it clear, by your voice and demeanor, that you are displeased. You don't have to overdo it—think "urgency," not "anger."

Urgently rush your dog outside—picking him up, if necessary—to the place you'd prefer that he go. But once you're there, change your demeanor—bye-bye urgency, hello patience and encouragement. If your dog manages to go potty again, this time in the right place, reward him with an outpouring of joy and a jackpot of treats, as you say, "Hurry up" in an impressed and happy tone of voice.

When you don't catch the mistake . . .

There's nothing you can do. Do NOT push the dog's nose into the pee or poop, or hit him with a newspaper. Neither of those acts communicates the real problem, which isn't the act itself, but *location, location, location.* All you'll be doing is teaching your dog to be more secretive about his business, training him to pee behind couches or in closets. Some dogs will even eat their own poop to hide the evidence!

Calling too much attention to a mistake can also create attention-seeking behavior—if your dog feels ignored, he can always go potty in an inappropriate place. Maybe it's not happy attention, but it's still attention. When I was a toddler and felt ignored by adults, I used to dip toilet paper in the bowl and use it as wallpaper. Even though it was clean toilet water, it worked like a charm.

So when you miss the mistake, the best thing to do is ignore it. If you've got the urge to hit someone, slap yourself on the nose with a newspaper and say, "Bad owner!" Next time you'll pay more attention to your dog's needs. (On Day 10, I'll show you how to use a chart to get a clearer idea of your dog's habits and needs.)

Be sure to clean up mistakes quickly, using a cleaner designed to neutralize pet odors. Dogs are all about their noses, and lingering smells just encourage a repetition of the same behavior. Just don't let her see you doing it—you don't want to draw any extra attention to the behaviors you're trying to eliminate.

DAY 2

THE POWER OF PAIN VERSUS PLEASURE

Today you're going to see how to use the concept of pain versus pleasure as the foundation for coaching new behaviors. You'll also learn the proper way to deliver treats, teaching your dog how to "take it."

PAIN AND PLEASURE

I have a relative who, while I love her dearly, is a big whiner. There is no aspect of her life that she's happy about, and she loves to call me and share her misery. But that's what caller ID is for! When I see her number pop up, I do the same thing I do for telemarketers—I let the call go to voice mail.

So what does this have to do with your dog? Well, everything! Dogs are just like people in that they're moved to action (or inaction) by pain and pleasure. When I associate "talking to my relative" with pain, I ignore her call. When your dog associates an activity with pain, he's likely to do the same. Of course, the opposite is true as well—when we associate specific people or activities with pleasure, there's nothing more we'd rather do than spend time with them.

You can see this all the time at dog parks. When the owner's ready to go, she'll call out her dog's name, and then get frustrated when her dog stops, takes one look at her, and runs in the other direction. The dog isn't being obstinate or dumb—he's just learned that when his owner calls his name at the dog park, he's rounded up, put into the car, and taken home—end of pleasurable activity. It's much easier just to ignore the request to delay experiencing the pain. You may know some teenagers who behave in the same manner.

(RE-)NAMING YOUR DOG

Of all the words you exchange with your dog, the one that's probably going to be used most frequently is his name. That's why it's incredibly important to ensure that he associates his name with pleasure, not pain.

I encourage all my clients who adopt their dogs from rescue shelters to rename their pets. Many of these dogs aren't in shelters because they had loving owners—there may be all sorts of negative baggage associated with the sound of their name. Give him a new start with a new name, one that you can associate with love and pleasure.

It's easy to do: Start using his old name with his new name, for example, "Rocky-Max." As your dog gets used to it, you can drop the original name and just say "Max."

The desire to please us is written into a dog's DNA. Dogs crave our approval, as being a valued part of a pack feels like the key to survival. The pack is where they look to fill their seven basic needs. As a result, our dogs are constantly monitoring us for signs that we're pleased with their behavior.

But dogs aren't mind readers. Nor do people always do a good job of clearly expressing their feelings, a complaint you'll often hear from men whose women seem to expect them to read their minds. Just because we're pleased with our dogs doesn't mean that we're conveying that information. In the absence of clear information—or guidance as to how they can please us—dogs will try to figure it out on their own. Most of the time that means reverting to what's easiest and most natural for them: their wolf instincts. And that's when the undesirable behaviors begin.

If we want to help our dogs learn good manners, new behaviors, resourcefulness, and how to make choices, we have to communicate our wishes clearly and make them pleasurable to follow. Here are a few things to consider.

Exaggerate important words and body language. There's a lot of evidence that dogs respond more to "prosody"—the way words are stressed and delivered—than the actual words themselves. According to professor and psychologist Alexandra Horowitz, author of *Inside of a Dog,* one of the reasons a lot of dogs respond to "baby talk" is "because it distinguishes speech that is directed at them from the rest of the continuous yammering above their heads." Using a singsong tone of voice when praising your dog may make him more confident that you're happy with him. "Good sit!" may work, but "Siiiiiiiit!" makes more of an impact.

Exaggeration also works well when you use gestures and hand signals—overacting works a lot better than subtlety. Dogs also like to look at your face to see how you are responding to their behavior, so avoid wearing sunglasses when you're coaching a dog. Let your face be an open book.

Use lots of repetition. The more your dog hears a particular word or phrase, the more deeply it will become ingrained in her vocabulary. And if you want your dog to associate a particular word with a particular behavior, object, or activity, make sure that you're using the same word every time to describe it. For example, don't just say, "Walk," a few times during a walk, say it often to help your dog understand what it means.

Use short words and phrases. Dogs can understand hundreds of words, but—at least at the beginning—they don't do very well with complicated sentence structure. "Hurry up?" is a lot more understandable to a dog than "Do you have to go to the bathroom?" (Later on in the book we'll talk about using more complicated sentences to ask your dog a question.) But do use words, as opposed to grunts or whistles—not only will you be teaching your dog to better understand you, but you'll also be expanding his brain.

Praise often, and be specific in your praise. Dogs respond best when you use a happy tone of voice. Try to praise every success, big or small, but be sure to associate that praise with a specific behavior. "Good boy!" may make your dog feel good, but he's not going to know the name of the behavior he performed to earn the compliment. You want your dog to be able to repeat the specific behavior the next time you ask for it, in order to elicit your approval again and again. If you want to praise your dog for sitting, say, "Good sit!" If you see your dog lying down, say, "Dowwwwwwwn." Look for things you can praise. Too often we ignore good behavior and give attention only to what is bad.

Use your voice as a tool. You can adjust the way you say certain words or phrases to indicate your level of joy or disappointment. I use three basic tones of voice—neutral, excited, and disappointed—and several degrees of gradation (i.e., excited, kinda excited, super-duper excited) within each.

Avoid yelling or barking commands. Imagine trying to learn a completely unfamiliar set of rules and customs from a teacher speaking a completely foreign language. Imagine that your quality of life depended on your understanding those rules and customs. Now imagine how stressful the experience would be if that teacher yelled at you throughout the lesson and every time you made a mistake.

Not only do you cause your dog stress when you yell or scream at him, but you also desensitize him to that particular tone of voice—not so good when you want to stop him from running into the middle of a busy street. Save the acting up and raising your voice for the times you *really* need to get your dog's attention. There are other ways to let your dog know when you're unhappy with him that don't cause him fear (see Day 11).

The whole idea of giving "commands" to your dog is kind of silly. Dogs respond way better when we simply talk to them in a clear way. The idea that they need to be "commanded" in order to get them to comply is another remnant from the Dark Ages. I prefer teaching "behaviors" to giving commands.

Be patient. Your dog is tuned in to your emotional state—if you're anxious, he's going to be anxious. If success is taking longer than you expected, don't let it get to you, and if it does, don't show it to your dog. Coaching works best when you're smiling and breathing normally. The breathing is particularly important—it's harder for your dog to relax (and learn) when you seem to be holding your breath. As a general rule, don't coach your dog when you're feeling angry, impatient, or pissy—wait until you're in a better frame of mind.

Don't be afraid of silence. How easy is it to concentrate on a task when you've got someone next to you, nagging you, not giving you any room to figure things out? In order to make the transition from wolf instincts to humanlike, conscious choices, your dog is going to need time and space to process what he is learning. It's not because he's slow or stupid—dogs (like many men) are wired to be single-focus hunters. They like to do one thing at time, assessing all of the angles, before they respond. And like men, if we give them the time and space they need, the responses are usually better than we expected! So when you ask your dog to lie "down" or back "off," give him some time to think about it before repeating the request again (and again). If he's confused or unsure whether whatever you're asking him to do is going to be pleasurable, you can repeat it again. Make sure that you are communicating properly with your tone of voice and body language, and that the environment is conducive to learning.

Silence is also a great teaching tool when your dog is not behaving the way you want him to. Turning your back on a dog can send a much more powerful message than screaming and yelling—the "cold-shoulder treatment" works on almost every social creature and is a lot more effective than physical corrections or the infliction of pain.

Reward success with a "jackpot." When your dog does something for the first time, or does it faster or better, or responds to you under tough or distracting circumstances, reward him with a series of treats, maybe five or six or twelve in succession. He'll know that he hit the jackpot and will be eager to improve on his success. We'll talk more about using jackpots on Day 3.

Make a party. If you're a parent, then you've probably already done this with your child, maybe when she brought home an art project from preschool. Even if it's obscure, you may have made a big fuss, said "wow" a lot, hung the project on the refrigerator, pointed it out to whoever's around. Kids love to feel really appreciated in this way.

So do dogs. When they do something we love, like catching a ball, they bask in the pleasure that we show. "Wow! Catch! Catch!" Clap your hands, smile wide, repeat the name of the behavior, and go all out with your enthusiasm. Your dog will be dying to repeat whatever it is that earned him such praise.

TEACHING NEW BEHAVIORS

When I coach a dog, I'm not trying to get him to obey me or to become subservient. There's a huge difference between leadership and dominance, the same way Gandhi inspired his people in a different way than, say, Saddam Hussein. Besides differences in style, one was elected, the other wasn't. You want your dog to elect you, so that he'll want to be with you, seeking your company and approval. It should be fun for the dog and fun for you. I want each dog to behave in a certain way not because he's afraid that I'll punish him or yank on his choke chain if he doesn't, but because it feels good. I want to put the dog in a resourceful state of mind. Not only is a resourceful dog a faster learner, but he's also more likely to surprise me with behaviors and talents that I never would have expected.

In fact, teaching a dog to be submissive can be hugely dangerous. Submissive behavior can mask warning signs, preventing our dogs from telling us when they're scared, overwhelmed, or annoyed. A dog who isn't showing us what he's really feeling is a ticking time bomb of potentially nervous aggressive behavior.

You'll see that I use the word "behavior" instead of "commands." This isn't the army, and we're not in boot camp! I want to create an environment in which a dog loves to learn and is always eager for more. The Loved Dog Method doesn't use screaming or push-ups as teaching tools. We don't tie dogs to treadmills to get them to exercise. Instead, we use games, toys, food, treats, and lots of fun!

We'll get into the games and toys later—today we're going to focus on treats. Treats are an incredibly powerful training tool for two reasons. First, they're situation specific: If you reward a dog with a treat at the precise moment he's behaving the way you want him to (or no more than three seconds later), his brain will begin to associate pleasure with that specific behavior. The stronger that link becomes, the more your dog will want to repeat the behavior because it feels good.

THE STORAGE HAND

For treats to be effective, they have to be delivered no more than three seconds after your dog is engaging in the behavior you're trying to teach. When I'm doing a coaching session with a dog, I use one hand to communicate. The other is a "storage hand," where I've got a supply of crumbled, raisin-size treats (but never actual raisins, which are toxic to dogs) ready to be delivered: one or two when he takes a step in the right direction, and a "jackpot"— three, four, six, or more—when he makes huge progress. When outdoors, I carry the treats in a fanny pack for easy access.

The second great advantage: Treats are quantifiable. You can adjust the power of your "message" with both the quantity and quality of treats you use as a reward. We'll go more deeply into this concept on Day 3, but for now, let's see how we can use treats to teach a simple but deceptively powerful behavior: "take it."

TAKE IT

This is an easy one to teach: Just put a treat in your hand, hold it out to your dog, and say, "Take it." Let him eat the treat. Then move your hand and have your dog move with it to "take it."

Simple, right? "Take it" is actually a powerful tool. As he begins to associate the phrase with the good feelings he gets from the treat, you can use it whenever you want to put your dog in a happy mood, one where he's certain that something good is coming.

I use this phrase daily. It's very useful when you're trying to help a dog overcome any anxieties he might have about new people, dogs, objects, or situations.

DAY 3

TREATS FOR TRICKS

They say that the fastest way to a man's heart is through his stomach; I say that the fastest way to a dog's brain is through his stomach as well.

USING TREATS

As I said on Day 2, you can fine-tune the emphasis you want to put on any particular lesson by adjusting the quantity or quality of the treats you use to reward your dog. Quantity is pretty self-explanatory—one treat means you're pleased, while a "jackpot" of two, four, six, or more treats means you're *really* pleased. A jackpot delivered at high speed means you're out of your mind with joy. As long as you remember to repeat the name of the behavior that earned him the prize, your dog's brain will create and reinforce a powerful connection between that behavior and the immense pleasure that comes with it.

When I talk about quality, I like to break treats down into three different categories: gold, silver, and bronze.

Gold treats are your dog's most beloved foods. They're going to vary based on your dog's individual tastes. How do you know if something is a gold treat? Give your dog a few different options and see which ones drive her wild with excitement. You can even do your own version of the "Pepsi Challenge," asking your dog to pick between two treats you've placed on the floor to see which one she prefers. Just remember that dogs, like people, are left- or right-handed and may consistently look at one side first—make sure to switch the treats between the left and right sides so you know that she's picking her favorite instead of the one she looks at first.

My dogs love the food I bring them from restaurants. Although I'm a vegetarian, I clean up my friends' plates to bring my dogs a bit of steak or chicken (from which I'll wash off any spices) and they're in doggy heaven. Your dog may love hot dogs or rotisserie chicken; experience will soon teach you which foods are most exciting to your dog. Just remember that you'll have to mix it up from time to time. No matter how much you might love lobster, you wouldn't feel the same way for long if you ate it at every meal. Don't ruin a good gold treat by overdoing it. Dogs love the element of surprise that comes with tasting something new.

I use gold treats to reward a dog when he learns a new behavior for the first time. I will also use them when I'm trying to coach a dog in a difficult environment, i.e., one full of distractions, like screaming kids, other dogs, or an unexpected visit from a cat. It's a way of acknowledging that you know there were a lot of other things your dog could have been focusing on instead of you, but he overcame his instincts and chose to do what you asked.

I was doing a coaching session at a client's pool with Sasha, his golden retriever. We wanted to teach her not to jump into the water without permission, even if my client's kids were jumping in and having fun. So we practiced "leave it" (a behavior we'll cover on Day 6), asking Sasha to ignore the toys we were throwing into the pool, or at least not to jump in after them. She did a great job, so we "made a party" and rewarded her with a jackpot of eleven gold treats.

We repeated this process a few times. When the session was over, we relaxed with some lemonade by the side of the pool. One of my client's kids arrived and, unaware of what we'd been teaching his dog, said, "Sasha, look!" as he tossed a toy into the pool. Sasha looked, but decided not to go after the toy. We went crazy with excitement, rewarding Sasha, "making a party" with a jackpot of about twenty treats!

Silver treats are the reward for repeating a behavior your dog has already learned, or while learning a behavior in a medium-stress environment. I use crumbled hard-boiled egg or healthy commercial dog treats. Some dogs are really enthusiastic about bananas, apples, and carrots. Many also love the coconut chips you find at the health food store, which are doubly great—coconut oil is beneficial to a dog's digestive system.

Bronze treats are your dog's steady paycheck, the reward when coaching challenges are at a minimum. They should also be healthy—you don't want to fatten up your dog by overdoing it with the gold and silver treats. I'll often use the dog's regular food as a bronze treat—we work for our paychecks, so why can't our dogs? Many dogs like cut-up pieces of fruit or vegetables dipped in olive or coconut oil. Crumbled pieces of commercial dog treats or dry dog food that you've tossed in a Ziploc bag with a piece of crushed, freeze-dried liver both work well.

You'll have to keep experimenting to find out which treats your dog likes the best. You can reward him with just about anything he likes, with a couple of exceptions. DO NOT feed your dog onions (which cause damage to his red blood cells) or grapes and raisins (which are toxic to his kidneys—we'll cover these and some other foods to keep away from your dog when we discuss diet on Day 23). Here are a few suggestions:

Gold Treats	Silver Treats	Bronze Treats
Chicken, beef, salmon (just be sure to wash off any spices or barbecue sauce), cold cuts, moist dog treats, string cheese, hot dogs	Yogurt, cottage cheese, wet dog food, healthy commercial dog treats, lung treats	Dog kibble (which you can mix with freeze-dried liver powder in a Ziploc bag or just use plain), fruit, and vegetables (no raisins, grapes, or onions)

THE LAS VEGAS METHOD

Imagine that, during a trip to Las Vegas, you receive a visit from a gambling genie. He grants you a magical power: Every time you play a slot machine, you're going to win. And you're always going to win the same amount.

What would you do next? You'd probably run down to the casino, full of excitement, and pull the first lever you saw. You might jump up and down as the bells ring and the coins pour out of the machine. As soon as you collect your winnings, you might run to the next available machine to try it again. And again. You might even stay up all night playing.

But after a few days (okay, *weeks*), the machines wouldn't seem as exciting. You'd move on to other activities, maybe spending some of your newfound riches.

Pretty soon, you'd hardly want to play the slots at all. Behavioral research shows that you'd probably settle into a pattern where you played just often enough to fill your bank account and spent the rest of the time doing other things.

The same reasoning applies to giving treats to a dog. If the pleasures become too predictable, your dog may start to ignore the rewards, making coaching less effective. In fact, as he starts to look for new ways to create the old excitement, his behavior might wind up getting worse.

The famous behaviorist B. F. Skinner discovered that when training animals, regular rewards gradually lose their effectiveness over time. The key to keeping the training going is to provide *random* rewards. It's the same principle that makes slot machines so effective—once you've won (or even seen someone else win), the memory of the jackpot is enough to keep you going back for more. I use the same thinking when coaching dogs. I call it the "Las Vegas Method."

Over the years, I've noticed that many dogs turn away from their owners after three treats. Why? Because their owners have fallen into the habit of giving three treats at a time. If you want to keep your dog interested, it's *critical* to vary the number of treats according to the difficulty level of the behavior and the dog's execution. Don't fall into the "three treats trap"!

As soon as a dog has learned a particular behavior, I'll stop giving him treats every time he repeats it. I'll keep smiling and praising him, but only occasionally will I reward him with a "jackpot." The chance that his behavior might result in a jackpot is enough for your dog to keep that behavior going. (Remember: A jackpot is an unpredictable amount of an unpredictable treat.)

The key is not to make the switch from steady rewards to the Las Vegas Method until your dog has really mastered the desired behavior. Some will catch on in a few minutes. Others may take a few days. You'll know he's ready when you get him to repeat that behavior with regular consistency.

By the way, just because your dog can repeat a behavior in a certain place doesn't mean he's mastered the behavior. You may teach your dog to sit on the rug in the living room, only to find that he's unable to transfer that behavior to a spot only a few feet away. If you've taught your dog to sit in the living room, try getting him to sit in another room, in the yard, or in the street. Teaching your dog to repeat a behavior in different places improves his mastery over that behavior.

Finally, no matter how good your dog gets at a particular behavior, you never want to stop rewarding that behavior altogether. If a dog (or a person) stops getting acknowledged or rewarded for doing something good, chances are he's going to realize that the particular behavior doesn't pay off anymore and will look for opportunities to do something that does. Everybody wants and needs a little acknowledgment, even if it's just once in a while, as long as it's in the form of a jackpot.

"SIT" (LEVEL ONE)

"Sit" is the first of three behaviors—along with "come" and "leave it"—that I consider to be the core behaviors that every dog should master. "Sit" is the foundation of nearly every other behavior you'll teach your dog. It's the equivalent of teaching a toddler to say "please." Almost all of the other behaviors we'll teach your dog will require him to sit first.

The fastest way to teach a dog to sit is to use the "magnet" method. First, test the "magnet" by holding a treat in front of your dog's nose and moving it from

Testing the "magnet"

right to left. Your dog should start following it with his nose. (If he's jumping at the treat, you're probably holding it too high—bring it down to his nose or mouth level.)

Now slowly raise the treat away from your dog's nose,

Moving the doggy into a "sit"

just an inch or so above his head, moving toward his tail. As his eyes follow it upward, his head will move backward, and his body will naturally drop into a "sit." (If he's backing away from the treat, try practicing the behavior in a corner.)

Quickly say, "Siiiiiiit," and reward him with the treat and a small jackpot. You'll be amazed by how quickly he'll catch on! Be sure to practice it in different rooms throughout the house, particularly by the front door, which can be a very distract-

"Sit": hand signal

ing and exciting place for most dogs.

DAY 4

CHEWING, NIPPING, AND THE POWER OF PLAY

Today, we'll learn why, for dogs (and children), play is serious business. I'll also show you how to use toys and treats to help prevent nipping and chewing, and you'll teach your dog the second important core behavior: "come."

THE POWER OF PLAY

"Tamar, do you know your hair is decorated in snot?"

The question came from a friend of mine who had just entered the hut in Fiji where I was playing with a group of young girls. Or rather they were playing with me. My blond hair must have seemed quite exotic to them, because they couldn't keep their hands out of it. Except when they were wiping their noses, which seemed to be perpetually running. The snot that wasn't crusting around their nostrils was being rubbed straight into my hair. My friend was clearly horrified by the sight.

I wasn't exactly pleased either, but while my instincts told me to jump up screaming, I made a conscious decision to smile. I didn't want to correct the kids for having such a good time taking care of me, their guest, and I knew that they were only exhibiting a healthy curiosity (well, maybe *healthy* is the wrong word) about the world. There'd be plenty of time to take a shower (or six!) later. Right now, the girls and I were sharing a moment of connection through the power of play. And there was no way I was going to let a little thing like hygiene cut it short.

There's nothing more natural to intelligent creatures than play. It's a safe context for trying out new things. There are rules to keep us safe, and mistakes are tolerated. We learn to connect with one another, and to reconnect when our relationships become strained or tense. Play leads to laughter, which (to paraphrase the old expression) cures just about everything.

Playfulness is a vital part of who we are as human beings. But for many of us, "playtime" is something we had as children. Now we are adults, with jobs, responsibilities, and stresses. We've forgotten how to play, at least with the kind of passion and consistency we had as kids.

Dogs, like kids, love to play. Clyde—my thirteen-year-old Doberman mix—is never too tired for games. He loves catch, fetch, and tug-of-war, three great ways to connect with your dog (we'll cover these on Days 7 and 16). Clyde has even invented his own game to play with me when I'm too tired to get off the couch: He lets a ball hang loosely off the side of his mouth, and when I try to flick it out, he squeezes it tightly to stop me. When I do manage to knock it out of his mouth, he kind of cracks up and happily retrieves the ball and starts again. We can play this way for hours.

As I said earlier in the book, play isn't a mere game or pastime for dogs. It's the way that wolf cubs learn how to survive, discovering their place in the pecking order, the social rules, and the skills they need to hunt. When we play with our dogs, they learn how to make humanlike choices, feel safe, and experience so much joy. When we don't, they may start to feel lonely, empty, and bored. They revert to their survival instincts—their wolf instincts. They start to look for other ways to get attention that aren't necessarily appreciated by most people.

I received a call from an owner who was worried that his dog, a sheepdog mix, was becoming increasingly anxious and "out of control." The owner felt that he took good care of the animal, feeding him well and grooming him once a week, but every time he walked through the front door, the dog jumped on him. And no matter how much he yelled at him, or how many times he punished him by sending him outside or to the garage, his dog just wasn't getting the message.

When I hear about scenarios like this one, my heart breaks. It was the owner who wasn't getting the message! The dog was looking for a connection with the most important figure in his life, greeting him in the playful way that dogs instinctively greet one another. But instead of celebrating a joyous moment with his owner, he was rebuffed. Of course the dog was anxious—he was being punished for exercising his most vital instincts. He was never shown any proper outlet or given any alternatives for taking care of his seven basic needs. He just got a "No!"

It's not always easy to play with our dogs. The games our dogs (and kids) want us to play sometimes seem boring or as if they make no sense. When we get home at the end of a long, exhausting workday, the last thing we want to do is something silly or nonsensical. The idea of "playtime" might make us even more stressed, tired, or cranky.

The truth is that playtime requires its own set of "muscles" that, for most of us, aren't as strong as they used to be. But they're still there, waiting for us to learn (or remember!) how to balance real-life demands with silly ways of playful connecting. Dogs can be a catalyst for us. Tuning into their hearts and minds, tuning into their needs, can help us to tune into our own. Which, in the end, may be one of the greatest gifts that dogs give their owners: a chance to reconnect with their spirit of play.

DOG TOYS

Human beings usually associate the word "play" with toys. This isn't true for dogs, at least not instinctively. There aren't any toys in the wild but many objects become toys. When a dog comes across an unfamiliar object, her first impulse is often to do what a wolf would do: pick it up and chew on it, or if necessary, "kill it." It's no wonder that the first few days with any new dog are littered (literally) with torn-up shoes and stuffed animals whose synthetic guts have been spilled all over the floor. Or curtains and couches—many dogs are natural-born interior decorators, albeit with questionable taste. Many unsuspecting owners discover that their arms and legs are also fair game, receiving war wounds from their playful puppies.

These are all great reasons for teaching your dog how to play with toys. Toys are also a great vehicle for helping you to connect with your dog. And when you're not around or are too busy to play with your dog, toys can help keep her happy and mentally stimulated.

Dog toys fall into two basic categories: chew toys and play toys.

CHEW TOYS (OCCUPIERS)

I can't tell you how many clients ask me how to get their dog to stop chewing on things. "You can't!" is my short answer.

My longer answer is that chewing is an important part of a dog's built-in wolf instincts. They chew when they are teething. They chew to relax, release anxiety, express joy, or just pass the time. But while you can't make her stop chewing, you can redirect her, letting her exercise her instincts in a way that saves your couches from total destruction. That's where chew toys come in.

A chew toy is anything your dog can chew on—and, in some cases, even eat—without hurting herself. (Stuffed animals are *not* chew toys.) "Bully sticks" are long, rolled strips of dried meat that they can chew on for hours—just take them away when they're chewed down to a stub that can choke a dog. Pig ears are a beloved favorite, but full of fat—use them infrequently. Many dogs also love to chew ice cubes, especially on a hot day. You can make a special treat for your dog by freezing chicken soup into cubes.

My favorite chew toy is a classic: the soup bone. You can get an uncooked, heavy-duty hip or knee bone from almost any butcher. I lay them out on a big bath towel or blanket that I can wash afterward. Under no circumstances, however, should you ever give your dog a chicken bone—especially if it's been cooked.* They're too brittle, snapping apart into sharp pieces that can really cause your dog serious injury should she swallow one. In fact, to avoid danger, you should avoid any bone that has been cooked.

Not all chew toys are meant to be eaten. There are plenty of excellent durable rubber toys designed to hold treats. (Avoid toys made of vinyl or PVC—they can release chemicals that could cause serious health problems for your dog.) Your dog may not know what to do at first with a new rubber toy, but if you stuff it with a bunch of small gold treats in a way that leaves part of the food sticking out, it won't take her long to figure it out. I love the Busy Buddy line of toys that you can squeeze open and fill with treats. Some, like the Twist 'n Treat and the Squirrel Dude, allow you to manage the difficulty level—your dog will spend hours problem solving, trying to get

---

* Some in the raw foods movement contend that it's okay to give a dog a chicken bone as long as it hasn't been cooked.

the treats out of the toy, a great way to keep her occupied if you're going to be out of the house for a few hours. Get a few of each to keep your dog occupied—it's much cheaper than a babysitter!

A FEW OF THEIR FAVORITE THINGS

Some of my dog's favorite chew toys include:

Real raw marrow bones from the butcher
Busy Buddy Twist 'n Treat (by Premier)
Busy Buddy Squirrel Dude (by Premier)
Bully sticks (braided or unbraided)
Cow hooves
Antlers

Please DO NOT use rawhide bones. Dogs can chew them faster than they can digest them. Many vets have told me that one of their most common surgeries involves cutting open a dog's tummy to remove rawhide, which can obstruct the gastrointestinal system. These treats may be inexpensive to buy, but they can wind up being super expensive to get rid of!

It's important NOT to leave all of the chew toys lying around on the floor, as your dog will get bored with them and will look for random opportunities to chew on something new, usually something that costs a fortune to replace. Let your dog play with one or two at a time, regularly rotating both the toys themselves and the treats you use for stuffing them.

When I'm leaving for a while, I like to set up a treasure hunt game for my dogs. I ask them to "stay"—you can ask someone to hold your dog on a leash (or tether her to something) if she hasn't learned "stay" yet—and hide a few rubber toys filled with treats around the house. Then I praise the dogs for staying and, as I walk out the front door, tell them, "No more!" and "Take it!" As I close the door behind me, I'll see them sprinting off to find the hidden treasures. It's a great feeling knowing that they're playing a fun game instead of whining, crying, or stressing out because I'm gone.

Best of all, it helps to associate my departure with something pleasurable (a game) instead of painful (separation anxiety). Many dogs associate their "parents" departing with pain—the treasure hunt game helps to build an association with pleasure. Stuff a few toys with treats, "torturing" your dog by not giving her any, and instead of thinking, "Please don't leave me alone," she'll be begging you to just go already!

WHAT TO DO WITH A DOG WHO CHEWS FORBIDDEN THINGS

Make sure that the seven basic needs are being met, especially exercise and mental stimulation.

Make sure that your dog has interesting chew toys. Rotate them regularly, vary the kinds of treats, and choose ones that are of high quality.

Observe your own behavior. When you grab an object out of a dog's mouth, you're not necessarily teaching her not to chew that object—you're showing her that having that object is the best way to get your attention. (Or worse: that she needs to be sneaky!) When your dog is chewing on something forbidden, it's usually for one of three reasons: out of boredom, to get your attention, or because she doesn't like any of the chew toys she has. If it's attention-seeking behavior, ignore her, turn your back, or literally leave the room until she realizes that she's not getting your attention and drops the object. When she does, quickly replace the object with a suitable chew toy. More often, however, she's simply lost interest in the chew toys she has: Vary the selection and improve the quality. I've been to homes that have enough bully sticks in different shapes to open their own pet store, but no other toys!

Set booby traps. Spray an old shoe with something that tastes terrible, like bitter orange, and leave it on the floor next to a proper chew toy stuffed with treats. Let your dog come to her own conclusions.

Don't let your dog use an old shoe as a chew toy. She won't be able to distinguish it from a new shoe. Also, a rope that has fringe can confuse a dog who lives in a home that has rugs with fringe.

Use a pheromone calming collar and a few drops of Rescue Remedy if you think the excessive chewing might be stress-related. (We'll talk about these products, which you can get from many pet or health food stores, on Day 17.)

PLAY TOYS

These are the toys that will really allow your dog to express her inner wolf and bond with you via games like tug-of-war and fetch (which we'll come back to on Days 7 and 16 respectively). Play toys should only be used under supervision, when your dog is playing with you or another dog. When the game's over, make sure you say, "No more," and put the toy away. You want your dog to know that this is your toy, one that you're kindly allowing her to play with—later, we'll talk about what these games mean to a dog and why you don't want to leave toys lying around until you're certain she's "elected" you as her leader.

NIPPING

Nipping is a completely natural and instinctive wolf behavior that doesn't translate well to the human world. Dogs nip at one another as an invitation to play (and while they're playing), unaware of just how painful their teeth can be for us. Particularly those sharp puppy teeth!

I generally won't address nipping until I'm sure a dog has had the chance to exercise her wolf instincts, whether through a good run/hike or playing with other dogs. Nipping is often just an invitation to wrestle, your dog's way of telling you that her basic need for physical and mental stimulation, as well as companionship, isn't being met. However, playing wrestling games with your dog actually teaches her that it's fun to nip people, something I highly discourage for obvious reasons.

Once I'm sure that a dog has had plenty of exercise, I deal

with nipping by introducing her to activities that guide her instincts into humanlike choices, such as:

- Redirecting her teeth toward an exciting chew toy
- Asking her to "leave it" (see Day 6)
- Asking her for "kisses" (see below)
- Playing a fun, vigorous game of tug-of-war (see Day 7)

Sometimes nipping is a serious problem, as it was with Koda, a five-month-old German shepherd who nearly bit off her owners' fingers every time they held out a treat. The owners instinctively responded by jerking their hands away, holding the treat high above Koda's head where she couldn't reach it. Unfortunately, they were only exacerbating the problem: Koda became so anxious that she wasn't going to receive the treat that she began jumping aggressively to grab it, resulting in even more painful nips and bloody scrapes!

We wanted to teach Koda that when we gave her a treat, all we wanted to feel was her tongue, not her teeth, as if she were in church taking Communion. (I love this metaphor!) So we took turns dipping our fingers in cream cheese, holding them together below her mouth. Every time we felt even the slightest hint of teeth, we said, "Ouch!" and quickly moved our fingers away from her. We were careful not to use an angry tone of voice that might make her feel bad, but one that communicated pain, like, "How could you do that to our fingers?" We coached Koda to want to make us feel better, tapping into her built-in instinct to crave acceptance from her pack.

When she licked the cream cheese off of our hands without using her teeth, we praised Koda by saying, "Gentle," in a happy tone of voice. It took only an hour to find a solution to a serious problem that had been going on for three months. Koda's parents were going to have to practice "gentle" many more times before the behavior would become ingrained, but at least, in just one hour, they were on their way!

On the other hand, if you teach your dog "gentle" *before* there's a problem—something you can do in less than an hour—the odds are that there will never be a problem.

Sometimes "ouch" alone won't do it. If your dog repeats the biting behavior, get up immediately and leave the room, closing the door behind you in a huff. The separation and isolation will send a clear message to your overly mouthy dog. After a couple of minutes, you can try again. It may take a few repetitions before your dog connects the nipping behavior with losing you, but if you stay patient and consistent, and give your dog some time, it will work. (Make sure your dog does get plenty of exercise and is not frustrated for lack thereof.)

Once you've taught him not to bite your hand, you can use the same trick with your bare feet and, eventually, your face!

"KISSES"

Another similar method is to teach your dog "kisses." Find something spreadable that your dog loves to eat, like yogurt, butter, or honey. Spread a thin layer on the back of your hand and hold it out for your dog. As your dog licks the treat off your hand, repeat, "Kisses! Kisses!" in your happiest voice. If she nips at you, pull your hand away and say, "Ouch!" in a way that communicates your shock at the pain she just caused you. Then move your hand or foot back in for more kisses.

NIPPING AND KIDS

When it comes to nipping, children are often the biggest victims. Their usual reaction—high-pitched screams and/or running away—can confuse a dog into thinking it's a game.

I don't want any kids in the vicinity when I start coaching a dog to stop nipping, but once she's at least 75 percent of the way to understanding "gentle," I like to let the kids get involved in the process. In another room, away from the dog, I'll role-play with the children, playfully air-nipping at their fingers. I teach them how to say "Ouch!" in a stern voice instead of screaming and running away. In severe cases, I'll "arm" the kid with a small spray bottle filled with water (or watered-down baby shampoo if the dog likes being sprayed)—if the dog doesn't respond to the "ouch," the child can spray the dog and say, "Leave it."

"COME"

"Come" is the second of the three most important core behaviors. It's my favorite behavior to teach when kids are involved because it's so much like a game of hide-and-seek, giving children a chance to communicate with a dog in a way that's familiar.

The best time to teach this game is before feeding your dog breakfast or dinner, so you know she'll be hungry. All you have to do is approach your dog, say, "Come," and give her a treat. After you've repeated this a few times, move a few feet to the side and call your dog by her name only until she approaches you. When she gets right next to you, smile big and enthusiastically *repeat* the word "commmmme" as you quickly reward her with a jackpot. When you're done, say, "No more!"

"No more": hand signal

Now move to a different place in the same room and call your dog's name. It's super important to use a tone of voice that your dog registers as "Come and see the surprise I've got for you!" instead of "Get your butt over here now!" Your dog will want to reexperience the earlier jackpot and will come running over to you. When she does, say, "Commmme," and give her another jackpot until there's "No more." Keep changing locations.

Look for more challenging opportunities to practice "come," like when your dog seems interested in something else. It's a good idea to keep stashes of treats around the house so you can reward your dog during these spontaneous sessions. (When your dog sees you carrying treats, she'll usually know that something's up and will probably be paying close attention to you. You want your dog to come when she's NOT paying close attention to you.) "Come" is also a great game to play with a (human) friend—each of you can "hide" in different spots throughout the house/apartment/park/wherever and take turns calling your dog. Just make sure each of you has a handful of treats ready when she arrives.

As you'll see throughout the book, it's great to practice a behavior in as many different environments as you can because you'll help to generalize that behavior, teaching your dog that it's something you want her to do everywhere, as opposed to something she associates with a specific place.

If you're having trouble getting your dog to come to

you when you call, she's probably still undecided as to whether you represent pain or pleasure. When I was on a tight schedule with Oprah's two dogs, I sped up the process by doing all of their feeding by hand—they came when I called because they were hungry. Once they started to realize that I was calling them for fun reasons—to go for a walk, to get a toy, to have a drink of water, etc.—and began to come without hesitation, we moved their feedings into bowls.

NAMES ARE SACRED

It's crucial to remember to use your dog's name *only* when talking to him. When you use it in situations where it's not meant for him—like when you're talking about your dog on the phone to a friend—you are teaching him that he doesn't need to jump to attention when he hears you say his name. It was the cutest thing to see little Sunny or Lauren Winfrey rolling in the grass or sniffing something on their mom's flowing property, only to stop whatever they were doing on a dime the moment they heard me calling their names and dash over with big smiles on their gorgeous faces.

In order to avoid saying the dog's name when talking about him you need to give him nicknames. When you're talking *about* him and he's in earshot, use nicknames— "the puppy," "the hairy one," "the tornado," and "my son/daughter" all work. Sunny and Lauren Winfrey were "the spotted one" and "the explorer."

When you say your dog's name, and he immediately lifts his head to look at you, eyes full of expectation, you know you are in great shape!

DAY 5

SOCIALIZATION, PART I

You should continue to practice sit, come, take it, kisses, ouch, and no more whenever you can, but today is the first of two that we'll dedicate to socialization, probably the most important thing you can do with a dog.

BASIC SOCIALIZATION

I was in Fiji, sitting with Taiyo, my friend's eighteen-month-old boy, and his nanny Jo. We were playing with blocks, but Taiyo seemed much more interested in the Band-Aid on Jo's leg. "No!" Jo kept repeating as Taiyo reached out to touch it, but that didn't stop him from trying again and again.

Many of us might be inclined to see Taiyo's behavior as stubborn or annoying, but in this particular moment, he reminded me more of a curious puppy.

"Band-Aid!" I announced in a singsong voice and with a smile. "It's a Band-Aid!"

Taiyo looked at me, the wheels in his brain clearly whirring, trying to digest this new information. He pointed at the Band-Aid again. "Band-Aid, Taiyo," I repeated. "Band-Aid." Content with my answer, Taiyo went back to playing with Jo and me, his curiosity sated . . . about the Band-Aid, anyway. I continued to call out the names of the different shapes and colors of his blocks, a simple interaction that seemed to fill Taiyo with delight.

On the surface, it might seem like Taiyo was simply learning new words. But on a deeper level, he was engaging in "socialization," the process we use to learn how to give meaning to our world. As I named each object, Taiyo was registering my attitude toward it. The singsong voice told him it was something good and that I was pleased by his curiosity, his desire to explore and learn. If I had said no or otherwise discouraged him, I'd miss an opportunity to help Taiyo create a positive association with this particular object, so I grabbed two Band-Aids and placed one on Taiyo's foot and one on my foot. It's also incredibly important to reward exploration—we want our children and dogs to want to learn, a much tougher task if curiosity is associated with rejection and pain.

For dogs, the stakes are even higher: Socialization is their most important survival tool in human society. Every time your dog encounters a new person, object, or situation, he's asking himself a simple question: What is the meaning of this? Will this new person/object/situation cause me pain or pleasure? Oftentimes, dogs—like many people—assume that the unknown is going to be painful.

Without proper socialization, a dog may grow up to experience anything new or unknown as a potential source of pain. For most dogs, that fear manifests itself as nervous aggression, a defense mechanism ("offense is the best defense") that is often tragically misdiagnosed as "dominance." When a conventional trainer or alpha-minded owner tries to "correct" that dominance with power or fear, he actually reinforces the dog's anxieties instead of curing them. Socialization can change a dog's sense of meaning and point of view from pain to pleasure. Corrections, on the other hand, encourage a dog to strengthen his defenses, turning him into a ticking time bomb with a one-way ticket to the animal shelter.

When a dog who hasn't been socialized to children is suddenly introduced to a tiny humanlike creature who doesn't respect his personal space, tugging on his tail or poking at his eyes, the dog tries to warn the child in the only way he knows how—through body language. He licks his lips, yawns, looks away, tries to walk away, or freezes. Still, the child—who doesn't know how to read a dog's body language—continues to provoke the dog, so the dog growls. That's when all hell breaks loose—the dog gets yelled at, or worse, smacked, and sent away to think about his behavior. The next time the dog encounters the child, he knows that he's not supposed to growl. So the next time the situation begins to escalate, the dog—who's now even more stressed because he doesn't have any way to ward off the toddler or alert an adult to the situation—may bite the kid instead.

Just today, I talked with a woman about Jake, her fifteen-month-old German shorthaired pointer, who had been barking and snapping at people. The previous trainer, who had visited her home, advised her that Jake was exhibiting dominant behavior and that she needed to exert more control over her dog.

Here we go with the dominance nonsense again, I thought, taking a deep breath. "Has he ever been aggressive toward your family?" I asked her.

"No," she replied.

"How about the people he knows well?"

"No. It's really just the gardeners and the pool man. Sometimes when we have guests."

"Is he acting as if he's lunging aggressively, but mostly he's actually backing away?"

"That's exactly what he does," she said.

"Let me ask you something," I continued. "Imagine that you see a woman on the street, screaming like crazy and kicking a man. Would you call her 'aggressive'?"

"I don't know. Probably."

"Now what if I told you the man was trying to steal her purse and that she was only trying to defend herself. Would that change your opinion?"

"Of course!" she replied.

I explained that if Jake was really "dominant," he'd be acting aggressively toward everyone and certainly wouldn't be backing away. The fact that he was only behaving that way with strangers suggested that he was acting out of fear or self-defense; strangers represented the unknown, the possibility of pain. Like most dogs, he'd probably tried aggression a few times—barking at gardeners who, wisely, backed away from him—learning that he could use this kind of fake aggressive behavior to make disappear whatever was causing him anxiety.

We socialized Jake in the manner described in Day 10, and within two weeks he was so nice to the people he previously acted aggressively toward. Socialization is all about alleviating these anxieties before they cause a dog to act aggressively. Exposing your dog to anyone, anything, and everything that he might encounter in his lifetime while you give him his favorite treats and toys helps him to associate these situations with good, pleasurable feelings instead of anxious, worrying ones. If your dog is raised to believe that children aren't annoying, unpredictable, or dangerous, but to love kids, to associate them with the best feelings in life, your dog will probably never behave aggressively toward children.

The more you socialize your dog, the more he'll begin to associate *anything* new with the possibility of pleasure instead of pain. It's the most important thing you can do to help nurture a happy, well-balanced dog who can handle whatever life throws his way. The best way to get started is by simply narrating the things you do, giving names to household objects, new activities, and startling noises in a happy and enthusiastic voice, and following up with treats. (We'll get more into socialization on Day 10, when we'll talk about preparing your dog for more specific situations.)

Narration isn't just important for socialization; it's also a great coaching tool. Naming specific behaviors, objects, people, and places for your dog, even when you're not in an active coaching mode, helps "prime the pump" for teaching new behaviors and reinforces the ones he's already learned. For example, saying "down" every time your dog is lying down or "drink" every time he's drinking water makes it easier for your dog to associate that word with the behavior.

Socialization is an incredibly important and ongoing process that lasts a lifetime. When dogs live in a state of habitual fear or stress, their nervous systems become strained, which weakens their immune systems. In other words, not socializing your dog is literally dangerous to his health. We'll come back to this concept again, in a lot more detail, on Day 10.

DAY 6

NONVERBAL COMMUNICATION

Today you're going to teach your dog the third core behavior, "leave it," and how a "shallow waters" approach can make any coaching more effective. But first, we're going to take a quick look at the importance of good nonverbal communication.

YOUR FACE IS AN OPEN BOOK, BUT WHAT ARE YOU READING?

I was in the Hamptons at my friend Kristina's house, working in the kitchen with her three-month-old Australian shepherd puppy, Holden. It was a gray, drizzly day, and Kristina was tired. She'd begun the morning with an early wake-up call—Holden, jumping on the bed—and now, as she tried to get him to engage in even the simplest behaviors, he seemed to have less interest than usual in the coaching process. Kristina was normally a sweet, smiling, and energetic woman, but her spirits were low that day, as she was obviously exhausted. "I just don't know what's wrong with Holden today," she said.

So I gave it a try. Almost immediately, Kristina and I could see a huge difference in Holden's behavior. The dog was acting superbly. "No, I didn't sprinkle magic fairy dust on your dog," I later said to Kristina. "It's not the dog. It's what the two of you are like as a team. And you're sixty percent of that team."

Holden's "problem" was a response to Kristina's exhaustion. She was having a low-energy morning. Her normal happiness and enthusiasm were missing. Even if she wasn't aware of the difference in her demeanor, Holden was. He didn't understand why she wasn't smiling. He'd become a little anxious, worried that he'd perhaps done something wrong, and he tried to do all that he could to engage her in play, which is the way dogs connect with one another.

Dogs don't only react to the things we say. They are much more aware than any human observer of our body language, facial expressions, tone of voice, the way we're breathing, and even our silent pauses. When a dog behaves in a way that's different from what we hoped or expected, it's possible that he's reacting to something we're not aware of doing—or something we're *not* doing.

Human beings are often unaware of their own body language. I was once at a seminar where I noticed that many of the people in the audience looked bored or angry. During a break, I asked a few of them if there was something about the seminar that they didn't like. All of them were surprised by the question. They weren't bored or angry in the slightest, they told me, but focused on what the speaker was saying.

I began to realize that a lot of people, when listening to information they think is important, actually look upset. I took a few pictures with my cell phone of people listening to the seminar and showed them the photos during the next break. They were surprised by the disconnection: Their facial expressions conveyed something completely different from what they were actually feeling.

Try this exercise: Stand in front of a mirror and try to look like you do when you're deeply focused on something. Now try to look as if you're seeing something that really meets your approval. Are the facial expressions different? Try it again looking thrilled.

Dogs look to our faces for cues—do we approve of what they are doing? If it looks to them like the answer is no, many dogs will try something else in an effort to make us happy or, at the very least, engaged. Often that means giving us a "buffet" of all the behaviors they've learned from us, or reverting to their wolf instincts. This is the reason I never wear sunglasses when I'm coaching a dog. Sunglasses are great for the Secret Service, military personnel, and professional poker players who want to keep their feelings to themselves. But you wouldn't wear them when going on a date, would you? When you're coaching a dog, you *want* him to tap into your feelings. And your eyes are one of the most powerful ways of communicating those feelings.

More important, when you're happy with your dog, remember to smile! Your clear approval will make your dog feel more secure in his connection to you.

THE POWER OF SILENCE

One of the best nonverbal techniques you can use with your dog is exactly that: nonverbal. It's much harder to figure out the solution to a problem when someone is standing over your shoulder and nagging you. That's exactly how your dog feels when you repeat the same command over and over without offering any new information or space in which to think. Silence is a sign of respect for your dog, especially when he's trying to figure out a new behavior. Dogs—like people—appreciate time to think, to process, to put two and two together. We all learn in different ways, but everyone needs a little peace and quiet when he or she is trying to connect the dots.

"LEAVE IT!"

Many owners try to teach "leave it!"—the third of the three most important "foundation" behaviors—the hard way. It's usually introduced in a frustrated or angry tone of voice, as the dog is running off with a favorite shoe or nosing around a dead animal, when we're asking him to give something up. That dead animal might look nasty to you, but to the wolf part of your dog, it's GREAT—something he can roll around in to get rid of that "new-bath smell." Losing it feels painful to your dog. We want him to associate "leave it" with pleasure, not pain.

It's important not to confuse "leave it" with "drop it" (see Day 7), which I say when I want a dog to let go of something that he's already holding. "Leave it" is a request to your dog to override his wolf instincts—to choose not to sniff a person or a dead animal, or put something in his mouth, because you've asked him not to—by moving his head away from whatever it is he finds interesting. It's very useful when taking a dog on a walk.

Teaching this behavior couldn't be simpler: As long as you remember to make it fun. Kneel down in front of him and place a treat on the floor without saying anything. When your dog goes to inspect the treat, cover it with your hand. Don't say a word to your dog until he looks away, looks at you, or shows any disinterest—even if it's accidental. The instant he does, say, "Leave it!" and reward him with a jackpot of tiny treats from your storage hand, NOT the treat on the floor (which you should quickly cover again if he makes a move for it—it may feel scary to lift the hand that covers the treat in order to reward him with a jackpot, but you're faster than you think. When standing, use your foot if you really don't think you can cover it again in time, but it's very important to expose the treat while you're rewarding him with the jackpot so that your dog understands the decision that he's made).

While it may be a simple behavior to teach, "leave it" has profound implications. When a dog makes a decision to look at our faces instead of a treat, we are witnessing a huge triumph of choice over instinct. He is letting go of thousands of years of DNA programming just to see what it is we want him to do. It's a great opportunity to recognize how much dogs want to understand us, how much they are willing to sacrifice for us, how badly they want to be on "our" team, and the extent to which they look to us for guidance.

After a few repetitions, you can start saying "leave it" before your dog turns his focus away from the treat on the floor. You'll be amazed by how fast he catches on once he realizes that it's much more pleasurable to look at you than to nose around a treat he's never going to get anyway— some dogs will master the behavior in less than five minutes. Your dog is going to learn to love "leaving it" because when he does, an even better experience is waiting for him.

Once your dog gets the hang of it, move from kneeling to a standing position (unless you were already standing) and repeat the game a few more times. It's also great to get the kids involved—even dogs who live in a kids-free household should learn to "leave it" when asked by kids.

As with other behaviors, the more you generalize it, the more powerful it will become. Practice "leave it" whenever you can with toys or household items, people, and—the ultimate challenge—keeping your dog away from other dogs while you're on a walk. I use this behavior more than any other when dealing with aggression toward other dogs during walks. The dogs I'm working with absolutely love it! Maybe they're feeling the triumph of nurture over nature.

THE "SHALLOW WATERS" APPROACH

Imagine you want to teach a child how to swim. Is the best way (a) to place her in the middle of the ocean or the deep end of the pool and show her how to move her arms and legs; or (b) to introduce her to swimming in shallow water, build a comfort level, and gradually encourage her to move toward the deep end?

When you're trying to teach something to a child, a dog, or even an adult, you're going to get your best results when your student is in a relaxed and relatively undistracted environment and state of mind. Neither of those things is going to be true for a novice swimmer in the middle of the ocean, who will probably be too concerned about survival to pay careful attention to your lesson. You've got to be compassionate—six feet of water may not seem like a big deal to you, but a non-swimmer might find it absolutely terrifying.

You can use the same logic to tailor your approach when you want to get a dog to stop barking at a squirrel, digging up a flower bed, or chewing your curtains. You want him to "leave it," but unless your dog has already mastered this behavior, you're expecting him to perform while he's highly distracted and emotionally invested in whatever activity you're trying to prevent. So why not start him in shallow water instead?

Here's an example, using the "leave it" behavior.

1. **Introduce "leave it" when your dog is relaxed and undistracted.** Practice in a quiet room when your dog is well rested after exercising, well fed (the opposite of the condition I like to use when teaching "come"), and eager to learn. Start by teaching your dog to leave a treat alone, then use the behavior to get him to ignore other objects, like shoes or a ball.

2. **Add distractions.** Involve your dog in something moderately distracting. Ask your dog to "take it" a few times, then surprise him with a "leave it." When he does, "make a party" and reward him with a jackpot.

3. **Move to the deep end.** Ask a friend to walk your dog, someplace where you can see them, near that flower bed he likes to dig in or the squirrels he always barks at. The moment your dog starts to dig or bark—don't let him work himself into

a frenzy—say, "Leave it," reward him, call his name in an inviting voice, and ask him to "Come." When he does, reward him with a humongous jackpot of gold treats, and keep repeating "Come" until the flower bed or squirrels are forgotten.

HAND SIGNALS

I was visiting with Brad Paisley and his wife, Kim Williams, who had taught Huck, their (human) one-year-old, how to "speak" using sign language. I was blown away. Huck was very expressive, telling us so many things, and seemed free from the frustration that comes with being misunderstood.

When you think about it, dogs don't use words to communicate with one another—they use body language. As a result, they have a keen eye for hand signals, which you can teach your dog in conjunction with the words you use to describe particular behaviors. Not only are the hand signals easier to understand, but they also provide extra mental stimulation for your dog and are really useful if you've got a sleeping baby in the house, or you're in the middle of a conversation and don't want to interrupt whoever's speaking.

Hand signals can't replace words—just try signaling your dog to "come" when you're standing behind him at the dog park—but they're often easier to teach and will help you and your dog to better communicate with each other. You can follow the hand signals that come with some behaviors as I describe in this book, but you can also have fun and come up with your own hand signals.

DAY 7

THE BEST GAME OF ALL

Parenting has changed a lot over the years. Ever watch the TV show *Mad Men*? When we see depictions of life in the 1960s, we realize it wasn't too long ago that most parents believed "children should be seen, not heard" and relied on fear and punishment to maintain order in their households.

Nowadays, many experts in childhood development have completely changed the script. Parenting isn't just about discipline, but also about development and empowerment. We want our children to explore, to feel encouraged, and to have secure attachments to their parents and the world around them. Gone are the days of despots and tyrants—now it's all about play, getting down on the floor with your kids and engaging them in games. Play gives us the ability to coach in a way that's pleasurable—children learn to act the right way because it's FUN to act the right way.

Dogs benefit from the same strategy. They don't have to be taught how to play—all you have to do is observe wolves in the wild to see how they use games to teach critically important survival skills. Long before the cubs join the hunt, they've learned how to chase their prey (by chasing one another), wrestle it to the ground (a skill they've learned by playfully wrestling with one another), and tug at the prey to break its neck and get their fair share of the meal (by practicing on fallen tree branches, roots, or dried bones). It's no coincidence that most dogs' three favorite games are chase, wrestling, and tug-of-war.

Unfortunately, the first two games don't really help us to teach our dogs "human" manners; in fact, they can interfere with the process. When you play "chase" with your dog, you are actually teaching that it's fun to run away from you. Wrong game if you want him to dash over to you when you call. And wrestling with your dog can be dangerous—like wolves, dogs like to use their teeth. If a dog thinks that wrestling is a behavior he's rewarded for, he might also think it's appropriate to wrestle with a child or a stranger who he wants to befriend.

But the third activity—tugging at prey—couldn't be a better tool for teaching your dog manners. I'm not suggesting you get on the floor and fight your dog for his food. But tug-of-war is one of the best games—if not THE best game—for developing a strong bond with your dog, teaching important manners, maintaining total control when he's at his "wolfiest," and, of course, having fun. Tug-of-war will:

- Help your dog to release his pent-up energy
- Allow your dog to safely express his wolf instincts
- Give you total control over your dog when he's at his "wolfiest"
- Show your dog that you are a coach who can be trusted
- Get him to give something up willingly
- Make your dog fall madly in love with you!

Some trainers believe that tug-of-war should be avoided, as it encourages your dog to be aggressive. That's the 1960s *Mad Men* way of thinking. We know a lot more today about what makes dogs tick and how to work with them more effectively. If you play the game properly, you'll actually be helping your dog to become calmer, more relaxed, and more likely to behave in a well-mannered way by making conscious choices. Tug-of-war helps a dog to channel his natural wolflike instincts into a controlled, socially acceptable activity. While I don't recommend playing tug-of-war with dogs that seem abnormally aggressive—they may be "resource guarding," a problem behavior we'll address on Day 10—most dogs will quickly become addicted to the game, transforming the tug toy into a remote control (particularly if it has a squeaker) that allows you to gently take command of almost any situation.

Playing tug-of-war correctly involves following a few basic rules:

1. YOU must initiate the game. Don't force your dog to play—invite him! Lay a sturdy plush squeaky toy on the ground next to him. Most dogs are more interested if the game starts on the floor, where your dog is hardwired to look for prey, than in the air around his head. Imagine that the toy is a rat, and wiggle it around on the ground using jerky motions. Keep your eyes on the toy, not your dog, and make happy noises, the way you would with a baby. Act as if nothing would bring you more pleasure than catching that pesky rodent.

As soon as your dog tries even the lightest tug, even if you barely feel the pressure from him, let go of the toy. Tell him, "You won!" in a praising tone of voice. You want your dog to feel like he's so strong that even a mild tug is enough to "win" the toy from you. Give him the toy and start again right away, but this time the toy will be in your dog's mouth, not on the floor. You can gradually build to tougher and tougher pulls, and he'll get it in no time.

If your dog seems completely disinterested in the "rat" on the floor, you may have to build his enthusiasm first. Keep the toy with you in any situation when your dog is naturally excited, like when he first sees you coming home through the door. "Make a party" and reward him with a treat the moment he shows any interest in the toy. Some older dogs who were taught that it's wrong to play with kids' toys or to hold things in their mouths will take a little longer to become comfortable with a toy that they're actually allowed to use.

2. **You have to win the game (about 90 percent of the time).** However, during the early coaching phase, it's essential to let your dog win most of the time. Why? You're trying to show your dog that you're a fun person to play with. Dogs, like

kids, will quickly become frustrated or bored by a game that they feel they can't win. On the other hand, they'll be excited to play with someone who makes them feel strong and smart.

Once you've established yourself as a fun and trusted coach—and your dog is hooked on the game—you can start to win a little more often. Tug-of-war isn't just a meaningless game—in the wolf pack, it determines who gets the largest share of the meal and helps to define the pecking order. Eventually, you're going to want to win most of the time, giving you a pleasurable way to establish your benevolent leadership without rubbing your dog's nose in it. Ideally, you're going to want your dog to get to a point where he's happy to relinquish his resources to you, whether it's the tug-of-war toy or a juicy bone. (We'll get to "drop it" in a minute.)

Even then, however, you must let your dog win about 10 percent of the time. No one likes to play a game he or she can never win. Lose just often enough to keep him happy and interested, but not enough to challenge your supremacy as the coach of the team.

3. Repeat the words "play, play, play." You want your dog to know that this fun activity has a name—you can use it whenever you want your dog to come to you to play. Make sure to smile, moving your hand (with the toy) from side to side, not in a jerky motion that can hurt a dog's neck. It's a great way to teach your dog good manners while building great arms for yourself— just make sure to switch hands to get an even workout.

4. Teach your dog how to DROP. While grabbing at a toy might come easily to your dog, giving it up again may be a little harder for him to do. Once again, he needs to be patiently coached away from his instincts toward making a conscious choice. You can make it easier by teaching your dog to "Drop!" throughout the game. You'll do it in the same way that you might tell a child that she'll get ice cream . . . after she's finished her veggies. Your dog will get to play this fun game again, but he'll have to "drop" first.

"DROP"

While your dog is hanging on to the toy, silently hold a bronze or a silver treat near his mouth. Most dogs will drop the toy immediately—they'll want to make room for the treat. (Some dogs will only do it for a gold treat.) When he does, say, "Drop," and give him a treat. Then immediately ask him to "Sit" and say, "Take it," as you give him back the toy to start another fun game. You're making sure that your dog associates "drop" with pleasure (a treat and the chance to keep playing) instead of pain (the loss of his toy and the end of the game). After a couple of tries you should be able to get him to "drop" without the treat—the real reward will come when he's got the toy back in his mouth and is playing the game again.

You may find that your dog isn't interested in the toy once you've given him a treat. In that case, try the "bridge method." While you're playing the game, keep repeating "Play, play, play" with a big smile and a happy tone of voice. When you want him to "drop," stop moving your hands from side to side, erase the smile from your face, and, using a neutral tone of voice, ask your dog to "Drop." Give him a few seconds to think about it, then tell him "Drop" again. Chances are your dog will just resume the game with extra vigor, but don't despair, this is normal. He's telling you that he's having so much fun playing the game that he wants to encourage you to keep playing by going at it with extra energy. This is one of the rare times when I think it's okay to touch a dog during coaching. If he still refuses to release the toy, use your middle finger and thumb to create what I call a "bridge," which you can position over his muzzle. Applying gentle pressure against the skin on the sides of his upper lip in the little space between his front and back teeth, pull downward in a way that makes him feel like he's (lightly!) biting the inside of his own mouth. The discomfort will cause him to stop biting down so hard. His mouth will open. Gently remove the toy, enthusiastically say, "Drop," then say an immediate "Take it" while you offer the toy again with a big smile. When your dog starts to get the hang of it, you can move to the "drop, sit, take it" routine.

The point of the bridge method is never to cause your dog any pain, but to teach him this important game while showing him that dropping the toy isn't the end of the world. It usually only takes a couple of times to get your point across, and as long as you change your facial expression from a happy, singsong "play" to a deafening silence, the light touching won't make your dog dislike you or the game. If you can show your dog that he can trust you, that you'll always give him back the toy for another session of play, he will actually learn to love giving away his resources. You want to be able to use "Drop!" the way a coach uses "Time out!" when his players seem like they're getting too emotional. It's an opportunity for your dog to stop what he's doing, connect with his coach, and return to a calmer state of mind.

5. At the end of the game, you wind up with the toy. This is another instance where you need to think like a wolf: If you allow your dog to hold on to the toy at the end of the game, he is going to think that he's "won." This may sound a little petty, but it's important.

The wolf instinct part of your dog is playing for points, as it represents what will probably happen in a real-life situation after a successful hunt. If two wolves tug for control of a piece of meat, the one that winds up with the meat wins. If you leave your dog with the toy at the end of the game, he's going to think that you gave in, that he won the prize. Your dog might wonder what other privileges he can win, encouraging him to look for other opportunities to do things his way and not yours.

But don't forget that the experience is supposed to be

pleasurable. Hopefully, by the end of the game, your dog sees "drop it" as something pleasurable.

6. End the game *just before* your dog is ready to quit. As they say in show business, always leave them wanting more!

7. When you do end a game—or any other activity—it's good to have a "release word." Whether it's tug-of-war, a walk, or a handful of treats, when I decide that the activity is over, I like to hold out my palms, facing upward, and say, "No more" (even if I have more treats). It's a simple act, but it allows you to "remove the batteries," giving you a useful off switch when your dog wants to keep playing and you're ready to collapse, or when he's using his cutest face to try and convince a guest to give him food from a plate. Having an off switch allows your dog a lot more freedom to play out his wolf instincts—you know that you can stop him and redirect his focus with one word.

DOGS' EMOTIONAL COMPLEXITY

Some trainers seem to think that dominance and submission are the two most important traits to consider when you're trying to make sense of a dog's emotional state.

I think that this is a ridiculous way of looking at dogs—it's a caveman's approach, like trying to understand a person's behavior by asking only if they're happy or sad. We have a huge range of emotions—from elation and anticipation to frustration and envy—that we use to understand how people are feeling.

Recent research suggests that dogs have a similarly wide range of emotional responses. Big dogs will "handicap" themselves when playing with smaller dogs, demonstrating a sense of fair play. When Duke, my seventy-pound Labrador mix, wrestles with Biscuit, Larry King's fifteen-pound Cavalier King Charles spaniel, Duke lay on the ground to even out the playing field. When games involve nipping, dogs will let one another know when the biting gets too hard, and will even exclude "cheaters" who don't take the hint.

Dogs get jealous when they see another dog receiving what seems like preferential treatment. They get embarrassed when they make mistakes. At times, they feel hope, joy, resentment, and fear. There's even evidence that dogs know how to get a joke: When they're excited and pant rhythmically, their brain activity looks a lot like a human being who's laughing.

The more you listen to your dog—studying and empathizing with him instead of blindly demanding his obedience—the more you'll see that dogs have a surprisingly rich and complicated emotional life.

WEEK 1 REVIEW

This has probably been an exciting week for you and your dog! Hopefully you've enjoyed your fair share of successes, whether it's new learned behaviors or quiet moments of love and contemplation. You've probably encountered a few frustrating moments as well: accidents on the carpet, a favorite pair of shoes torn to shreds, a new behavior that your dog just can't seem to master. It might even feel like these frustrating moments could outweigh all of the positive experiences you've enjoyed together. You might even be afraid that there's something wrong between you and your dog. You might wonder why you haven't fallen in love.

Let me tell you: Even if you feel like you're head over heels for your dog right now, it isn't *love*. It's infatuation. Excitement. But love—*real* love—takes longer. It's a gradual process that involves two spirits growing closer to each other, learning what makes the other tick, developing a rapport and a connection.

This is the main reason you don't want to get a dog "for the kids"—children can't be expected to have the patience and follow-through for the gradual process of falling in love (not to mention the long road involved in coaching a different species to choose a completely foreign set of behaviors instead of its instincts). Once the infatuation and excitement are gone, so is their attention.

If you already feel like you're falling madly in love with your dog, then you're probably feeling great. But if you're not, here are a few things to keep in mind:

1. It's not personal. There's something about a dog who has trouble with the "come" behavior that strikes a raw nerve in many owners. When your dog doesn't sprint toward you, it hurts. If you're in public, it might feel embarrassing. Regardless of where you are, you may feel betrayed or dismissed, as if your dog doesn't love you.

You may have felt the same way—as I have—when your man comes home from work and ignores you. It's (usually) not because he doesn't love you, but because he needs what Alison Armstrong calls "transition time." Single-focus hunters need downtime to shift from the mentality of the hunt to that of the loving family man.

Just keep in mind that when your dog (who is a hunter by instinct) doesn't run toward you, he isn't rejecting *you,* he's just focusing on something that—in the short run—seems to be more pleasurable. The longer he has to get to know you, and the more he comes to associate *you* with the most pleasurable parts of his life, the faster he'll come running to you when you call.

2. **"Love" is a verb.** If something your dog is doing—or isn't doing—is making you tense, you probably won't be the most resourceful coach in the world at that particular moment. We'll get into coaching theory a lot more in Week 3, but for now, here's an easy technique that you can try when you want to reconnect with a more loving feeling toward your dog: During a good patch, make a list of all the things you love about him, the things he does to make you smile, all of the times that you want to kiss him, like when he's sleeping. Revisiting that list during the bad patches can help you to recapture the love.

3. **BE PATIENT.** I've given you a lot of information to process and exercises to practice this week. How many times a day do you want to do them? At any free moment you have. This is the time to make sure that you are building a solid foundation for an amazing relationship between you and your dog. Keep listening to your dog, looking for opportunities to connect through play, through teaching him how to understand what you are saying, and through praise. Before you know it, you're going to be in love. The kind of love that only gets better over the years, with no chance whatsoever for a breakup or a divorce. The kind of love where whatever you give, you'll get back ten times as much. Your dog, unlike kids, boyfriends, or spouses, will ALWAYS be appreciative.

Dogs don't go through puberty or have stress at work. One of the most amazing experiences in life is waiting for you if you just put in the effort.

LETTING THE IDEAS SIT

By the end of the first week, you may have discovered that you have a genius for a dog. Congratulations! (You also have my sympathy—"brilliant" dogs need nearly constant stimulation.)

More likely, you'll probably have a dog who excels in some areas and needs work in others, no different from most students in school. If your dog isn't quite a genius yet (or even if he is), keep in mind that some ideas take time to settle in. While many of the manners you're trying to teach your dog will get better with repetition, some are going to require your dog to do some quiet reflection before the light goes on in his brain. If your dog doesn't seem to be catching on to a particular behavior, and you've tried to teach it in a few different ways, the best bet may be to forget about that behavior for a while. When you come back to it again, you may be surprised by how much your dog has learned during the time when you weren't actively teaching.

When I first got Duke, I could NEVER get him to "sit." He had a good excuse—his previous owners had used him as a practice dummy for fighting pit bulls. Duke's feet were too broken and deformed to let him sit comfortably. He couldn't focus on the "magnet," and usually just ignored me no matter how I tried to teach him the behavior.

Instead of fighting with him or diagnosing him with what I call "SDS"—stubbornness, dominance, and stupidity (which I don't believe even exist in dogs)—I waited. Every time he sat down on his own, I narrated his behavior—"Sit!"—and "made a party" with enthusiastic love and an occasional treat. In a few weeks, he was sitting happily whenever I asked him. In fact, he got so good at "sit," I could use the behavior in any situation that reminded him of his painful past, like when he encountered a pit bull. I'd ask him to "sit" and "take it" and he'd immediately comply, forgetting the pain of his memories and living in the more pleasurable present with me. Allowing your dog time to process new information is vital to the training process. It's also a sign of respect from you, the parent, acknowledging that you trust your dog to use her own mind.

WEEK 2

The supreme happiness of life is the conviction that we are loved; loved for ourselves, say rather, loved in spite of ourselves.

—Victor Hugo, *Les Misérables*

WEEK 3

DAY 8

RELEVANCE COACHING

I believe that all dogs should start with the three foundational behaviors: sit, leave it, and come. They're easy for you to teach and for your dog to learn, giving both of you the chance to start right away with a success on which to model all your future coaching. These three behaviors are also the basis for all of your dog's good manners, in the same way human toddlers start with "please" and "thank you." They aren't just arbitrary words—they create a mind-set, a world in which good manners and minding one's parents are both expected and rewarded.

But as most parents know, just because your child learns good manners doesn't mean that she's going to use them. Those manners have to become ingrained so that they're almost automatic. So how do you make sure that your dog's foundational behaviors become second nature?

Treats are great for rewarding your dog's successes. But

they're also just that: treats. Imagine if you had to give your dog a piece of Kobe beef every time you wanted him to come over to you, or steak every time you wanted him to "sit." You'd quickly have a fat dog and a skinny wallet. Eventually the treats would lose their value altogether, as your dog came to see them the way a spoiled rich kid looks at a new car. Treats are like training wheels on a bicycle—at one point they have to come off.

This is where "relevance coaching" comes into play, allowing you to integrate the coaching you've already worked on into your dog's everyday life. Once your dog understands a specific behavior, you can build that behavior into his daily routine. For example, ask him to "Sit" before he has breakfast, has a leash put on, begins a game, or is allowed back in the house. Over a short period of time, usually just a couple of days, "sit" will become an important part of your dog's life, as natural as it is for well-mannered humans to say "please."

I will usually begin to incorporate relevance coaching with a dog after the first session of "sit." Before I allow him to come back inside, I'll ask him to "Sit," followed by a hand signal if I've taught him one. I use a nonchalant tone of voice and keep my face expressionless. Usually the dog will stare at me as if he doesn't have a clue. And he probably doesn't. All he knows is that he really wants to go back inside, but it seems like I'm expecting him to do something first.

So I'll give him some time to think about it—to *generalize* the behavior. When he does figure it out and sits on the ground, I immediately open the door and "make a huge party," telling him what a good "sit" he's done. (Opening the door only works if your dog *loves* coming inside the house— if your dog doesn't, attach the "sit" to something else he does find pleasurable, like going to day care, the dog park, or jumping into or out of your car.)

Besides reinforcing the behaviors your dog has already learned, relevance coaching can also be used to get your dog to do things he doesn't really want to do. I call it "VBD"— veggies before dessert. Most of us were told as kids that if we wanted to eat ice cream, we had to finish our vegetables. Unless you were particularly creative—I had a friend whose parents, when they moved, discovered a very old stash of lima beans in the storage bench beside the kitchen table—you began to understand the concept: The pleasurable activity— eating ice cream—was tied to the thing you had to do—eat your veggies.

My dog Duke used to hate being brushed, but he *loved* to go on hikes. So before we left the house, I'd give him a very short, quick brush—five or ten seconds!—then we'd set off on an incredible hike. It didn't take long for Dukie to begin associating the brush with the hikes. He began to tolerate the brush and, eventually, looked forward to it, knowing that there'd be fun as soon as it was over. As a result, the brushing sessions got longer and longer.

Make a list of the things your dog loves, whether they be treats, massages, chasing and catching tennis balls, or invitations onto the couch, and look for ways to sneak in the "veggies"—practicing your dog's conscious choice behaviors—

before the dessert. Use relevance coaching with all the new behaviors that you teach your dog, looking for ways to reduce the pain and make what's pleasurable the reward, and you'll be amazed by how well mannered your dog will become without a constant reliance on treats, but only an occasional jackpot. (But be sure to keep the jackpots coming during these early stages of training!)

After only three days of working with Sunny and Lauren Winfrey, I had people believing I was a magician—the dogs were sitting every time I said their names or, in some cases, just when I looked at them. It wasn't any magic on my part; in fact, the dogs thought they had trained *me* to reward them for sitting without me having to ask them. They were happy to be dealing with such a trainable and coachable human being. I can't tell you how many wives and mothers ask me if I can coach their husbands and kids!

DAY 9

SHAPING BEHAVIOR

Shaping is the theory that you can teach a dog (or a horse, a dolphin, a person, etc.) to do just about anything by breaking the new behavior down into small parts. Animal behavior is "variable," a scientific way of saying that animals aren't programmed like robots or computers—they don't do things exactly the same way every time. If you want to "shape" a new behavior in your dog, reward him every time he takes even the smallest step in the right direction. You can stack these small steps on top of one another, like Legos, eventually building the desired behavior.

Shaping is a very powerful tool that works best (and fastest) when you keep a few important principles in mind:

Visualize the result. Whether you want your dog to lie down (which I'll show you how to do later in the chapter) or ring a bell to let you know when it's time to go for a walk (see

Day 21), it all starts with visualizing the end result. Once you know precisely what it is you want your dog to do, you can start breaking the process down into incremental steps.

Go backward. Once you've broken down a behavior into small steps, teach the last step first. For example, dogs in agility classes (see Day 25) are taught to climb up and down an A-frame. If you started at the beginning—asking your dog to climb up a ramp then slide down the other side—many dogs would be too afraid to try. So they start with the end instead—getting comfortable with sliding down the ramp in small, incremental steps—and then they already know exactly what to do when they reach the top of the ramp.

Take small steps. The easiest way to get your dog to improve is to make it easy for him to improve. Make sure each bar is set low enough for him to reach it. Allowing your dog to experience a series of small victories is a lot more effective than punishing and using harsh corrections in the hope of reaching some major milestone. You'll also be making the process of learning something that is fun, pleasurable, and addictive for both you and your dog.

Make sure that your dog has really mastered a step before moving on to the next one. This may seem like a paradox, but slow, consistent progress (in many different locations, when applicable) will get you where you want to go faster than a series of quick breakthroughs. Your dog needs time to process each step in order to really integrate it into his behavior. You'll know your dog has mastered a particular success when you can get him to repeat it without having to reward him with a treat each and every time (but still use occasional jackpots).

Stick to your plan . . . The goal is to always be one step ahead of your dog, anticipating his next move before he does. That way, if your dog masters a particular step faster than expected, you'll be ready to coach the next step.

. . . **but be flexible.** Good coaching—an idea we'll get to during Week 3—sometimes means thinking like a GPS navigation device. As long as you have the destination in mind, your dog can't really make any "wrong" turns—all you have to do is adjust the route to find a new way there. If the approach you're taking with your dog isn't working, try something else. And if your dog offers you a behavior that you weren't expecting, but is a good behavior to know, reward him and teach him the new behavior instead!

End on a high note. It's not where you start, but how you finish. When you end a coaching session on a success, the memory of that success has a better chance of carrying over into the next session. It's better to quit while you're ahead than to push the coaching, especially if your dog seems like he's getting tired, overwhelmed, or distracted.

"DOWN!" AND "STAY!" (LEVEL 1)

According to those trainers still stuck in the Spanish Inquisition, "down" is one of the toughest behaviors to teach, as most dogs want to resist. Nonsense! The Loved Dog Method will have your dog feeling like he's relaxing on a lounge chair, someplace fabulous, with his favorite person in the world there to wait on him hand and foot. "Down" is also an easy behavior to shape into another supposedly difficult behavior, "stay." Ask your dog to "Sit" on a carpet, rug, or dog bed. Place a treat next to his nose and draw it in a *straight* line down to the floor. Keep your eyes on the floor, not on your dog, so it's clear where you want him to direct his attention. A lot of trainers make the mistake of

staring into a dog's eyes when they're trying to teach this behavior, confusing the dog. Don't say anything—if you keep repeating "Down" while your dog is sitting and staring at the floor, your dog is going to think that "down" means sitting and staring at the floor!

After pulling the treat from your dog's nose toward the floor a few times—making sure to keep your eyes focused on the floor as well—he'll probably do something to try to get closer to the treat. You may need to adjust the angle when you get halfway down, moving the treat away from your dog's front legs, using it like an invisible cord to guide your dog

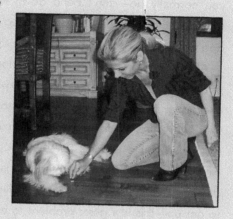

into the right position, or backward to encourage your dog to collapse in an inelegant "down." Whatever style gets him to "down," that's where you're going to start. Remember to smile and keep breathing (I don't know why, but a lot of people unconsciously hold their breath while coaching this behavior), and eventually your dog will lie down on the floor. Do not—ever—push your dog into a "down."

Once he is lying down—not before—say, "DOWWW-WWN" in the happiest, most impressed, singsong voice you can muster. Immediately reward him with that treat, but don't put it in his mouth—place it on the floor between his front legs, closer to his chest than his toes. You want the floor to be the place where he *chooses* to stay because that's where the treats are. Keep placing treats on the ground in front of him, while repeating "Down" about ten times. It's important to straighten up, standing up the way you normally do—don't bend down in some feeble attempt to block your dog from getting up, because your dog will learn to ignore you when you stand up normally.

After about ten times, reward your dog with a small jackpot and say, "No more." Don't walk away from him, however, as you may teach your dog to associate walking away with "no more," making it more difficult to teach him to stay while you're walking away. (We'll get to this shortly.) Finish the coaching session with a big jackpot and tell your dog that he's free to go, "no more." Many dogs won't want to get up—this is a *great* problem to have. The more you can make your dog feel appreciated while he's lying on the ground, the more bummed out he'll be to get up and return to his boring "normal" life. If you really want him to get up, crouch on the ground—using your body language to say, "Let's play"—or just ask your dog to "Come."

If your dog does get up, don't correct him. We didn't (and shouldn't) ask him to "stay"—we asked him to lie down—and he's done exactly what we asked him to do. However, you can show him that you're disappointed. Turn away, doing your best to look defeated, as if you're completely drained of energy. I recommend that you huff and puff or moan. Don't laugh (and if there's anyone else around, ask them not to laugh at your act either). You want to connect with a very powerful part of your dog's wiring: his desire to make you happy.

When you have a good relationship with your dog, he'll usually respond to your "disappointment" by trying to do something that pleased you in the past. Many dogs will offer you a "sit." Some will just look confused. Start the process again from the beginning. But if your dog happens to return to the "down" position on his own, "make a party." The same goes for any effort by your dog, once he's on the ground, to shift his weight so he's less like a sphinx—he's committing to getting comfortable on the ground, so reward him with a jackpot!

Once your dog remains on the ground for about ten "downs" and you've given him his jackpot, release him by saying, "No more," not because you've run out of treats, but because *you* are done with playing the game.

Once he's mastered this first step, you're ready for the next—getting your dog used to seeing you in motion. Smile and move from side to side *in front* of your dog. Say "Down," and give him a treat right after you stood to his left, then do it again right after you stood to his right. The point is to teach him that his job is to remain "down" even when you are moving around.

You don't want him to abandon the "down" because he thinks he needs to follow you. Just don't move more than a few steps away—you're NOT trying to test your dog's will, you're coaching him through a game. It's important to face your dog so that it looks like you are walking from side to side and not walking away from him.

It will take most dogs only a few minutes to catch on, but don't correct your dog if he rises—just do a little more huffing and puffing to let him know that you're disappointed. Nonchalantly take him back to the spot where you started and ask him to "Sit" again. Concentrate on helping your dog to understand when you're thrilled with his "down," and when you're disappointed—huffing, puffing, and avoiding contact when he gets up too soon. Just remember that it's all new to your dog and he really wants you to be proud of him. (And, of course, to get that special treat you're holding.)

As your dog masters each step, add more distractions: Act silly, do some jumping jacks and 360-degree twirls, make funny noises, open and close a door, kick a toy in front of him. If he gets up, act disappointed and try it again. You can also use quiet distractions that are tough for a dog to ignore—sit on a chair or a couch for a few seconds and exhale deeply. When most dogs see their owners relax, they think the session is over and may want to join them for a cuddle. You can even lie down on a bed. Just remember, you're not testing your dog; you're trying to teach him, little by little, to remain in the "down" position until you release him. Start by practicing these sessions for a few seconds at a time, then slowly make them longer. Don't forget to give a jackpot and say "No more" when you're done—many owners get so relaxed they forget that they're in a coaching session. Your dog may look content lying next to you, but she's actually super focused on the matter at hand.

You'll also want to practice in different parts of your house, generalizing the behavior. Just because your dog knows what "down" means in the kitchen doesn't mean he's going to get it in the living room. It may even feel like you're starting over, but don't worry—your dog will catch on very quickly.

It's also a good idea to teach this behavior after your dog has mastered "leave it." I made the mistake of flip-flopping the two with Sunny and Lauren Winfrey. When I held my hand to the ground to cover a treat, they thought I was asking them to lie down, which they happily did. I had to stop practicing "down" with them for a few days and coach them to "leave it" by using my foot instead of my hand to cover the treat.

DAY 10

SOCIALIZATION, PART II

Much of what we consider "bad behavior" in dogs comes from our failure to communicate. We're judging their behavior by using human values instead of making the effort to understand what that behavior means from a dog/wolf point of view.

Wolves are actually incredibly well-mannered animals, with a remarkably sophisticated code of conduct. Unfortunately for dog owners, this wolf code of conduct—our dogs' hardwired, factory specs—incorporates behavior that humans don't like, such as jumping, nipping, and chewing whatever they can get their teeth on.

We'll get into addressing some of these "problem" behaviors on Day 12. For now, I want you to consider the idea that dogs face exactly the same obstacles we do, only in reverse: A lot of what passes for normal in human society looks very weird to a dog. For example, people like to look one another in the eyes—a behavior that's considered rude, even threatening, among wolves—and show their teeth by smiling when they're happy, a behavior that has very different meaning in wolf society.

The world is a very different place when you start to see it through a dog's eyes. How would you feel if you were introduced to potentially dangerous animals while you were tethered to a leash that prevented you from escaping? Or if people you'd just met started touching you on the head and face without asking? People talk about a dog's life as if it's the easiest thing in the world, when in fact it's full of all sorts of stressful situations.

It's never too early to start the socialization process. In a perfect world, dog breeders planning to sell their puppies would begin introducing them to household sounds and children as early as possible—there's a lot of evidence to suggest that dogs form most of their ideas about the world during their first four months of life. But most puppies don't get this kind of treatment, meaning that it's our responsibility as parents/owners to socialize our dogs.

You can start right away with any dog of any age by naming the people, objects, and activities around him in a happy tone of voice, as I did with Taiyo and the Band-Aid (see Day 5). As our dogs begin to encounter new and stressful situations—strangers, loud noises, unruly kids, other dogs—we can help them to socialize by desensitizing them to these experiences.

It's important to distinguish "socialization" from "exposure." Just exposing your dog to something he may perceive as scary isn't socialization, as it won't teach him not to be afraid of it. Let's say you're afraid of spiders—do you really think the best way to overcome that fear is to have someone drop a spider on your lap? Or to place you in a room full of spiders? I happen to be afraid of snakes. If someone tacked a hundred-dollar bill on the opposite end of a pit of snakes and said, "Go get it, Tamar!" I can promise you, that hundred-dollar bill is going to stay right where it is.

But let's say that it's not a pit full of snakes, but one snake, safely housed in a securely locked, glass-enclosed aquarium. And it's not a hundred-dollar bill on the other side of the room, but a hundred thousand dollars. Would I walk across the room? Gladly!

This is the mind-set you want to get into when you're socializing your dog to potentially stressful situations. You're going to expose your dog to a variety of these situations, in very small doses, then reward him magnificently for his bravery. Or as a psychologist might say, you're going to minimize the fear element as much as possible while increasing the pleasure element associated with that particular fear.

When I'm starting the socialization process, I like to give a dog a variety of gold treats every time he's introduced to a new person, a new dog, or a startling new sound like a vacuum cleaner or a garbage truck. No, you're not rewarding your dog for being a coward; you're helping him to build a pleasurable association with anything that might seem like a threat. Repeat this association a few more times—you can switch to silver or bronze treats after the first few exposures—and your dog will stop thinking, *Aaaah!!!* and start thinking, *Where's my treat?*

No matter where you are or what you are doing, if you see your dog having an adverse reaction to someone or something, stop what you're doing and try to link whatever it is to pleasure. We were filming a segment for Oprah's show with her two puppies when Lauren became frightened by a man with a big straw hat—the gardener. I immediately stopped in midsentence, gave the gardener a treat, and asked Lauren to "Take it" from him. After a few more "take its," Lauren was happy to be petted by the nice gardener. We resumed the filming. The point is to never ignore a fear signal from your dog—*immediately* go into coaching mode and change the association from pain to pleasure.

The more distinct stresses you introduce your dog to, the easier socialization becomes. Introduce him to all kinds of people—male and female, tall and short, old and young, bearded and unbearded, from different racial backgrounds. Be sure to include children, the source of all kinds of unexpected physical behavior.

Socialize your dog in different rooms of the house, at different times of the day and night—a lot of owners forget just how much scarier a strange noise or person can seem in the darkness. And as your dog gets ready to face the world, take your socialization game on the road: new places, new faces, and, of course, other dogs.

WHEN IS IT OKAY FOR A PUPPY TO MEET NEW DOGS?

There's no real consensus among veterinarians as to when it's okay to introduce a puppy to other dogs. While it's never too early to start socialization, it's also never too early to catch any of several diseases that your dog is ultimately going to be vaccinated against over the first sixteen weeks.

My personal take on this is that there are a lot more dogs put to sleep because they lack socialization than there are dogs dying from diseases. That said, for caution's sake, I think a puppy should be kept in the house, away from other dogs, until after the second set of vaccinations (usually when he's around eight weeks old). At that point, you're probably safe inviting over or visiting other dogs in their homes, as long as they've been properly vaccinated. After the third set of shots (usually around twelve weeks), I feel that it's safe to take your puppy out for a short walk, avoiding contact with other dogs (and the feces they've left behind) until the fourth and final set of vaccinations.

TOUCH PROOFING

Human beings touch one another all the time—we shake hands, pat one another on the back, give hugs and kisses on the cheek to people we barely know. In the wolf pack, however, touching is a very big deal: Lower-ranking dogs don't touch higher-ranking ones without an invitation. It's up to you to make sure that your dog associates physical contact with the people in his life—especially veterinarians, groomers, and curious kids—with pleasure instead of fear.

The easiest way to build this positive association is to give your dog a treat every time he's touched by a new person or in a new way. You can start the process yourself, touching him on his back, on each ear, and his paws, tugging (gently) on his tail, massaging him gently in the sensitive spot between his toenails. Make sure to give him a treat immediately, saying, "Take it," and that you're smiling, breathing normally, and otherwise communicating to your dog that you're having fun. He'll quickly start to connect all kinds of human physical contact with pleasure.

It's also worth making a quick trip to the veterinarian's office, before your dog's first checkup, just to give him a treat and get him comfortable with the surroundings. He'll be much better prepared for his first "official" visit. (We'll talk more about veterinarians on Day 28.)

BABY AND CHILD PROOFING

A lot of dog owners treat their dogs like they're the center of the universe—until a new baby arrives and turns the world upside down. The birth of a child can be very confusing and scary for a dog, as his "parents" are suddenly distracted by a new living creature, one who is tiny, uncoordinated, unpredictable, noisy, and easily injured. Without socialization, many dogs will respond to a new baby with feelings of "pain": abandonment, resentment, and at times, even nervous aggression, especially when the baby starts to crawl.

It's important to start socializing your dog to babies and toddlers the moment you get your dog, even if you're not thinking about having children. Your dog is going to encounter kids on the street, at friends' homes, and in veterinarians' offices, so you want to make sure your dog *loves* children. Once your dog has happily begun to associate being touched, hugged, and squeezed with a jackpot, look for any opportunity to introduce your dog to young kids (one at a time), making sure that you have plenty of treats on hand (and that you can manage the kids' behavior) to define the experiences as "pleasure."

If you're planning on having children and there are going to be any significant lifestyle changes for your dog, like the loss of a play area, the loss of a spot in your bed, or a lack of exercise time with you, try to get him accustomed to them months before the baby arrives. Try to find alternatives where you can, like a new play area, a comfy dog bed for your bedroom, or someone who can take your dog on long walks and hikes. Give your dog treats while listening to a recording of a crying baby and you'll create a positive association that most parents wish they had!

When you do bring a baby home for the first time, try to set your dog up for success by putting him in a positive frame of mind. Make sure his seven basic needs are being attended to and that he's had plenty of companionship and exercise leading up to the arrival. You can bring home a blanket with the baby's scent in order to let your dog get accustomed to the new smell, giving him treats to help him associate it with yummy things—just don't let him chew or paw at the blanket, which might reinforce some wrong ideas. When you arrive home from the hospital, try to include your dog as much as you can in the celebration. Sending him out to the backyard while the rest of the family cheerfully dotes on the new addition is just asking your dog to associate the baby with "pain." Not a good idea.

Finally, make sure that you never leave your dog alone with your baby or young child until you're absolutely certain that *both* of them can be trusted around each other. I wouldn't leave an unsupervised child under six years old alone with a dog for any length of time. A lot can happen in just a few minutes, and past behavior doesn't guarantee safety—studies show that two-thirds of the dogs who bite children have never bitten a child before.

FOOD PROOFING

I can't tell you how many times I've heard nervous owners say, "Oh, you don't want to bother him while he's eating." Many dogs get nervous or aggressive when someone approaches their food bowl. "Resource guarding" is another example of an instinctive wolf behavior—defend your food or one of your littermates is going to snatch it from you—that doesn't jibe well with our human ideas about good manners. An aggressive resource guarder can endanger unsuspecting passersby. Fortunately, with a few applications of the pleasure versus pain principle, you can teach your dog to not only tolerate interruptions to his meal, but to actually look forward to them!

How do you know if a dog is resource guarding? When he's eating, he'll freeze as soon as he sees someone walking toward him, staring at the food while watching the intruder from the corner of his eye. If you're lucky, he'll growl, giving you clear notice that he's on alert—many people fail to see the body language and may not understand the severity of the situation.

Why do dogs do it? Once again, the biggest misconception is that it's because your dog wants to be the alpha. In reality, most dogs are resource guarders because they're afraid, worried that someone is going to take their food away. *Here we go*, he's thinking. *Time to defend my food. Offense is the best defense, so I'd better scare them away. I'll bite if I have to. Whatever it takes to protect my food and my survival.*

Harsh corrections or other attempts to make your dog submissive will only exacerbate his fears. He's likely to become even more stressed out and offer fewer warning signals, as the warning signals only led to punishment. That's usually when I get the call, hearing that the dog, from out of nowhere, just bit a small child who happened to be standing near his bowl. Using nasty corrections to scare your dog into compliance gets people hurt and dogs killed.

The Loved Dog Method is to coach a dog into seeing disturbances around the food bowl or next to his prized toy as something to look forward to instead of fear. Even if your dog doesn't have a resource guarding problem, it's a good idea to food proof him anyway—it's an easy issue to prevent and a difficult, potentially dangerous problem to have to solve later. For a dog, it can be a matter of life and death. You can do it in three stages, a little bit at a time.

BEFORE YOU BEGIN . . .

Here are three important tips to keep in mind while you're food proofing a dog with a resource guarding issue:

1. Don't give your dog treats at any time *other* than when you're specifically working on getting rid of or preventing fear around the food bowl or prized toy.
2. Keep the meals boring. If you normally mix dry food with wet food, give him only the dry food. The lesser the quality of the food he's guarding, the more receptive your dog will be to any improvements (i.e., treats) that come with being interrupted.
3. If you have other dogs in your household, keep them away from the dog with the resource guarding issue during the food-proofing sessions.

The first step—the "bronze stage"—is about getting your dog comfortable with allowing people to approach him during mealtime. Just walk up to your dog, while he's eating, quickly from above drop a bronze treat in his bowl, and walk away. You may need to toss it from a distance. The key is to do everything quickly: Drop the treat, turn around, walk away.

Repeat this a few times. The goal is to get to a place where your dog will remain relaxed—wagging his tail at midlevel or lifting his head to give you a silly smile—as you walk up to him and drop a treat into his bowl from above his head. It might take a few minutes or a few weeks, depending on the dog. It's also a good idea at this point, if possible, to include other people in this exercise to help your dog generalize these pleasurable feelings toward anyone who approaches his bowl.

Please don't rush the bronze stage. Take your time, even if it takes months. This method has an extremely high success rate and is used effectively in many shelters, but it has to happen at a pace that your dog finds comfortable.

When you're sure he's not just comfortable but actually happy, even thrilled when people approach, it's time to move to the "silver stage." Walk toward the bowl like you did in the bronze stage, only this time stick your hand in his bowl, just for a second. When you do, drop a jackpot of silver treats in his bowl and walk away. A little bit of cottage cheese works well. If your dog likes wet food that you normally mix before serving, you can wait until this moment to drop it in—don't worry about mixing it. You can also introduce a few new kinds of wet food as a silver treat—dogs love variety. Repeat this process until your dog is happy and thrilled to have you mess with his food.

For the final step, the "gold stage," you'll walk toward him and take his bowl away. Return it a few seconds later with a massive amount of gold treats on top—grilled chicken, ground beef, hot dogs, or small pieces of steak. It won't be long before your dog is practically begging you to interrupt his meal!

One note of caution: If your dog seems to be a seriously aggressive resource guarder—one who might bite—use gold treats throughout the process instead of starting with bronze. Make sure to keep kids away from him while he's eating. It also helps to place your dog's bowl on a raised surface, like a chair or a low table, so that he isn't able to hover over it so aggressively.

I used this method with a Cavalier King Charles spaniel. Usually one of the sweetest-tempered breeds out there, this particular dog was very fearful when it came to his food, guarding it ferociously. His owners, a pregnant couple, had many people visiting the household; in other words, we had a ticking time bomb on our hands. We didn't have the luxury of time. Normally, I'd never tether a dog while working on this issue—when a dog's in "fight-or-flight" mode and can't flee, that leaves only one option—to fight. But this particular dog was so focused on his food bowl that he didn't seem to mind. So we tied him to the heavy refrigerator, placed his food bowl between him and us, and, having removed any risk of his biting someone, practiced many sessions each day. By the time the baby arrived, a few weeks later, the dog was looking forward to being disturbed while eating.

DOG PROOFING

My older dog, Clyde, was very unhappy when I introduced Duke into the family. I tried to protect Clyde's feelings by sending Duke (who had learned to be pushy from his days as a victim of pit bull target practice) away whenever the younger dog started to annoy Clyde. Sounds logical, right? Only I was making a big mistake: I was reinforcing Clyde's association of Duke with pain without doing anything to build a more pleasurable association.

Once I'd finally come to this realization, I began rewarding Clyde whenever Duke approached him, ending the rewards as soon as Duke walked away. It didn't take long for Clyde to begin looking forward to Duke's approaches.

NEW PEOPLE AND EYE CONTACT

An important part of socialization is teaching dogs not to be afraid of new people. It's especially a problem for rescue dogs, many of whom have had nothing but bad experiences with the people who have tossed them away and broken their hearts. Other dogs may just be naturally shy and afraid of any new interaction.

Having a dog who isn't interested in being touched by strangers—or is even afraid when someone new looks at her—may sound like a difficult problem, but it's actually easy to solve as long as you're patient and remember that in the wolf pack, as noted earlier, direct eye contact is considered rude, even threatening.

Start by kneeling to the ground, body language that reassures the dog that you are not positioning yourself for an attack. Face sideways, eyes away from your dog (in her mind you can't attack if you are looking away), holding a treat out in your hand. It's important to let the dog come to you. Remember the snake example from earlier? If I was afraid of snakes (which I am) and I saw one coming toward me, it wouldn't matter if he had a million dollars tied to his head, I'd still run away. If I happened to be tied to a leash, I'd go on the offensive, trying to attack him first to get him to switch direction and leave me alone.

If your dog is too fearful to even approach, toss the treat to your dog without looking at her. By gradually dropping treats closer and closer to where you are standing, you can teach her to approach your hand. Be sure to say, "Take it," each time she takes the treat—and not, "Good girl." As I described on Day 2, hearing "take it" will help your dog learn that it's a pleasurable experience and not a painful one.

Once the dog is comfortable enough to approach and take the treat from your hand, you can introduce the eyes. Hold a silver treat between your eyes and, when she looks directly at you, for even a second, say, "Watch me," smile, and reward her immediately with the treat. Not only will the dog eventually overcome her fear, she'll also learn to forgive your rude human insistence on direct eye contact. As an added bonus, teaching your dog to "watch me" can be a huge help when you need to get her attention in a hurry.

Once your dog likes eye contact, try to smile whenever you catch her looking at you. Most dogs lose their wolf instinct to avoid eye contact with people they are familiar with and feel safe around. Despite the fact that we're from two different species, you and your dog will enjoy many long moments of soulful connection. My dog Clyde, who was once terrified of any eye contact, now sits and looks right at me for long periods of time. Whenever I happen to lift up my eyes from whatever I'm doing and catch him looking at me, waiting for me to look back, my heart skips a beat.

"SIT" (LEVEL 2)

Even when you're not teaching your dog a new behavior, you can always work on generalizing one that he's already learned. If you've coached him to "sit" while you're standing in front of him, make sure he understands that it means the same thing when you're sitting or kneeling down. Most dogs, when they see you lower yourself to the ground, see an invitation to play, forgetting their manners and jumping on you. We want them to learn that whether we're standing, kneeling, or lying down, we still expect them to sit politely. This is especially important if you have kids around, as they're naturally lower to the ground.

The method is the same as the one you used the first time—use a treat like a magnet in front of his nose—only this time you're sitting on the floor while you do it.

If your dog jumps on you, turn your face and body away from him and say nothing. You want him to understand that he'll get no attention from you if he jumps, but when you say "Siiiit" and he does, he will be rewarded by your love and a treat. Once he learns his manners, that treat will turn into an occasional jackpot.

When I began coaching Sunny and Lauren Winfrey, the two competed with each other for everything, each dog afraid that the other would get something extra from me if she didn't jump and tackle me first. So after I coached each dog individually, while sitting on the floor, I worked with them both together. At the end of the day, it all boiled down to trust. They began to believe that they'd get my love, attention, cuddles, and treats even if all five of Oprah's dogs were around, and even if they weren't sitting the closest to me. Watching them grow from wild wolf pups to well-mannered little girls made me want to gobble them up and kiss them to pieces.

PREPARING A HOUSEBREAKING CHART

The first few days with any new dog—especially puppies—can be difficult. You're both trying to get used to each other's habits and quirks. Much of what we've talked about so far is designed to help your dog learn new customs and get along in a totally strange environment. But a housebreaking chart is a great way to reverse the dynamic, helping you to get a better understanding of your dog.

SAMPLE HOUSEBREAKING CHART

	SUN	MON	TUE	WED	THU	FRI	SAT
7:00 A.M.	(1, 2)						
7:15 A.M.	W, F						
7:45 A.M.	(1, 2)						
10:00 A.M.	W (1)						
11:00 A.M.	[1]						
12:00 P.M.	W						
12:15 P.M.	(1)						
2:30 P.M.	W (1)						
4:30 P.M.	W, F						
5:00 P.M.	(1, 2)						
7:00 P.M.	W (1)						
9:00 P.M.	W (1)						
12:00 A.M.	(1)						

NOTE: Your dog should drink water every two hours or so up until three hours before bedtime. As above, highlight your dog's mistakes to see if there is a pattern of behavior.

DAY 10: SOCIALIZATION, PART II

165

It's simple to do. Look at the preceding sample chart—you can create your own in a notebook or spreadsheet program, or download it from my website, www.tamargeller.com. Every time you feed or water your dog, note the time in the appropriate column, adding an "F" for food and a "W" for water. Do the same for bathroom breaks—put a "1" next to the time when she pees and a "2" when she poops. If she does her business in the "correct" area, draw a circle around the number. If she made a mistake—going outside the assigned area—draw a square around the number.

Don't worry too much yet about evaluating the information on the chart—we'll get started on that next week. For now, you should think of yourself as a scientist, gathering data without making judgments. It's a good mind-set to have when you're coping with the inevitable accidents—there is no "good" or "bad," there are only results!

By now, after ten days of routinely taking your dog out, there might be a pattern in his bathroom habits. Certain times of the day when he's less likely to make a mistake, and certain times of the day when he needs extra supervision or extra bathroom breaks. Recording and reviewing a week of activity will make it easier to spot any trend.

DAY 11

NEGATIVE FEEDBACK

I went to Ricki Lake's home to meet Jeffie, her new golden-doodle puppy. The joy in the room made it feel like a baby shower. Many of her friends brought gifts, toys, treats, and other items to celebrate Ricki's new family member.

One of the gifts was a spray bottle that, according to the pictures on the packaging, promised to stop your dog from doing anything you didn't like. All you had to do was spray the poor dog in the face whenever she did something "wrong."

A lot of trainers rely on this kind of negative reinforcement to stop dogs from doing what they don't want them to do. What they don't do is take the time or effort to show dogs what they *would* like them to do. These negative methods of training contribute to an atmosphere of fear, confusion, and mistrust, instead of a deeper relationship built on security, communication, appreciation, compassion, and love. There's no coaching on how to behave using new, humanlike behavior instead of natural wolf instincts. Instead, many young puppies are simply expected to learn proper behavior by hearing "NO!" and getting sprayed in the face. This is lunacy. We could prevent millions of dogs from ending up with one-way tickets to the local shelter if, as people, we took the time to simply coach them in a clear and loving way instead of making them pay with their lives for what nature has made them.

The worst part is that an owner who uses the spray feels like she's following a trainer's advice. What happens when that advice fails? A lot of frustrated owners wind up taking their confused and scared dogs to an animal shelter. Another "damaged" dog with "behavior problems."

It wasn't too long ago that most dog training relied on negative feedback and punishment for results. Devices like choke chains and prong collars were used to (supposedly) help keep dogs' egos in check. The notion was that a dog who wasn't submissive to or afraid of his master would try to run the show; these painful devices prevented the dogs from making any unwanted moves. Owners were encouraged to use a stern tone of voice with their pets, never letting them forget who was in charge.

There are trainers today who spray Binaca into a dog's face in the hope of discouraging a problem behavior. Others insist on using "alpha roll over"—tackling your dog to the ground and staring menacingly into her eyes as a way of asserting a leadership role. How well does that work? Ask my friend Michelle, who wound up in an emergency room after her terrified Jack Russell terrier bit back. (We'll get into the misconceptions surrounding the "alpha dog" on Day 15.)

I find it disturbing that people who are supposed to be professional trainers focus so harshly on the symptoms rather than the root causes of "bad" behavior, completely ignoring the many behavior-modification techniques that are available today to everyone. In my world, choke chains and prong collars feel as anachronistic as any other medieval torture device.

Brad Paisley, the brilliant country singer I'd helped with his own dog, invited me to Nashville, Tennessee, to work with his best friends' two eight-year-old Malteses. The dogs were behaving very aggressively, biting the owners and guests, and even once when the husband tried to take a short bathroom break in the middle of the night. They wouldn't stop barking, and bit anyone who tried to shush them, sending several people to the doctor.

Brad's friends had been to see many local trainers, all of whom had given them the same answer: The dogs needed to be submissive. They were given the choice of using shock collars (keep in mind that these were tiny, five-pound dogs) or putting the dogs to sleep, as at age eight the problem was probably not correctable.

Brad accompanied me on the first session, warning me that the dogs would attack the moment they saw me. To make a long story short, I was never attacked. I had a super-yummy treat for the dogs as soon as the door opened, and they immediately began to associate me with pleasure. It was very clear to me that they wanted to be coached and that most of their seven basic needs weren't being met. I taught them to "take it" instead of running away barking, to "sit" when I asked, and introduced them to some light child proofing. I also forbade them, for the time being, from sleeping in bed with their "parents" or sitting on the bench next to the dining table when Mom and Dad were eating.

The change was so immediate that after about 30 minutes Brad started calling some of his friends—I jokingly asked him to become my publicist. When I returned to the house two days later, I was greeted by one of the dogs—he put his head between my legs, looking for a rub. We were all moved to tears. Two days earlier, this dog would have bitten you for accidentally rubbing his ear! The dogs were happy, and so were the owners, who could move around the house without triggering a symphony of barks and without fear of getting bitten. It felt so good to have saved these two little dogs from being put to sleep. Again and again I get the gratification that comes from coaching, not disciplining dogs.

As I hope you've gathered so far, The Loved Dog Method relies on fun, games, clear communication, and a deeper understanding of how dogs think. We want our dogs to want to behave based on our values because they feel good when they please us, not because they're terrified of the repercussions when they don't. Punishments stress out a dog, making her a less willing student. Would you really want to pay attention to a teacher who gets angry and hits you with a ruler when you make a mistake? Or would you look for ways to avoid that particular teacher?

That being said, there are a couple of situations in which

I'll use a *very limited* amount of negative feedback that is *very* different from any pain-causing device like a prong collar or a choke chain. It's also different from punishment, which I am against, as it takes place after the fact and doesn't give the dog an opportunity to do the right thing. As we'll see on Day 13, a few gentle sprays from a water bottle, or what I call a divine correction (because it appears to come from someone other than you), can help to break a barking habit. But the most effective forms of negative feedback don't require any props.

One of the most effective ways is simply to turn your back on a dog. In the wolf pack, unruly youngsters are "frozen out" by their elders until their behavior improves. Dogs crave connection, wanting to be a part of a pack; it's in their DNA. When you turn your back to them, you're taking that connection away. It's a punishment, but a gentle one that can be immediately remedied as soon as the dog returns to a more teachable state. On Day 12, I'll explain how to use this method to teach a dog to stop jumping on people.

You can also convey your feelings with your tone of voice. Normally I like to maintain a very happy, positive voice when I speak to a dog. I want them to enjoy communicating with me, eagerly waiting to listen to what I'm going to say next. When I'm rewarding a dog, I switch to an excited tone, making it clear that she's done something good. But occasionally, I'll use an unhappy tone of voice, or even a series of annoying "dolphin clicks," when I have to convey displeasure. And I do have an angry voice, or what I like to call my "Level 8." We'll come back to that on Day 24.

THE "STAY" GAME (LEVEL 2)

"Stay" is a variation of "down" that you can use when you need a dog to remain in one place for a certain amount of time. I'll use it when a dog is interrupting a coaching session that I'm trying to do with another dog, when I need to clean up broken glass on the floor and don't want him to step on the shards, or when I want a dog to join people in the living room without walking around and investigating everyone's clothing with his wet nose. I won't use "stay" to get a dog to stop jumping on guests (a problem we'll cover on Day 12), and I don't throw it around casually. It's always followed by a release phrase, like "no more," when it's okay for the dog to start moving around again.

As you can probably guess, we're going to make "stay" into a fun game, something your dog is going to associate with pleasure. We're going start by using a technique I call "the seesaw."

Begin with your dog in a "down" position. By now, your dog should see "down" as a welcome vacation, the equivalent of sipping piña coladas on a lounge chair during an exotic vacation—after all, he's getting praised and rewarded for *doing nothing*. Choose a place where your dog will be comfortable lying down for a while: a carpeted room, or if you don't have carpets, a bathmat, towel, or folded blanket.

Stand in front of your dog, but don't face him—your

head and entire body should be turned at a ninety-degree angle, as if you're staring at a wall to your dog's left or right. When your dog is in the "down" position, place a treat from your storage hand between your dog's front legs, allowing him to gobble it up, and say, "Down." Then hold your palm in front of his face—imagine a policeman saying "Halt"—and in a matter-of-fact (but never threatening) voice say, "Stay." Quickly place another treat between the dog's front legs on your opposite side—if your dog is on your left, you'll place the treat on your right—a couple of feet away from your dog. You want to make it clear that you're not inviting him to eat the distant treat.

Place another treat between his front legs, allowing him to eat it, repeating "Stay" with a slightly warmer tone of voice. Then "seesaw" back to the other pile, adding a treat and repeating "Stay" in the matter-of-fact voice. Keep seesawing back and forth between rewarding your dog (with a treat and a warm voice) and adding to the growing pile a couple of feet away (using the matter-of-fact tone and the hand signal).

Once there are about five treats in the distant pile, congratulate your dog for his patience with a huge jackpot between his front legs: Happily announce, "No more . . . Take it!" and invite him to dig into the pile of treats a couple of feet away. If your dog is regularly getting up before you're done, resist the urge to correct him. Forget about "stay" for a little bit and go back to coaching him on "down" and allow him to get used to any distractions in the room. You want your dog to want to stay, which is even easier when you turn it into a fun game of "treasure hunt."

As your dog starts to understand the routine, slow down the seesaw, increasing the time your dog has to stare at that growing pile of treats before receiving a reward. You can also increase the level of difficulty by moving the pile a bit farther away, spreading out the treats. Do it while you're doing jumping jacks or stepping away into a quick 360-degree twirl, making it clear that you want him to stay *regardless* of what is going on in front of him.

When your dog really gets it, it's time for a fun game of treasure hunt. Ask your dog to "Stay" patiently where he is while you hide treats around the room and later around the house, then release him with a "no more" so he can hunt them down. The more you can make a behavior seem like a fun game, the more your dog will start to ask you to play—in other words, he'll be begging you to "stay." This is the kind of coaching that the old conventional dog trainers could never dream of: Your dog is on your team, by choice!

A favorite "stay" game is the Chicken Tree. When outside, you ask your dog to stay and then stuff little pieces of chicken into the cracks in the bark at the base of a nearby tree. Then release your dog by saying, "No more. Take it," repeatedly until he's found all of the chicken, at which point you say, "No more."

DAY 12

PROBLEM BEHAVIORS— JUMPING AND DIGGING

JUMPING

I absolutely *love* to coach dogs who jump, because they make me look like a magician! I can usually cure a dog of jumping in just a few minutes, without uttering a negative sound. I'm no magician—it's just that easy and fun to do, a chance for you and your dog to work as a synchronized team.

Some trainers will tell you that a dog who jumps on people is trying to establish his dominance. They tell you that you've got to nip this behavior in the bud by yanking on his collar, driving your knee into his chest, or even stepping on his back paws. I'm so done with the nonsense of dominance theories. Not only are these trainers completely off base in their understanding of the situation, but if you take their advice, you may wind up seriously injuring your dog. You'll almost certainly injure your relationship, as you're teaching your dog to associate you with pain.

Jumping comes naturally to dogs—it's the way wolves greet one another when they're happy. For young wolves, jumping can also be a survival mechanism: When the mother wolf comes back from the hunt, her pups jump up and lick her face, causing her to regurgitate some of the partially digested meal. Sounds disgusting to us, but for a wolf pup, it's called dinner!

I get to see dogs greeting each other all of the time at The Loved Dog day care. It's so cute to see them stand on their back legs, their front paws on each other's shoulders as if they're dancing. While this kind of greeting is fun and instinctive for dogs, it's an instinct that isn't always appreciated in human society. Getting jumped on by a dog with muddy paws is no fun; a big dog who likes to jump can actually be dangerous.

Before you can teach your dog not to jump, you've got to take a look at your own behavior. It's important that you (or anyone else who interacts with your dog) aren't unintentionally reinforcing your dog's behavior. As we've already discussed, dogs don't communicate with one another by using words— they respond more to body language and facial expressions. Even if they seem incredibly cute while they're doing it, make sure that you or anyone else never pet or smile at a dog who is jumping on you.

Let's break the behavior down: Since a dog is jumping to

look at or lick your face, the easiest way to eliminate jumping is to take your face away from him. When your dog jumps on you, just turn away. You're not angry, just nonchalant. Don't say anything, not even a "no"—a jumping dog shouldn't receive any attention from you, not even negative attention. It can be tough to resist saying "no" at first, but the impact is much more powerful if you don't say a word to your dog when he jumps. The idea is to give him zero attention when he's jumping, then lots of attention when he's sitting.

If your dog jumps on you again, keep turning away. As soon as she's got all four paws back on the ground, ask her to "Sit," then "make a party" and reward her with a jackpot when she does. Chances are your dog will jump again right away, but if you're consistent, she'll soon start to feel like she's training *you* to reward her every time she sits. "What a great people coach I must be," she'll say to herself. "I've trained my mommy to give me a yummy treat every time I sit!" Just make sure that you switch from giving her a regular reward for each "sit" to a random jackpot as soon as your dog starts to catch on. Then you must raise the bar and reward your dog's sitting *only* if she *didn't* jump up first. You don't want to wind up teaching your dog a new trick: the sequence of jump, sit, and get a reward!

Simple, right? Children can coach dogs this way, and they feel empowered doing it, which makes them want to be involved in the coaching process.

Lots of jumping takes place near the front door. Use that area as the primary spot when teaching your dog how to sit.

A dog who likes to jump on guests presents a slightly different challenge. You're going to have to teach her that jumping on guests gets her nothing, but if she leaves them alone and comes to sit near you, you'll "make a party" for her. The easiest way to address it is to let your dog practice on "fake" visitors. Invite a few friends over (or use an otherwise planned social gathering) for some improvised theater. Explain the "turn your back" method to your friends, then have them take turns playing the part of the unsuspecting guest. Don't ask your dog to "sit" or "stay" before they walk in—you want your dog to jump on the guests so you get the opportunity to coach her. As she's jumping on the guest, who turns his back on her, you hold a treat to your dog's nose like a magnet, moving your dog away from the guest and into the sitting position. After a few repetitions, your dog will avoid the guests, and will come and sit for you instead. Just make sure your guests know that they're not supposed to do anything that will encourage your dog to jump on them, sabotaging the coaching. Make it fun, and remember to reward your friends as well as your dog!

DIGGING

Digging—along with barking and chewing—is one of the most common things a dog will do when his seven basic needs aren't being met. So before you even start to address a digging issue, take the time to consider the idea that it might be a symptom of a larger problem. Unless you take care of the root cause—in most cases, boredom or a lack of physical or mental exercise—your dog may wind up trading his digging for a barking or chewing problem.

A few weeks ago, I coached a wheaten terrier who was constantly nipping, chewing, and digging. When I looked into his seven basic needs, I realized that the poor dog was *never* allowed to be off the leash, had never been on a hike, and never got to play with other dogs. I said as much to his owners.

When I came back a week later, they told me they'd taken my advice, but nothing had changed. I asked them what they'd done differently. "We're taking him on longer walks," my client explained, "and when he meets another dog, we let them play for a few minutes." By "play," I discovered, she meant letting the two dogs nose around each other without ever taking them off their leashes and letting them play.

I asked my clients to let their dog spend a few hours at The Loved Dog day care. For the first time, he had the chance to play with other dogs without a leash, running, climbing, and rolling with them. When my clients picked their dog up, four hours later, he had a huge smile on his face. So did the clients, who for the first time felt like they had the dog they were hoping for. I convinced them to put their dog on a daily activity routine that alternated among off-leash hikes, visits to a dog park, and doggy day care. Lo and behold, the problems they'd been facing for a whole year just disappeared.

So once again, the first thing to do when addressing a digging problem is to make sure your dog's seven basic needs are being met. Don't assume that your dog is getting enough physical or mental exercise just because whatever you're doing worked for your last dog.

If you're confident that your dog's needs are being met, and he's still digging, how do you get him to stop? You probably can't—some dogs are just hardwired to love digging. But if your dog is tearing up your lawn or favorite flower bed, you can redirect his focus.

You can start by making sure your dog doesn't see you digging. If you garden in front of your dog, he's going to assume that gardening is fun and do his best to pitch in. Also, make sure that you're not using any fertilizers that contain bone marrow, which is way too tempting for a dog to resist.

Give your dog his own "digging pit" where it's okay to exercise his impulses. Sandboxes work well if you bury some goodies in the sand, like his favorite chew toys and treats. You can change the "treasure" from time to time to keep it interesting. Keep the sand damp, so it's easy to dig, and cover it up at night to keep cats and squirrels from using it as a litter box or messing with your dog's goodies.

You'll be giving your dog a choice: Why would he dig over *there* when digging in the sandbox means surprises and jackpots? If your dog happens to eat a little sand, don't worry—it all comes out in the poop.

If redirection doesn't work, you can try to get your dog to associate digging with pain, at least in the areas of your yard that are off-limits. Instead of goodies, bury bad things. Bury items that will be uncomfortable for your dog to touch, like lava rocks (aquarium rocks) or stereo wire that you've stripped out of its casing. Or bury things your dog won't want to put his face into, like fresh poop. You can even bury something to scare your dog, like a jack-in-the-box. (Make sure you don't laugh when he finds it, or he'll start to associate it with fun instead!)

Just remember that we're not trying to associate digging with *real* pain—I'm not suggesting you bury a bear trap—but that the point is to cause some mild discomfort that will make your dog think twice before he digs in that certain spot. And don't let your dog see you setting the booby traps or he may wise up and take his digging elsewhere.

Generally speaking, a tired dog is a happy dog. Take care of her seven basic needs and chances are the digging will stop.

"SIT" (LEVEL 3)

You've already taught your dog "sit" when you're standing, sitting, and kneeling on the ground. But how about when you're lying down? I want you to be able to ask your dog to "Sit" when you're doing yoga, sit-ups, lying on the grass in the backyard or on a sandy beach, or spending time on the floor with a new baby. It's also handy when you let your dog on your bed and want her to "chillax" without your having to get up.

In wolf language, if you're lying down, you don't really mean business. You want your dog to start paying attention to your words, not just your body language.

Just practice the behavior the same way you did with Levels 1 and 2, only this time lie on the floor while you do it. Concentrate on the hand signal, as your dog's nose might be too far above your reach to use the "magnet." If you've done a good enough job with the hand signals in Levels 1 and 2, your dog will be happy to comply.

DAY 13

BARKING AND GROWLING

As I said on Day 5, many people mistake nervous aggression—especially barking and growling—for dominant behavior. In fact, the opposite is usually true: A dog that is ready to attack will usually freeze, tensing his muscles, mentally and physically preparing himself to fight. Barking and growling can be annoying, for sure, but when we misdiagnose them as signs of defiance, we often wind up exacerbating the problem rather than finding a solution.

BARKING

There's nothing like the sound of a crying baby to get a person's attention. The sound always triggers a response. You might feel concern (if you're the mommy or daddy) or annoyance (if you're sitting next to the baby on a cross-country flight). But most parents will tell you that not all cries are the same. My friend Julyet's sixteen-month-old daughter, Rain, cries differently when she's feeling frustrated or looking for reassurance than she does when she needs something tangible, like food.

Just like with kids who cry, there are all kinds of reasons for why a dog might bark. It might be a cry for help or a warning. The act of barking actually releases endorphins, making a dog feel so good he may want to continue barking even after he's forgotten what he's barking about. Many dogs use barking the way people use drugs or even exercise: to alleviate boredom or loneliness. Sometimes they're barking to warn us against intruders, which of course isn't a problem unless they're still barking long after the intruder is already gone.

Unfortunately for most human beings, the sound of a dog incessantly barking doesn't release any endorphins—it can feel more like a direct path to insanity, for both you and your neighbors. It's a no-no for a well-mannered dog. But how do we take away something that, for our dogs, is instinctual and feels so good?

The answer is, we can't, not entirely anyway. We don't want our dogs to be mute—we want them to be able to bark to warn us, or to let us know when they need something. What we really want is for them to be quiet *most of the time,* especially when we ask them. I've got an agreement with my dog Duke—he's allowed to bark a few times when someone is at the door, but when I tell him to "Shush, I've got it from here" or "It's a friend," he happily complies.

If your dog seems to be barking too often, the first place

to start—you guessed it—is with the seven basic needs. Your dog may simply be barking because he's not getting enough physical or mental stimulation. Other dogs bark and growl because they're anxious or traumatized. When I first brought my dog Dukie home from the shelter, he was an emotional wreck. A falling leaf would trigger a barking episode so loud, high pitched, and urgent that you'd think the house was under attack. Not surprising for a dog who was once used as a practice target for pit bulls in a fighting ring! In Dukie's mind, potential dangers were everywhere. Barking was the only rational response.

By changing Dukie's situation, however, I was able to change the associations in his brain. Rather than react to his barking, I refused to acknowledge it. Slowly, over time, as Dukie saw my other dog Clyde and me ignoring the "dangers" he saw lurking everywhere, he stopped seeing them as dangers. He began to feel more secure in his environment, his anxiety levels decreased, and so did the barking.

Acknowledging the barking can often be part of the problem. Like a child who throws a tantrum, a barking dog who craves attention—then gets it from an aggravated owner—is being rewarded for his efforts. If you only acknowledge your dog when she's barking, you're going to raise a dog who likes to bark. I often tell my clients to simply turn their backs on a barking dog or leave the room altogether—sometimes it works like magic, as long as you're providing plenty of love and positive reassurance during those times when she's not barking.

I worked with Pat Sajak and his family, who rescued a five-month-old Australian shepherd named Stella with the most intelligent eyes. When she looked at Pat's wife, Leslie, and started barking, Leslie was sure that she was asking for something. She'd immediately start asking, "What do you need? What can I do for you?" As you can probably guess, the barking became more frequent as Stella realized it was the best way to get Leslie's attention.

Once we made sure Stella's seven basic needs were being met, I taught Leslie to turn her back when she started barking. A couple of hours later, the barking had all but stopped. Leslie also made a point to spend more quality time with Stella, filling her need for mental stimulation. As a brilliant Australian shepherd, Stella had a need more intense than that of most breeds, so she wasn't so hungry for attention anymore.

Some dogs, however, are so habituated to barking that it becomes difficult to stop—especially since it feels good to them. Telling these dogs not to bark is like telling a chocoholic to avoid candy. When I encounter dogs like these, I want to help them break their habit by replacing one positive association (the barking) with another, even more positive association.

The key is to get the dog to quiet down long enough to create a new association. The first step is to teach the word "shush!" I've got two different methods: "speak and shush" and spray bottles. I highly recommend starting with "speak and shush."

Let's say I asked you to turn off the lights. Easy to do, as long as the lights are already on, but if they aren't, you won't be able to do what I asked. Same goes for teaching "shush"— your dog needs to be barking before you can tell her to quiet down. So first, you're going to teach your dog how to "speak." Choose something that causes your dog to bark, like a person ringing the front doorbell. You can ask someone to wait outside your door, tell your dog to "Speak," which should be the signal for the visitor to ring the bell. When your dog starts barking, reward her with a bronze treat. After a few repetitions, your dog will start barking every time you ask her to "speak."

Now you're ready for the "shush" part. When you see your dog in a calm and quiet state, put your finger to your lips (the universal hand signal for "shush"), ask your dog to "shush," and reward her with a gold treat. After practicing "shush" a few times, ask your dog to "speak." When she does, give her a bronze treat. You're giving your dog a choice: "speak" and get bronze, or "shush" and get gold. If you were in her paws, what would you do?

You can also try to associate "shush" with something else that's pleasurable, like a toy. I don't mind when my dog Clyde barks to tell me that someone is at the front door, but I had to teach him not to bark at every single person who passed by the house. After telling him to "shush," I handed him his favorite toy, an old tennis ball. Now when I tell him to "shush," he immediately runs off to find the ball, focusing his attention on the toy instead of the passersby.

However, there are a few dogs who really get off on barking, even after you've eliminated attention-seeking behavior or boredom as a cause. This is one of the few situations where you have my blessing to use a spray bottle filled with water. You're not trying to prove your superiority or be malicious; you're just trying to divert his attention. (If your dog happens to loved getting sprayed with water, as some people do when relaxing at ritzy hotels in Hawaii, add a little baby shampoo.)

When a barking dog starts up, say "shush" and spray a cool burst of water at the back of his head. He should stop barking long enough to figure out what hit him, giving you the opportunity to use the hand signal, say, "Good shush!" and reward him with a gold treat. Repeat this over a few barking sessions and your dog should begin to associate "shushing" with pleasure. Just remember that you're not using the water bottle to shush the dog, but to create an opportunity to teach the word "shush." Use the bottle sparingly and, once your dog has learned to "shush," you shouldn't have to use it at all. The idea is to teach your dog if he stops barking when he hears "shush," good things happen. And if not, there will be negative reinforcement, which takes place *during* the unwanted behavior and stops as soon as the undesired behavior stops. Use the spray bottle *only* as negative reinforcement and not as punishment.

GROWLING

"My dog is growling," I hear from a lot of frustrated or scared owners. "How do I make it stop?"

I usually reply with a few questions of my own. What if a friend told you that her husband was "screaming"? Would you immediately assume that she was married to an angry or abusive husband? Or would you ask about the circumstances? He could have been screaming with joy because his favorite football team just scored a touchdown. Maybe he was screaming a warning to prevent your friend from falling off the edge of a cliff. Your reaction would probably be totally different if she told you "He was at a baseball game," "He was in his karate class," or "He was standing a hundred feet away," instead of "We were having a fight." The word "screaming" doesn't necessarily mean there was any kind of problem. The same goes for growling.

Many people mistake growling for anger when, in fact, dogs growl for all kinds of reasons. It's how they vocalize—their vocal chords don't give them too many other options. The average man uses 2,000 to 4,000 words every day, while women use 6,000 to 8,000. Dogs, on the other hand, have a relatively limited supply of barks, growls, howls, whines, and whimpers to get their points across. A growling dog might be preparing for (or trying to avoid) a fight, but he also might be nervous, scared, or just excited, like during a fun game of tug-of-war with us or when wrestling with other dogs.

Many owners make the mistake of responding negatively to their dog's growls. They'll yell, make hard corrections with the leash, or even hit the dog in an effort to make the growling stop. Unfortunately, all this does is (a) teach the dog not to growl when he's scared, eliminating a valuable warning sign; and (b) create an even more terrifying and untrustworthy environment for your dog.

On the other hand, if you allow your dog to growl at threats and those threats disappear—a stranger backing off, for example—then your dog will quickly learn to become an expert growler. That's not going to work for you either.

So what should you do when your dog growls? If your dog is growling during play, that's just normal fun, like kids screaming while they play at the playground—don't worry about it. But if your dog growls as a warning, take note of whatever is taking place at that moment. As calmly as you can, remove your dog from whatever situation is causing him to growl, and try to determine specifically what it was that scared him. If it's a kid, adult, or another dog, get your dog away from him or her. Then you can use any of the socialization techniques described so far (Days 5 and 10) to address the particular issue.

ANOTHER WAY TO THINK ABOUT "PROBLEM BEHAVIORS"

Let's say you're driving and, suddenly, your car comes to a complete stop. Would you immediately jump out of the car and start pushing it toward your destination without first trying to figure out what might be wrong with it?

Sounds ridiculous, right? But a lot of conventional dog training is based on exactly that idea: Without trying to discover the cause for the growling, trainers just react, or overreact, to the symptom. You get rid of a problem behavior by correcting the dog every time he does it, usually through punishment. The idea is that if you punish a dog for doing something, he won't be likely to do it again. Maybe so. But what these trainers often fail to realize is that they're addressing the symptom, not the root cause of the problem.

If your car stopped running, you'd probably go down a checklist. Is there gas in the car? Is any smoke coming out of the engine? Did I hit something?

There are probably dozens of other questions you could ask—cars are complicated, which is why we take them to mechanics. Dogs, on the other hand, are simple. You can almost always figure out what's causing a problem behavior by working through a short checklist.

It's an approach that will probably seem familiar to anyone who has raised a baby. I explained the checklist to a client, Helen, while we were working with Kallie, her mini Labradoodle. Helen's face immediately lit up. "That's just what we did when our daughter was a baby," she said. "Whenever she cried, we knew it had to be one of three things: She was hungry, her diaper needed to be changed, or she had gas. Using the process of elimination, we could always figure out which one was the problem."

Dogs are just as easy to understand. The first thing to look at is whether or not the dog is associating something with pain instead of pleasure. Usually, this behavior is connected to a lack of socialization.

When a dog associates an experience with pain, he's going to do whatever he can to avoid it. For example, if he learns that when he hears "Come here!" it's good-bye playtime, hello boredom and isolation, he's probably going to learn to ignore his owner. The same goes for having a chew toy taken away from him.

If your dog needs more coaching to associate pleasure with things that his wolf instincts tell him will be painful, then go back to Day 5 and Day 10 and socialize the heck out of your dog (with love, fun, games, and treats). If his wolf instincts are at work, provide your dog with an appropriate outlet so he can make better choices. If your dog associates a particular person, behavior, or activity with pain, find a way to connect it to pleasure.

The second question to ask is whether or not the dog is just exercising his wolf instincts.

Let's say you've just climbed out of bed, on your way to get your morning coffee, and suddenly, your dog is jumping and growling, clawing at your robe and biting your pajama pants. What the heck is going on? Is your dog on a mission to attack you while you're half asleep?

Not at all! After sleeping through the night, your dog is well rested and ready to play. And what's better than a good wrestling game with an unsuspecting "victim"?

Much of what we consider "problematic" about a dog's behavior feels perfectly natural to a wolf, who is taught from birth to use his teeth and claws while wrestling with his friends, and play whenever and wherever the mood strikes. To me, it doesn't make sense to punish a dog for exhibiting behavior that, in his culture, is accepted and encouraged. Instead, you can either engage in play, or if you are still sleepy or just don't feel like it, give your dog a yummy chew toy on which to focus.

BACK "OFF" (LEVEL 1)

I use "leave it" whenever I want to tell my dog to stop touching something, or not to touch something in the first place.

"Off" is a request to your dog to back off from someone or something. I literally want him to take a step back, and ultimately many steps back. For example, if your dog is staring with hungry eyes at a dinner guest's plate, "off" will let him know that you want him to allow your friend to eat in peace. (Later on, you can string it together with "go to bed" and really impress your dinner guests!) You can use it when your dog is taking up all the space on the bed, or you want to move him from point A to point B. I find it useful to give a dog as many words as I can in his vocabulary to make it easy to communicate with him.

Start by asking your dog to "Sit." Then stand really close to him, leaving less than a foot between you and his face. Hold a treat to his mouth and ask him to "Off." Your dog will put his mouth right on your hand, but after a few seconds will return his head to a normal position. Reward him as soon as he moves his head away from the treat. Set yourself up in the same position again, under a foot away, with a treat in front of his mouth, but this time take a step toward your dog. Because you're so close, he's going to have to take a step or two backward. (If he doesn't, you can shuffle your feet into him, a little at a time; eventually he'll take a big frog leap backward.)

As soon as he backs off, walk quickly toward him and

"make a party," repeating, "Off! Off! Off!" in an excited voice as you feed him a jackpot. Your dog may be a little confused—he won't know exactly what behavior is being rewarded—but he's going to be very motivated to figure out how to repeat it. Bingo! You've now got a dog who wants to learn!

As you keep practicing, the way you reward your dog will determine how "off" will look. Some owners reward their dogs for backing away in a graceful and elegant straight line. Others are happy with a dog who turns around and walks away. Some dogs do what I call "the sundial," their butts staying in one place as they move their front legs away in a circular motion.

On my DVD, *Celebrate Your Dog*, Mickie, a cute three-month-old golden retriever keeps backing up until she's about thirty feet away. It's fun to see all the different styles—dogs can be incredibly creative.

Regardless of the style, however, you've got to reward your dog while he's away from you. If your dog has to come back toward you to receive the treat, he's going to learn that "off" means walk away and return immediately. Make sure you reward the outcome you want by walking toward your dog quickly, rewarding him as far away as possible from your original starting point.

"Off" is a great behavior to practice with relevance coaching. If your dog knows how to catch, ask him to "Off" so you can throw him the ball. And don't forget to practice it in different places.

DAY 14

LISTENING TO
BODY LANGUAGE

Monty Roberts is one of the most successful horse trainers in the world, a man I admire for his insight, wisdom, respect for animals, and courage in challenging the accepted methods for "breaking" a horse. He's worked with and socialized "crazy" horses that others had given up on. The queen of England asked him on a few occasions for a private audience to get advice and be coached in his methods. His autobiography, *The Man Who Listens to Horses*, spent more than a year on the *New York Times* best-seller list. It's a fantastic book, one that makes you feel privileged to share your life with an animal.

Monty is a quiet, humble man with one huge ambition: to change the way human beings relate to horses. Growing up around horses, he came to believe that the "traditional" method of training—demoralizing the animal, breaking its spirit and will until it becomes subservient to a human master—was cruel and ineffective.

Instead, Monty has developed a technique he calls "join up." He uses gentle words and nonverbal communication to persuade the horse to enter a voluntary partnership. By first developing a bond of trust, Monty creates a situation in which the horse will willingly accept a human rider. He's even used "join up" with wild, untamed, flight animals like deer. His abilities seem almost magical.

Monty doesn't have any superpowers that allow him to speak with animals. "What I can do with horses," he says, "is the result of long hours observing them in the wild. It's essentially a simple thing based on common sense. There *is* something magical about it, but it's the magic of an undiscovered tongue—primitive, precise, and easy to read."

For example, stallions pin back their ears when they're angry. Dun mares "freeze out" unruly colts, exiling them to the edges of the herd until they start behaving. (Just like we do, in The Loved Dog Method, to unruly dogs who jump or bark.) Monty spent his teenage years "listening" to these and dozens of other behaviors. He learned to communicate with horses by reading their body language and responding in kind. He's not a "horse whisperer," because he doesn't do any talking. Monty takes pride in being a focused listener, and according to him, "Horses are great teachers."

I would highly recommend you read this book; you can learn to communicate with your dog in the same way. Anyone who tells you that dog coaching is "hard" or requires some special knack is a false prophet. I hope you've seen by now that most of what I'm offering is common sense, based on engagement and observation. If you take the time to listen to and learn your dog's language, you'll discover that you have a willing and enthusiastic partner who wants to be coached and be a part of your pack, not a creature who needs to be dominated.

BODY LANGUAGE

We've spent a lot of time so far talking about the best way to teach your dog. But what has your dog taught you? It's time to learn to listen to our dogs a bit more deeply.

As we said earlier, dogs are somewhat limited in their vocal communication. There are a few different kinds of barks, growls, and other sounds, but they're not always easy to tell apart. On the other hand, dogs are extremely expressive in their *non*verbal communication.

Have you seen your dog smile? Most dogs use several different kinds of smiles. The two most common are the submissive smile—a dog reveals his front teeth, but keeps the back ones hidden—and the happy and relaxed smile—no teeth at all. Your dog may stamp his front two paws when he wants to get your attention or tilt his head when he's curious, focused, or trying to figure out something you've said. His ears point forward when he's alert, backward and flat when he's nervous or submissive. Dogs bow toward one another when they want to play.

How does your dog use his tail? Fast wags often mean a dog is excited, while slow wags can be an indication that he's uncertain about something that's going on around him. A tail pointing stiffly upward means confidence (some might even call it arrogance!). Straight up and moving stiffly is often a sign of potential aggression. Dogs who are afraid will let their tails hang low, sometimes tucking them between their legs to cover their "business cards," the anal glands that advertise their special scent. When the tail straightens horizontally, your dog probably sees something interesting. Some hunting breeds or mixes may even lift one of their front legs, just like you see in photos from the old days of hunting foxes or birds.

When read in combination, these gestures can give you a sense of your dog's overall mood. For example, a dog who is stressed out may drool, yawn, lick his lips, and close or otherwise avert his eyes. A good, full-body shake usually means that he's released his stress, something you'll often see after he's met a new person or dog.

How else does your dog talk to you? Does he scratch at or pounce on objects he wants to play with? Does he lick his lips when he's hungry and no food is nearby? Your dog may not be able to speak, but he's always communicating. It's up to us to learn how to listen—being a good listener is the most important tool in building a good relationship.

A dog who is wagging his tail isn't necessarily friendly and may not want you to pet him. It's important to read a dog's body language correctly, particularly when kids are interacting with a new dog for the first time.

WEEK 2 REVIEW

A client, a very wealthy man with a family (including two young kids) and more than thirty people on staff, wanted me to work with his female rottweiler. I visited his house several times. The dog was always easy to communicate with and perfect in her manners. But neither the client nor his family was ever around for the coaching sessions.

A year later, I was vacationing in the south of France when I got a call from the client. "We're in Spain with the dog," he explained. "Can you come?" They actually flew me to Spain for an emergency session with the dog, who was (supposedly) behaving aggressively toward the kids. I worked with the dog for more than a week out on the streets, interacting with babies, toddlers, grown-ups, and many other dogs, and, once again, found her to be an easy dog. I never once, however, saw the kids, let alone had the chance to coach them on how to work with their dog.

Shortly after I'd returned to Los Angeles, another call—the dog is growling again. Could they send her to stay with me for a few days for another session? I suggested another idea. "I'll send you a person who works with me," I said. "They'll stay with you for at least a week, from the moment the kids get home until the dog goes to sleep, so they can not only give the dog feedback, but work with the whole household, family and staff. Everybody is going to get on the same page, giving the dog a consistent message. It's going to be kind of like that TV show, *Nanny 911*." I also came up with an exercise program for the dog that included more than just a daily, leashed walk around their property.

They weren't interested, and sent the dog to stay with me instead. Again, she was perfect. She returned home, was perfect for a couple of days, then went right back to the old aggressive behavior. Fourteen months later, I got another phone call.

I was angry and sad. I felt that they were being completely unfair to the dog. I told them that a rottweiler's instincts, in her DNA, were to protect her loved ones and her territory, and that with the ever-changing staff of more than thirty people coming in and out of the house, without even one person giving her the proper feedback or connection that she needed, there were too many unfamiliar faces for the dog to ever relax. I asked the owner to think about his own life, to try and relate.

We all know how differently we handle big problems when

we are calm and relaxed, and how little problems can seem like big problems when we are stressed and overworked. The dog never had any aggression issues when she was with me because her seven basic needs were being met—she was in a good place physically and mentally. I took her on daily hikes, allowed her to play with other dogs, stimulated her brilliant mind by teaching her new behaviors, and provided her with everything good in her life. She was connected to me and more than happy to abide by the boundaries I set for her. When she barked at the door, I thanked her and told her that I could take it from there.

But in her own home, the dog was living her life like a champagne bottle ready to burst. Without the attention, love, or coaching reinforcement from her owners, she had little to look forward to. When a stranger came into the house—the most exciting and surprising part of her day—her "let me protect my family" instincts overwhelmed her.

If the owner and his family weren't going to have the time or energy to become more involved in this dog's life, I suggested I'd help them find her a new home. Sooner or later, she was probably going to bite someone.

Apparently, that got their attention. I sat with them and explained:

"Your dog gets no exercise. She's locked up most of the day in one of the fancy rooms in your mansion. She has no connection with you. You never take her hiking; you never play games with her; you never do anything to show her who you are in her life. She is operating according to her wolf instincts, because there's no one to coach her on how to make human-like choices. How can you have any expectations of her?"

The Loved Dog Method isn't about teaching a dog tricks. It's about making a commitment to our dogs as treasured members of the family. It's about teaching our dogs to understand us, to trust us, to want to please us. It's not important how many behaviors your dog learns, or how well he performs; it's the relationship we develop, the role we come to play in his life, that bonds us.

Which is why we'll spend next week concentrating on our role in the process, developing the skills to become a world-class coach.

By the way, this story has a happy ending. After our talk, the family came together, each one of them (as well as the regular members of their household staff), to work with the dog. She began to get daily exercise and playtime with other dogs. The aggressive behavior disappeared. I'm happy to say that when I went to visit them, I saw one very goofy, very happy rottweiler playing fetch with her eleven-year-old human "sister." I hugged them both, tears of joy running down my face. (I'm tearing up now just thinking about it!)

As for homework, practice the sit, come, leave it, take it, off, speak and shush, child proofing, food proofing, and down and stay behaviors, as well as the housebreaking routine. Chart as much of the activity as you can and involve as many family members as possible. Look how far your dog has come in only two weeks!

WEEK 3

We make a living by what we get, but we make a life by what we give.

—*Winston Churchill*

DAY 15

BEING THE ALPHA DOG?

I hear a lot of trainers talk about "alpha dogs." They tell you that wolves always have a leader, one dog who uses aggression and dominance to command respect and submission from the rest. It's up to you, the argument goes, to be the alpha in your pack. Otherwise, your dog may think that *he* is the alpha, creating behavioral issues that are bothersome, possibly even dangerous.

In her book *Inside of a Dog*, psychologist Alexandra Horowitz points out that the idea of the alpha dog is, for the most part, based on myth. Wolf packs aren't "groups of peers vying for the top spot," she writes. They're families who sometimes behave in ways that seem "dominant" or "submissive" in order to maintain social unity:

The idea that a dog owner must become the dominant member by using jerks or harsh words or other kinds of punishment is farther from what we know of the reality of wolf packs and closer to the timeworn fiction of the animal kingdom with humans at the pinnacle, exerting dominion over the rest. Wolves seem to learn from each other not by punishing each other but by observing each other.

In reality, "dominant aggressive" dogs are *extremely* rare. The vast majority of aggressive dogs act that way because they're living in fear. Ever see a person overreact because they're scared? Or a "macho" man (or woman) whose facade is just hiding insecurity? When you exert your "alpha dominance" over a dog who is already fearful or insecure, more often than not you're just going to exacerbate those fears and insecurities.

When kids misbehave, they're not trying to run the show—they're just looking for more privileges or attention. Research shows that children crave good guidance and thrive when there are clear boundaries. The vast majority of dogs act up for the same reasons—to better their position within the family, not to take control of it.

Phil Jackson is the coach of the Los Angeles Lakers. He's not exactly what you'd call a conventional basketball coach—during the season, he suggests specific books for his players to read; encourages them to practice yoga and meditation; and even burns sage in the locker room, an old Lakota Indian tradition to ward off evil spirits, when the team is in a slump.

In 2010, Jackson won his eleventh championship, making

him the most successful coach in NBA history. Afterward, Lakers point guard Derek Fisher had this to say about his coach: "He doesn't try to control you. He empowers you to be who you are. He doesn't put himself in the way. I love that man."

Leadership comes in many flavors. At one end of the spectrum, there are tyrants like Saddam Hussein, who rule by fear and dominance. At the other end, there's Gandhi, who led by showing compassion and building trust. Gandhi convinced his people to believe in his nonviolent approach to change even though they were being shot at and killed. They listened, and won their ultimate wish: independence.

Imagine having the same relationship with your dog, one where he'll be willing to do whatever you ask him to do, even if it doesn't make sense to him at the time. While it's important to set boundaries, you shouldn't confuse good leadership with domination. I like to give the dog the option to elect me as her leader instead of forcing myself on her and calling myself the leader.

SETTING BOUNDARIES

Empowering others to "be who they are" doesn't mean letting them do whatever they want to do—a good leader has to set boundaries. One common mistake is to wait too long to create those boundaries.

I once had to fire an assistant who neglected her work. The problem started the day she called to say she wasn't feeling well and asked if she could work from home. I said yes, feeling grateful that she was willing to put in the effort, figuring it would be a one-time deal. Only she began to put in more and more hours from her home, and I started to wonder if she was really working. Rather than saying something, I allowed her to continue, until I received a notice that my credit rating was low because of many unpaid bills—paying the bills was part of my assistant's job. I became very upset and let her go.

I can't help but feel that if I had set clearer boundaries from the beginning—that I expected her to show up for work every day—instead of trying to avoid an argument with her, the incident never would have reached the point that it did. It was my fault for not wanting to have an uncomfortable confrontation. I did not do a proper job as the boss. I've learned, since then, to set clear boundaries by simply stating what I expect from my employees, what I can live with, and what kinds of behavior are not acceptable to me. And I've never had a problem since.

Even if you've never had this problem with an employee, you may have experienced it in a relationship. Many of us women don't feel comfortable communicating what it is that we want, or what our partners can do to make us happy. So we wind up testing our men to see if they'll "deliver." Or maybe you've felt it with your kids, getting upset with them for finding loopholes in your rules, when it was really you who failed to communicate the entire picture. I meet dog owners all the time who are experiencing similar situations. "I used to let my dog sleep on my bed in the morning, after I woke up—and now he jumps onto the bed whenever he wants!" Wouldn't it have been easier to teach the dog, from the beginning, that he only gets to jump onto the bed when he's invited? The same way that I should have said to my assistant, "Thank you for taking some work home today, but I want to make it clear that it's only a one-time thing—I need to have you here with me so I can supervise your work."

It's not always easy to set boundaries—most of us don't like feeling like "the bad guy" who sets the rules. We hope some issues will work themselves out. But when they don't, and a behavior persists to the point of driving us crazy, we may wind up exploding with anger. An anger that could have been avoided had we only been clearer about our boundaries from the beginning. Life is so much easier when we are upfront, communicating our needs and boundaries in a kind and respectful way to everyone in our realm. (At least when it comes to our expectations and relationships with our dogs.)

FETCH AND CATCH

Fetch and catch are two of my favorite games to play with my dogs. They remind your dog that you are in charge—after all, it's *you* who controls the ball—while making them feel lucky to have such a cool and fun person for a coach. In my experience, playing games like these (as well as tug-of-war) is the very best way to create a strong and lasting bond with your dog. When he sees you as a fun and playful leader, there's nothing he won't do for you! You are building goodwill that will pay back in buckets.

I meet a lot of frustrated dog owners whose dogs just can't seem to get the knack of these games. But almost any dog can learn as long as you're patient and able to identify the obstacles that are getting in the way.

Sometimes the problem is that your dog is *too* well-mannered. Many owners spend so much time correcting their dogs for "exploring" with their mouths that they've actually trained their dogs to think it's wrong to use them to pick up anything. They have unintentionally frogged their dogs!

My friend Chaz Dean has a brilliant yellow Lab—appropriately named Hunter—who likes to surprise his "daddy" by retrieving all kinds of random objects, including a huge knife delivered proudly on one occasion! Luckily, Chaz never yelled at or tried to correct Hunter's behavior, which might have discouraged the dog from fetching, but gently guided him toward his toys to redirect his focus. He also took extra time to teach Hunter the names of different toys to keep him mentally stimulated and happy. Another example of why having a brilliant dog means more work for the owner—the dog always needs to learn new things and, if we're not there to teach them, he'll take matters into his own paws in ways we may not appreciate.

When a dog doesn't seem interested in fetching, I like to start off with a squeaky toy or a tennis ball. Pick a time of day when your dog is at his highest level of joy—maybe it's right when you first get home (before you've even had a chance to put down your keys), when you're on a walk, or at mealtime— and introduce him to the toy. Toss it in the air, bounce it on the floor, and (of course) make it squeak. If your dog still isn't interested, try ignoring him for a minute or two, focusing all of your attention on the squeaky toy. Talk to it like it's an animal, pet it, and treat it like it's the most interesting object in the world. It doesn't take long for most dogs to become interested in figuring out what all of the fuss is about. (If that *still* won't work, try cutting a little opening in the tennis ball with an X-Acto knife and shove a few treats inside—your dog won't be able to get at the treats unless he brings the ball to you.) Be patient and repeat until your dog masters the behavior that you've named "fetch." If your dog has a favorite bed or resting area, sit there and have him fetch the toy back to that spot, as he already likes to go there.

The second, more common reason some dogs don't like to play fetch is because they associate the game with a feeling of pain. Many owners accidentally create this association when they grab a ball or a toy out of their dogs' mouths and throw it again the moment it's been retrieved. Imagine how you would feel if you gave someone a gift, only to have that person rip it from your hands and toss it aside without even a thank-you! When a wolf brings prey back to his pack, he's expecting a fun game of tug-of-war, or at least some acknowledgment that he's done something good. By immediately tossing it again, you are sending your dog the message, "I do not value this gift," causing your dog to associate the game with a feeling of pain and, therefore, leading him to stay away from you or try to engage you in a game of chase.

Instead, when your dog retrieves the ball or toy, take a minute to pet and praise him with a "Good fetch!" Touch him on his back or near his tail—away from his head—communicating that you're not coming near his mouth and he can keep the toy for as long as he wants. You can even reward your dog for dropping the ball in front of you by saying "Take it" and giving it back to him.

Sadie Winfrey, the cocker spaniel, liked to run away after fetching and tried to get me to chase her, but I had a couple of opportunities to scratch the velvety fur by her tail and happily say, "Fetttttch." The first time she dropped the ball, I gave it right back to her and you could see the surprise on her face. A week later, she was playing fetch, dropping the toy not because I asked her to, but because she wanted to, running away in the hope I'd throw it for her again. The point is that whatever you do, don't turn fetch into a game of chase—you'll just be teaching the dog that it's fun to be a thief.

The positive reinforcement will transform fetching from a simple instinct into a fun game that he'll want to repeat again and again, while deepening the relationship between you.

CATCH

Catch is a little easier to teach, but is harder for some dogs to learn. Dogs' eyes are structured differently from humans, making it difficult for them to see objects that are right in front of them. And not all dogs are born with equal mouth-eye coordination, any more than every human being is born with the same skills as Michael Jordan.

You can help your dog by giving him a target that's easier to see. Start with a two-tone tennis ball, or use a dark marker to color half of a regular tennis ball. Aim the ball at your dog's mouth and be gentle with your tosses. Be sure to reward the baby steps, praising him happily even if he lets the ball bounce a couple of times before grabbing it. But save the big praise—"making a party"—for the first time he actually catches the ball: "Catch! Catch! Good catch! Wow! Good catch!" As your dog becomes more coordinated, you can increase the distance of the throw by asking him to "Off."

A lot of dogs love to play Frisbee. Start as you would with catch—short, easy tosses into his mouth—gradually throwing it higher and farther. You'll make your dog so happy and even more in love with you!

THE MAGIC TENNIS BALL

As I mentioned on Day 13, my dog Clyde loves to fetch and catch his tennis ball. I use it to give him extra exercise when we're out on a hike and as a reward for making humanlike choices instead of acting on his instincts. Instead of feeling criticized when I tell him to "shush," he runs off to find the tennis ball.

The great thing about his relationship with the tennis ball is that I can use it to change Clyde's frame of mind. If he seems nervous or stressed, or is focusing on something other than me, all I have to do is pull out the ball. His mind will immediately go to a happier place.

I'm not the only one who uses this trick—many search-and-rescue dogs are not actually looking for people in peril, but for a tennis ball. During their coaching, whenever they found a lost person, drugs, or explosives, they were rewarded with their favorite toy—more often than not, a simple tennis ball and a fun game of fetch, catch, or tug-of-war!

DAY 16

OBSERVATION AND LEVERAGE

We're spending a lot of time this week talking about all the things that will allow you to be a brilliant coach for your dog, but don't forget to practice, every day, the fun behaviors she's already learned. By now, your dog should be sitting at Levels 1, 2, and 3, coming to you when called, lying down, staying, leaving it, backing off, playing tug-of-war, and dropping. She should be starting to get the hang of fetching, catching, and housebreaking, "kissing" instead of nipping, and chillaxing when you tell her "No more." Even if your dog is not yet perfect, keep up the good work and have fun coaching her!

A lot of trainers make it seem like coaching a dog is hard work. Sometimes it can be. (Only rarely!) But it's not the kind of work that requires special training or skill. Most of what you'll need to know you'll find out directly from your dog, as long as you're willing to listen.

We know that students perform better when they have great teachers. The best teachers don't just talk "at" their students, assuming that each of them will understand or approach the lesson in the same way—they listen, responding to their students' specific preferences and needs. The students feel like they're being heard, putting them in a more positive, more receptive, more resourceful frame of mind.

Before you can become a good coach to your dog, you have to learn what makes him tick. I have two managers at The Loved Dog Center who have entirely different ideas about their days off. One loves to decompress, neither thinking nor doing anything related to work. The other can't relax without knowing what's going on at the center. Whenever managerial issues arose, the first manager never thought to check in with the second—why would she bother her on a day off?—while the second manager got upset with the first—why wouldn't she let me know what was going on?

As a result, I instituted a system at the center where I asked each manager to list the things that had to happen in order to feel "heard" and supported by her coworkers. It's an approach that will also work with your dog. The better you know your dog, the more you'll start to anticipate his next move or desire before he does, keeping him resourceful and receptive and in the best mood possible to learn a new behavior or modify an old one.

WHAT DOES YOUR DOG LIKE TO DO?

It's hard to believe, but I've met a few children who don't like to eat sweets. There's nothing wrong with these kids—in fact, some parents would probably be overjoyed to have a child who didn't want to have chocolate cake for dinner. But you aren't going to convince one of these children to clean their room by promising a trip to the ice-cream parlor!

One of the fastest ways to get anyone—your dog, your child, your spouse—into a receptive frame of mind is to use "leverage." For a child, it can be a fun activity, as big as going to Disneyland or as small as playing a video game; your wife might prefer a day at home when the kids are gone, the house is empty, and she can sleep in. For your dog, it might be his favorite, most yummy treat (or a lot of yummy treats!). Any reward that makes someone happy can be used as leverage, keeping him or her in a positive and resourceful state of mind.

Not all dogs, for example, like meat or treats, preferring toys and games. Some dogs don't like being touched in certain spots or situations. There are dogs who love to sit on the couch all day, while others, like border collies, would rather die—they want to be "at work" herding sheep.

The more you understand what your dog likes and doesn't like, the more you will be able to empower your dog to be the best that he can be. Take a few minutes to think about the foods, activities, and places your dog likes best, dividing them into gold, silver, and bronze categories:

	Favorite Foods and Treats	Favorite Toys and Games	Loving Attention	Favorite Locations	Favorite Activities
EXAMPLES	sauteed meats, grilled chicken, cold cuts, salmon, coconut chips	tug-of-war, Frisbee, fetching the "purple bunny," chewing on a soup bone, treasure hunt with a tennis ball	places (if any) he likes to be kissed, likes to be petted slow/fast, petting in a special spot on her belly, relaxing touch on the bridge of nose, ears, or above tail, high-fiving you	on your bed, under the covers, on the couch, on the living room carpet, under the dining table, in the backyard	ride in the car, dog park, hikes, doggy day care, the beach
GOLD	grilled chicken	tug-of-war	kissed on the face	under the covers	hikes! beach!
SILVER		Frisbee			
BRONZE	coconut chips			backyard	

THE INTERVIEW

Psychologists try to understand human behavior by asking lots of questions. So why not use the same technique with your dog?

No, he's not going to be able to answer you directly. But by observing and thinking about his behavior, you'll discover that your dog is actually a very good communicator. Here are some good questions to "ask" your dog:

1. Would you rather spend time together with me or would you rather be alone to explore in the big backyard?

2. How much time do you like to spend with me?

3. How much of that time would you like to use for play? How much of that time would you like to use for rest, or just hanging out?

4. Do we play enough games together? Am I providing you with enough activities in your life for you to think of me as a fun parent/coach and to keep you stimulated?

5. At what times of the day are you happiest? At what times of the day are you "low energy"? Are there times of the day you like to be left alone?

6. What are the most fun and wonderful things I've done for you during our time together?

7. Have I done anything in the past that might have caused you pain or mistrust?

8. Do you like to be touched? Are there times you don't like to be touched?

9. Am I a good communicator? Do I confuse you by using too many (or too few) words?

10. Do I clearly name the behaviors that please me, or do I use "Good boy!" too often? Do I give you enough time to figure out what I'm asking you to do, or do I repeat my requests too many times?

11. Can you understand my tone of voice? Do you know when I'm thrilled, content, or unhappy with you?

12. Am I clear in my facial expressions and body language? Do I ever scare or confuse you, like laughing when I'm actually upset with you?

13. What do I do that makes you glad to see me? What would you like me to do more of? What do I do that makes you afraid of me?

14. Am I able to understand when you are scared or hurting?

15. Am I fulfilling your seven basic needs? Are there any I could be doing a better job of fulfilling?

16. Am I helping you to grow and learn new things?

17. What is your favorite part of our relationship?

18. What would you change about me if you could?

19. What are some of the ways that you show your love for me?

THE POWER OF LISTS

There's something very powerful about making lists, whether we're using them to define our lives' most important priorities and goals or just remembering to pick up milk at the grocery store. They make our lives clearer and more organized. Some psychologists claim that the act of making lists actually reduces stress.

You can harness the power of lists to become an even better coach to your dog. Here are a few to try:

1. Three things that make your dog happy
2. Three things that make your dog leap out of his skin with joy
3. Three sounds that will get your dog's attention
4. Three things that make your dog uncomfortable or fearful
5. Three things that put your dog in fight-or-flight mode

By making these lists, you'll start to see the areas where you're doing your best to meet your dog's needs. You'll also notice a few areas where you might want to improve. Your dog will love it if you do. You may even find yourself getting addicted to the feeling you get from having a really happy, loved dog. You might think about making a similar list for your husband or wife, boyfriend or girlfriend, parent or child. (We can learn so much from our interactions with dogs!)

DAY 17

COMMUNICATION
AND RAPPORT

Before we continue exploring the best ways to understand and connect with your dog in order to turn him into the amazing, well-mannered dog of your dreams, take a moment to test the consistency of your coaching by reviewing this list of questions:

- Does your dog "sit" and/or "off" for everything that he wants?
- Have you had enough "fake" guests visit so that your dog associates a stranger at the door with pleasure (getting a treat from you) and, therefore, has stopped all unwanted jumping?
- Does your dog *love* to play tug-of-war with you, and does she "drop" willingly when asked?

- Have you gotten your dog to kiss you or play tug-of-war with you instead of nipping?
- Have you identified your dog's favorite chew toy?

If the answer to all of these questions is yes, then you are well on your way to having a well-mannered dog.

Around the start of the twentieth century, a German math teacher announced an amazing breakthrough in animal training. He had taught his horse, Hans, how to count, spell, multiply and divide, and even tell time! Whenever Hans's owner asked him a question, this brilliant horse would tap out an answer—almost always the right answer—by clopping his hoof.

Soon people around the world were talking about "Clever Hans." A lot of very old ideas about humans being the only thinking creatures in the universe were suddenly in serious dispute, until a psychologist noticed something interesting. When Hans's owner knew the answer to the question that was asked, the horse got it right almost every time. But when the owner didn't know the correct answer, the opposite was true: Hans got it wrong almost every time.

A group of scientists eventually figured out that Hans wasn't answering questions with his brilliance, but his animal instincts. Like most horses, Hans was highly attuned to human anxiety. His owner was subconsciously tensing up whenever Hans reached the correct number of taps with his hoof, causing the horse to stop tapping. Clever Hans didn't know how to do math; he just knew how to read his owner.

For the next hundred years, Clever Hans was a cautionary

tale for anyone who argued that animals were thinking, reasoning creatures. An animal's instinct to please might look like "smarts," but it wasn't what we humans would call intelligence.

In the 1990s, however, an animal psychologist claimed to have taught Rico, a border collie, to understand more than two hundred words and phrases. Rico could also retrieve specific objects when asked. More important, the psychologist organized a set of experiments that proved the dog's intelligence wasn't just another example of the Clever Hans effect: Rico was actually capable of using logical reasoning to figure out which object the experimenters wanted him to retrieve.

Since then, there have been cases of even more intelligent dogs—an Austrian border collie named Betsy has learned more than 340 words. Other studies have demonstrated that dogs are capable of joy, guilt, even moral reasoning. Animal researchers have been forced to completely rethink the old ideas about dogs and intelligence. They aren't rats who can only be trained with behavioral conditioning, wired by positive or negative reinforcement to run through a maze in a particular way. In fact, the average dog has the brainpower and reasoning abilities we expect to see in a two-year-old human being. From my experience, I'd argue that there are times when dogs behave with more maturity, thoughtfulness, and humanlike manners than some grown-ups I know.

So what does this mean for you? You already knew your dog was a genius, right? Well, for one thing, it means we can teach our dogs to understand a lot more words than we thought we could.

CREATING RAPPORT

Tony Robbins is one of the most amazing coaches I've ever met. I've had the good fortune to study his methods for more than fourteen years. He is a big believer in the idea of "rapport," that truly powerful people don't get that way through intimidation or going it alone, but by creating connections, building trust and empathy with others. And the best way of building these kinds of relationships is by building rapport.

When was the last time you had a really great conversation? I'm not talking about "talking," which a lot of the time means thinking about what you're going to say next, before the other person finishes his or her sentence. I mean real communication, when you and the other person are really listening to each other, when you feel so "heard" and so connected to that other person. Do you remember how it made you feel?

Great communication—rapport—puts us into a positive frame of mind. When we feel that someone really "gets" us, that they like and have something in common with us, we're more receptive to new ideas. Sometimes we even feel like we're more resourceful than usual. It's the reason better teachers produce better students.

We build rapport in many ways. The easiest is when we take a genuine interest in what someone else is saying or something they're interested in, maybe even participating in that interest. Parents do it when they play with their kids; husbands can do it when they agree to see "chick flicks."

There are all kinds of ways to create rapport with your

dog. We've already spent a lot of time talking about how important playing games can be to developing a strong bond of trust. What these new ideas about dog intelligence tell us is that we don't have to depend on games alone. Our dogs are capable of understanding a lot of what we say to them, as long as we're clear in our communication.

There are times when I apologize to dogs. Every time I accidentally step on their feet or I feel like I've made a mistake, I will say a sincere "I'm sorry." If it's a more dramatic mistake, I'll hold the dog's face, kiss him on the forehead, and say, "I am *so* sorry." Not all dogs like being held or touched this way, but I believe that most are able to understand and appreciate our intention in those moments.

The most important idea is that you don't have to limit your verbal communication to just a dozen or so "commands." Your dog, whether it's a purebred collie or a mixed-up mutt, is capable of learning so many words and phrases. Once your dog recognizes these words, you'll be able to use them to create rapport in all kinds of situations, immediately putting him in a positive frame of mind.

I was very fortunate that my "son" Duke understood "rest your head," which I used to repeat every time he rested at home, rewarding him with a light and slow scratch behind his ears or on the bridge of his nose, up toward his forehead (his two favorite ways of being touched). Later, when I had to spend seven hours with him while he underwent a blood transfusion at the veterinarian's office, I could ask him to "Rest your head." He recognized the words and rested his head on my lap, and whatever stress either of us felt seemed to melt away.

Here are a few other helpful words I've taught to dogs. Feel free to come up with your own!

"Chillax." I say this in a singsongy way whenever a dog is completely relaxed, like after a good run or an active game. Once he understands the word, I can use it later when I want to "take the batteries out," winding him down when he's restless or agitated.

"I love you." I say this whenever I can, using a sincere tone of voice and looking lovingly into their eyes. It's a great way to comfort dogs when they are stressed out, and it feels good to say it.

"A friend." I repeat this whenever dogs meet someone who is nice to them. It's a very helpful phrase to have when they encounter people they might not trust right away. By hearing that the person is a friend, it helps the dog to associate him or her with a feeling of pleasure.

"Take it." I don't only use this as a behavior (see Day 2), but as a key word for anything yummy or fun. My dogs know they have my permission to jump right into whatever it is!

"Go to bed." I practice this when the dog is in bed; later, when I'm sending her to bed, she understands.

"Get in the car." I began saying this each time my dogs jumped in the car. Now I can say it from inside the house, and they immediately run outside and climb in (after I've opened the door, of course).

"No more." Easy to teach when your dog has finished

eating or you've stopped giving him treats, and great to use to end a game or activity.

Names. My dogs like to learn the names of their friends, whether human or canine. It's fun to gauge a dog's affection for particular people by his response to hearing their names.

Toys. I teach dogs the names of their favorite toys so they'll look for those toys when I ask them.

Places. "Home" is an important one, but so are the names of places that they love. Many of my clients' dogs love going to "day care." My dogs think that every beach is called "Malibu."

USING COMPLETE SENTENCES

When you begin coaching your dog, it's important to keep everything as simple as possible, using short and consistent phrases to tell him what you want him to do. But as your dog grows more comfortable with the English language, you may discover situations in which one-word sentences are actually harder for your dog to understand than more complicated ideas.

One morning, while I was working on this book, I asked my assistant Erich to feed breakfast to Clyde, who was lying by my side. Erich walked into the room and said, "Clyde, eat." Instead of jumping up to grab a meal, Clyde appeared confused. What was Erich talking about? Was there something to eat right here?

I told Erich to rephrase the statement. "Clyde," he said,

"do you want to eat?" Clyde licked his lips in agreement. "Let's go and eat!" Erich announced, to which Clyde leaped up, shook himself off, and happily trotted into the kitchen for a meal.

Once your dog understands individual words, don't be afraid to put them into sentences. Anyone who's ever tried to have a conversation with a surly teenager or tired husband who'll only give one-word answers knows how difficult it can be to communicate this way!

NONVERBAL COMMUNICATION

On Day 14, we talked about the ways a dog can express his feelings through nonverbal communication. But people also send all kinds of messages without being aware that they are sending them.

I once worked with a Chihuahua who freaked out every time his owner, a busy film producer, left the house. So the owner and I began creating "fake" departures. The woman did all of the things that she usually did when she was getting ready to go: brushing her hair; putting on makeup, her shoes, and her coat; taking her bag and keys; walking to the front door. It was a lot of effort, but the woman was committed to reducing her dog's anxiety. We hoped these rehearsals would help make the process feel less stressful for the dog, showing him that just because she was going through the ritual didn't mean she was going to actually leave the house.

The plan worked—sort of. The Chihuahua stopped getting stressed out during the rehearsals. Sometimes the dog would be okay during the actual departure. But sometimes it didn't work, and the dog would freak out as soon as the owner started getting ready to go. "I feel like she knows when I'm faking it," the owner told me.

So I asked her to videotape her normal leaving routine so we could analyze it. Can you guess how the little Chihuahua knew when she was faking it? When the owner was leaving for real, she'd usually put on an expensive perfume, one that she didn't want to waste on rehearsals. The smell of the perfume was triggering the dog's stress.

The human nose has five or six million receptors that it uses to detect smell. A dog has two hundred to three hundred million! Scientists estimate that a dog's sense of smell is between one thousand and ten thousand times better than a human being's. They can use their noses the way people use their eyes, pinpointing the location of certain smells the way that human beings shift their gaze.

It's important to remember that dogs perceive the world in a very different way from people. When you take your dog for a walk, and you see him sniffing everything in sight, remember that he's just checking his "p-mail." His nose is being bombarded by all kinds of information that is invisible to us.

You can use your dog's heightened sense of smell to your advantage. Let's say you have a dog who likes to lick the garbage or go "shoe shopping" in your closet when you aren't around. Any time you respond with negative feedback, add a certain smell into the mix, like a specific perfume (one that you'd never use on yourself) or air freshener. Soon enough, just smelling that particular smell will be enough to let your dog know that an experience is not going to be pleasurable. Spray a little on the garbage or near your shoes, and he'll stay away.

THE POWER OF PHEROMONES

You've probably heard of pheromones before: chemical signals that can be passed from one animal to another, sending messages that range from warnings to sexual attraction. Because they trigger a dog's amazing sense of smell, pheromones are a huge part of any dog's life. Ever hear of a dog "marking" his turf? It's the pheromones in the excrement that cause our dogs to spend so much time reading their "p-mail."

There are more and more products that put pheromones to work in a positive way. For example, a pheromone collar gives off synthetic pheromones that mimic the ones emitted by nursing canine mothers. I've combined it with a few drops of Rescue Remedy (which you can get at almost any health food store) to reduce stress and decrease barking with around a 90 percent success rate.

There are plug-in versions you can use at home, but I really like the pheromones that come in a collar—they go with the dog, not just the wall. There are also pheromone sprays that you can use on people or other dogs who might scare your dog. Combined with behavior modifica-

---

tion (like giving your dog his favorite toys or treats only when strangers are around), it's an almost surefire way to decrease anxiety or get rid of it completely.

THE HOUSEBREAKING CHART: FIRST REVIEW

If you started the housebreaking chart on Day 10, then you should have a week or more of results to start analyzing. By now, you can probably start to see some patterns.

Do accidents happen more frequently in the morning or afternoon? You may have to pay extra attention (and maybe add an extra potty session) to the times of day when your dog has trouble holding it in. You can relax a little more during the times when your dog hasn't shown any need to eliminate.

Is he getting enough food? Dogs should be eating three meals a day until they're twelve weeks old, when you can switch them to two. Is he getting enough water? Dehydration can damage a dog's kidneys, so make sure that there's plenty of water available during meals and at regular two-hour intervals (right before you take him out to the designated bathroom area). This will change later on when he has free access to water.

Does your dog have a favorite spot to go potty? Does he prefer to go at a certain time of day? Does he go all at once or more than once? Have you noticed any change in her mannerisms around that time? Dogs have many different ways of letting us know when they have to go to the bathroom—some walk in circles, whine and cry, sniff, or scratch at the door. Some don't do it much at first, but give us subtle signals, little by little. Pay close attention to your dog during "potty prime time" and you'll start to decipher some of these cues.

If you notice that there are certain times when your dog behaves particularly well, start increasing his "free time." You want to get to the point where he has 100 percent free time because he knows how to "hold" it and lets you know when he needs to go, or goes out on his own.

DAY 18

BLUEPRINT, ENVIRONMENT, AND STATE OF MIND

A few years ago, my friend Greg and his wife, Alex, purchased Cheri, a beautiful nine-month-old schnauzer from someone they thought was a professional "breeder"—after all, he was showing dogs like Cheri in national competitions and had quite a few awards to show for his efforts.

By the time they brought Cheri home, she was demonstrating aggressive behavior. By age four, it had become *seriously* aggressive behavior. She barked menacingly at any strangers in the house, especially males. She routinely bit both people and dogs, sometimes deeply enough for them to require stitches. The last straw—or so Greg and Alex thought—was when Cheri smashed through a glass French door to go after someone doing some work outside their house.

They began putting Cheri into doggy day care whenever strangers visited, only to receive reports that she spent the whole time hiding in some corner, trying to be invisible. Greg and Alex were losing faith that they'd ever be able to socialize their dog. They called me and asked me if I could help.

As I've mentioned earlier in the book, it's been my experience that the majority of the aggressive dogs I've encountered were behaving that way because of extreme nervousness or insecurity, mostly because of a lack of proper socialization and, on rare occasions, a traumatic experience. It sounded to me like Cheri was one of those dogs. She wasn't trying to dominate Greg and Alex or run their household; she seemed like she was getting rattled by the unknown, associating new people and new experiences with pain. So I got to work using another idea I'd borrowed from Tony Robbins—thanks, Tony!

At one of his seminars, he drew a triangle on a whiteboard that looked like this:

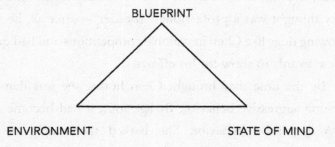

The idea is that these three concepts—blueprint, environment, and state of mind—are interrelated, combining to determine the way we react to stimuli. In other words, it's an attempt to answer the question of why certain events—a driver cutting you off in traffic or a piece of bad news, for example—will cause completely different responses in different people, or even different responses in yourself.

BLUEPRINT. When you experience something consistently enough times, especially at a young age, that association, good or bad, gets "locked" in place, forming a "blueprint" that helps define how you identify yourself in relation to the world.

Although I'm a woman, as a child I really connected to my father, who showed me a lot more love than my mother. Years later, I can see that my "blueprint"—my worldview, my values, and my sensibilities—are very much defined by that relationship. I tend to see things, for better or worse, as if I'm looking through my father's eyes.

In Cheri's case, I thought that she had probably been neglected or abused by the "breeder" who raised her for the first nine months of her life, a critical period of time. At the very least, she wasn't socialized to new situations or new people, leading her to associate them with pain, uncertainty, and fear instead of pleasure and excitement. In other words, she developed a blueprint that told her new people and new situations were going to be painful.

ENVIRONMENT. Hearing an unfamiliar noise while you're at the office, in the middle of the day, may not cause you any stress. Hearing that same noise when you're alone, in the middle of the night, might make you terrified. Your environment plays a major role in determining how you will respond to a certain situation.

Your perception of your environment is not always rooted in reality—sometimes it's affected by your blueprint. If something really terrible happened to you on a rainy day, you might begin to associate all rainy days with a feeling of terror. You might be stuck with those feelings until you learned how to change your perception of rain, associating that particular environment with pleasure instead of pain.

Greg and Alex were clearly trying to create a loving environment for Cheri. But Cheri's blueprint was so strong that it dominated the way she experienced her immediate surroundings. Any change to her environment triggered feelings of pain and anxiety and a deep need to protect herself.

STATE OF MIND. Your current state of mind greatly affects the way you respond to stimuli. The world seems like a much different place when you're tired, busy, hungry, or impatient than it does when you're relaxed and well rested. Your physical state plays a big part in determining your state of mind. How well do you focus when you feel sick or have a huge headache? In my previous book, I wrote about a dog who refused to "sit" and wound up biting a trainer who tried to physically force him into the position. It turned out that the dog was in immense physical pain that the "trainer" failed to notice. Under pain-free circumstances, the dog probably would have been able to tolerate this kind of bullying. Just not on that day.

Cheri wasn't in physical pain, but she had managed to learn that an aggressive state of mind was an effective way of "managing" her environment, scaring off strangers she expected to bring her pain. (BTW, you may know people who do the same thing!)

After evaluating Cheri's behavior using these three ideas, I knew I had to start with her environment, making it seem less threatening. That would lead to a change in her state of mind, which, if repeated often enough, could change her blueprint just enough so that she no longer associated new people or new situations with tremendous pain.

But first I had to walk through the front door. You'd have thought Cheri wanted to kill me. She barked ferociously and lunged at me—but Alex was holding her tightly on a leash.

I asked Alex to show me the way she normally handled this kind of situation. She asked Cheri to "Down!" and "Stay!" But Cheri completely ignored her, continuing to bark at me.

I completely understood where Cheri was coming from. Her wolf instincts told her there were three ways to deal with a potential threat: She could freeze, hoping I passed by without seeing her, fight off the threat, or run away (flight). I'd clearly already seen her, so freezing—hoping to remain inconspicuous—wasn't going to work. Alex asking her to stay "down" made Cheri feel like flight wasn't an option. Imagine how you would feel if you were tied to a tree and saw volcanic lava oozing toward you, or an angry bear rushing at you. You would do whatever you had to do to get out of your restraints. But Alex was telling her not to run away from the danger that had just walked through the front door. Would you listen to a person who told you not to try and escape from the rushing lava, even if it was the person you trusted most in the world?

It was no wonder that Cheri wanted to stop danger from ever coming close to the house, busting through the French doors to scare it away before it made its way inside.

One "trainer" used a shock collar on Cheri when she refused to stay, which only increased Cheri's level of stress and fear.

Fortunately, I knew there was another way: The Loved Dog way. I asked Alex to skip Cheri's last meal. As soon as I saw what was going on, I took a few super-gold treats from my pocket, broke them into tiny pieces, and tossed one on the floor in front of Cheri. "Take it!" I said in my happiest singsongy voice. I didn't look at her and angled my body sideways in a way that communicated to her I had no intention of attacking.

Cheri sniffed at the treat suspiciously—if she picked it up, she'd have to take her eyes off me. But after a few seconds, Cheri finally decided that the treat was worth the risk of ignoring me—my body language let her know I wasn't a threat—and she gobbled it up. It was a huge first victory, one that gave me hope. If a dog is too freaked out, she won't eat. The fact that Cheri ate the gold treat was a wonderful sign.

Three treats later, I asked Alex to loosen Cheri's leash, giving her enough slack to move closer to me (but not enough to reach me). This time, I dropped the treat a little closer to me, so that Cheri would have to make the decision to move toward me to get it. Rather than approaching her, I wanted Cheri to *choose* to approach me. Sure enough, she grabbed the treat and immediately retreated back to Alex.

Alex had justifiably been tense throughout, fearing a bloodbath, but I noticed that when she loosened the leash, Cheri seemed to become a tiny bit more relaxed as well. So I asked Alex to take a deep breath and let it out loudly, an exaggerated sigh of relief. Cheri picked up on Alex's cue and began to relax even more. This time I held the treat in my hand, still making sure not to look directly into Cheri's eyes. Cheri finally stepped toward me and touched my hand, momentarily overcoming all of the risks the blueprint in her mind had been programmed to warn her about. She took the treat. "Take it!" I said immediately in a calm and happy voice, then rewarded Cheri with a jackpot.

I moved to a spot about four feet away. At first, Cheri seemed to regress to her old behavior—what seemed like a small distance for us meant "Uh-oh . . . Here we go again!" for her. She could trust me by the window, but could she trust me by the chair? But a few repetitions later, I'd regained her trust. Slowly we moved toward the front door, which for Cheri was ground zero.

Greg's arrival home broke the spell of tranquility, as Cheri reverted to her old pattern of barking intensely at whoever was coming through the door. I calmly stood next to Cheri and did a "take it" with another treat. Now, it might seem like I was rewarding an unwanted behavior. But scolding Cheri would only have increased the tension—and if I could return her state of mind to something pleasurable, I could help her to feel better about the situation. Not only did Cheri stop barking, but we could see her relax. Greg entered the house and repeated the same sequence of "take its" that I had earlier, while we all intentionally exhaled loudly.

At the time, the family was having some work done in the guest bathroom, and had two workers—whom Cheri had been barking at aggressively for days—waiting outside. I wanted to show Greg and Alex that Cheri was manageable, but didn't want the dog to feel like she was being tested. With Cheri on a loose leash, we invited one of the workers inside and repeated the same series of "take its." Five minutes later, Cheri was eating out of the worker's hand as he walked up and down the hallway between the door and the guest bathroom.

We repeated the process with the other worker. By the end, Alex had tears in her eyes. In just two hours, we'd conditioned a supposedly untrainable dog to eat out of a stranger's hand.

"We're just getting started!" I told them. I wanted to show Greg and Alex that their supposedly dominant, aggressive dog wasn't interested in controlling the roost or being leader of the pack, as other trainers had told them. All she wanted was to feel safe. So I got on the floor, my head five inches from Cheri's face, and taught her to "leave it," covering the treat with my hand until she moved her head away. It felt great to connect with her that way, and it was amazing to see her leave her instincts behind and make a conscious choice to do things in a new way.

When I got off the floor, I walked over to the door and opened it quickly. Cheri immediately reverted to her old barking. Greg and Alex finally understood the psychology behind Cheri's aggressive behavior. She needed to be socialized, to learn from her parents that people were trustworthy. That there was nothing to fear from the postman, from simple household objects, or from imaginary boogeymen.

"Please forget everything you ever learned about dog training," I told them. "You've been doing it the conventional way for four years and you saw no improvement. If anything, things only got worse. If you want to modify your dog's behavior, you've got to modify your own behavior as well."

I helped Greg and Alex create a list of "triggers" that led to Cheri's aggressive behavior, then suggested ways to help socialize the dog to those situations. I also asked them to practice the "take it" game with four people a day, teaching Cheri that there's no need to be afraid of strangers.

"Most of all," I explained, "you need to be patient with Cheri. Desensitizing her is going to be like a vaccine where you dilute the disease to such a low level that the body has a chance to build an immunity to it. Let Cheri experience the things that scare her at a very low threat level, and little by little, you can help her to build an immunity."

"And she'll learn to obey?" asked Greg.

"It's about trust," said Alex, causing me to smile. I was thrilled that she understood, and that Greg was on his way. They put a pheromone collar on Cheri, began applying a few drops of Rescue Remedy each day, and did some TTouch (see Day 26) with their dog. The problems began to fade away. However, it took months before we saw some real and consistent change, as it takes a long time to overcome trauma. That is why socializing a dog at any age is one of the best gifts you can give her, as well as a great insurance policy for you.

DON'T DRIVE WHEN YOU'RE ANGRY

We all know that you shouldn't drive when you are drunk or while text messaging. But did you know that drivers who are *angry* are twice as likely to get into accidents? They are more aggressive, more impulsive, and more anxious than normal drivers, and cause thousands of accidents and injuries every year. Why? Because they aren't in a good state of mind to respond properly to stimuli. They tend to overreact.

Your dog's state isn't the only one you have to worry about when you're coaching him—you're not going to be a good coach when you're angry, hungry, or tired. If your feelings toward your dog—or your life—are getting in the way of a happy, fun, and compassionate coaching session, take a break and get the time you need to take care of *your* needs before returning.

DAY 19

THE POWER OF BELIEFS

In 2008, my nonprofit The Loved World Foundation launched a program called Another Chance at Love. We take shelter dogs to juvenile prisons, where they're coached by inmates. The idea is to create another chance for both of them. The dogs return to the shelter as "certified" well-mannered Loved Dogs and have much better odds of being adopted into permanent homes. The prisoners, most of whom will be released by their twenty-fifth birthdays, experience a sense of connection with another living creature, while getting a chance to see themselves in a different light, in some cases helping them to see their lives in new and exciting ways.

Before we take the dogs into the prison, we spend a few weeks coaching the prisoners. One of the first things we do is teach them how to speak in baby talk. Imagine me, standing there in front of a room full of tough-looking teenagers and young adults—with tattoos, shaved heads, and menacing expressions—asking them to say, "S-i-t, g-o-o-d s-i-t!" in the highest voices they can manage. It's a great way to get them relaxed and laughing.

These teenagers are not the cuddly kind, at least not on the surface, but I believe that for most of them, the tough exteriors are just shields to hide behind. (It takes much more courage to be soft!) It's so heartwarming to see a class with teenagers who have been coaching with us for a while. When they learn to feel the joy of effective communication, it can change the way they communicate with everyone around them.

One of them—an eighteen-year-old named Kwami—shocked me when he told me that he became a dad at age thirteen. Do you remember what you were doing when you were thirteen? We set Kwami up with an older, overweight cocker spaniel girl. Afterward, I asked him if he'd learned anything. Without hesitation he said, "I now have more patience and I know I need to be playful with my kids!"

Another student, Anthony—a muscular Hispanic whose shaved head was covered in tattoos—started tearing up when he confessed that he'd never understood that dogs have feelings. Where he grew up, people kept dogs for two reasons: protection or dog fighting. But after spending a few weeks with a cuddly little dog, he began to see how smart and emotionally vulnerable they were.

A former drug dealer told me about how the environment he grew up in led to his imprisonment. "The way everybody was talking about me, that I will always be bad, I decided to be the worst," he said. "I joined a gang and made a name for myself as a good moneymaker." His story reminded me of just how powerful beliefs can be in shaping our lives. We believe in the goodness of these young adults and want them to believe in themselves again.

If you want to see a video of this amazing experience, it's on my website, www.tamargeller.com, in the section on my nonprofit work.

THE BELIEFS WE HAVE ABOUT OURSELVES

In 2009, we started another program called Operation Heroes & Hounds, taking shelter dogs to be coached by wounded marines in Camp Pendleton. I wanted to contribute something to the amazing people who were fighting in Iraq and Afghanistan, having myself served in the Israeli army during the first Lebanon war, where I saw the horrors of combat.

My experience didn't prepare me for what I saw at Camp Pendleton. It wasn't the injuries that disturbed me, but the losses some of these soldiers had suffered in terms of self-esteem and self-image. As one of the guys said to me, "Now that I got shot and can't fight anymore, I'm just a broken, useless piece of machinery." It would be an understatement to say those words broke my heart. I know that the healing power of the shelter dogs has helped to improve this particular veteran's perspective on his value as a human being and his future.

It's no wonder that there's such a high rate of suicide and domestic violence among those who have experienced the horrors of war. When soldiers go to war, they have to put aside compassion, sensitivity, and empathy in order to be able to kill others. In his book *From Baghdad, with Love: A Marine, the War, and a Dog Named Lava,* my friend Jay Kopelman, a lieutenant colonel in the U.S. Marines, writes about his experiences trying to rescue a stray dog he'd found in Fallujah. Jay found himself constantly at odds with the rules of war, which wanted him to follow orders, see the world in black and white, and deny many of his basic human emotions. Lava, the dog, helped him to reconnect with those emotions. It's an interesting read with a happy ending.

Operation Heroes & Hounds has been a great program. It's incredible how fast these shelter dogs get under the marines' hard skins and into their hearts. (You can see a video on my website, www.tamargeller.com.) Dogs have a magical ability to heal the soul that is nothing short of miraculous. The program was just as rewarding for the dogs, getting them out of the shelters and into forever homes. We're currently expanding the program to a national level, giving many more of the wonderful warriors who've fought for our country and the dogs who have found their way into shelters a better quality of love and life. Once again, we saw how our belief in these wounded marines' ability to redefine and reinvent themselves changed their own belief in themselves as well. (Of course, there was a lot of work to be done with and for all of them, but the immediate change we saw thanks to the program was undeniable.)

Most people feel, on one level or another, that they are not enough. There are many ways of dealing with these feelings of inadequacy. Some hide them with bravado, shyness, anger, or sarcasm. Others look to build an image with "success"—cars, clothes, money, or titles. But even then, success becomes an unobtainable goal: There's always another promotion, a newer car, ten pounds to lose, a better relationship that they'll need before they can feel good about themselves.

One of the greatest gifts we get from living with dogs—maybe *the* greatest gift—is that they see us for who we are. They don't care about our money, our jobs, our cars, or any of the ways in which we might feel we're not living up to some incredible ideal. They just love us, with unwavering consistency. Let me tell you from experience: Oprah's dogs don't know that she's one of the most powerful women in the world; for them, she's "Mom." Charlize Theron's dogs don't know that she's one of the prettiest women in the world—they know her as the best cook any dog could wish for. Ben Affleck's dogs don't care if he's acting or directing, and Mabel and Wolfie DeGeneres don't love Ellen even more now that she hosted *American Idol*—she's already the best mother in the world.

If only we could see ourselves the way our dogs see us! Your dog is a canvas that allows you to see your success. Every day you see your dog grow, whether he's surprised you with a new behavior, mastered an old trick, or learned not to dig up your flower bed, you've gained some success. These little victories add up over time, creating an even more powerful feeling of success.

GRATITUDE

It's so much easier to focus on what is missing than on all the things that are great, which is why I like to see gratitude as a muscle. Every night before I go to sleep and each morning when I wake up, I take a moment to tell my "sons" that I love them and thank them for being healthy and in my life. Instead of giving them attention only when they're doing something wrong, I always try to look for something that they are doing right, some reason to tell them that I am happy with them. These habits have helped me to build a "gratitude muscle" that allows me to see my relationship with my dogs—and every other aspect of my life—as juicy, passionate, brilliant, and fun.

My dog, my "son" Duke, recently died unexpectedly from cancer, and I can't tell you how grateful I am now for having been so grateful and appreciative of him during his life.

Take a moment to look at your dog and identify something positive in whatever he's doing. Is he "shushed" instead of barking? Lying "down" and not jumping? When out for a walk, is your dog "close" to you and not trying to run away? Take notice—and express it out loud.

Here's a crazy thought: Try it with the people you love. It's like the lyrics of that great James Taylor song, "Shower the people you love with love / Show them the way that you feel." It sounds so obvious—of course you want to shower the people you love with love—but in reality, research shows that most of us do the opposite, taking the people we love for granted. When we do show love toward the people in our lives, they sometimes feel uncomfortable—while almost everyone wants to feel loved and appreciated, not everyone knows how to receive those feelings.

The good news is that our dogs are *always* ready to receive our love! They are great and willing subjects for our gratitude target practice. Give it a shot. Find something to be grateful about and tell your dog each time there's a commercial break on your TV, every ten minutes, every hour, every week. If you can develop a propensity for seeing the good in another living creature, you will open yourself up to a sense of gratitude that feels absolutely amazing!

YOUR BELIEFS ARE THE KEY TO EVERYTHING

My friend Scott Hamilton is an Olympic gold medalist. You might think, as I did, that Scott was born with some sort of God-given talent for figure skating. But as he wrote in his book *The Great Eight,* nothing could be further from the truth. He was shorter than average, and skating was the only sport he could participate in where his size wasn't a total hindrance.

After a few successes, he came to believe that he could be a good figure skater. He became one, through focus, perseverance, hard work, and excellent coaches, but it all began because he believed in himself, not because it was natural or easy for him to skate.

Your dog does not have to come from an incredible bloodline in order to be great. Start with any average shelter mutt that has no obvious talent or skill, and with the proper coaching from you, the dog's brilliance and character will shine through. It's like sculpting—you don't need great materials to create an unbelievable sculpture. A good artist can figure out how to bring out the best in whatever piece of wood or stone is put in front of him. Just look at the TV show *Project Runway*, where the contestants create masterpieces on a shoestring budget.

Of course, dogs have certain physical and mental limitations—we all do. But the most important factor in your dog's success is your belief in him. Your dog will only be limited by his breed, his temperament, or his age if you think he is incapable of learning.

It's been proven that most people make up their minds about another person, assigning them an identity, within thirty minutes of meeting him or her. We spend the rest of our time with that person looking for the reasons that initial assessment was correct. Do you think your dog is stubborn? Aggressive? Stupid? Settle on one of these adjectives and you're likely to spend all kinds of time "proving" just how stubborn, aggressive, or stupid your dog seems to be. In the more than twenty-two years I've been coaching dogs, I have never met even one dog that fit the derogatory description someone gave him. Not once. (But I can think of a few derogatory terms for the people who insult their dogs!)

It's also important not to get caught up in the idea of the

"ideal" pet. You don't want to "frog your dog" by expecting him to live up to some unattainable standard.

I've heard a lot of my friends, especially my female friends, talk about how badly they want a husband or a baby. But when they get the man or have the baby, when their "dream" comes true, they are suddenly plagued by doubts. I hear them counting the minutes until the nanny arrives or the next girls' night out. It's not that they don't love their husbands and babies— they're just disappointed by the unrealistic expectations they had about how perfect their husbands and babies would be.

What kind of expectations do you have for your dog? Do you want him to be like Lassie? There's nothing wrong with that, as long as you remember what I told you in the introduction: Lassie was actually played by five different dogs. Each of these dogs was trained all day long by professionals, then swapped in and out of the show according to their moods and abilities.

How do you manage your expectations without limiting your dog's potential? By adjusting your sense of the behavior you'll accept as "success." Success is not the same thing as 100 percent perfection. If you can hit a baseball 30 percent of the time—failing the other 70 percent of the time—you'll probably be a multimillionaire. You can make a small adjustment to the way you see your dog and start to see how great he already is.

For example, it's unrealistic to expect that when you say "Come," your dog will sprint toward you at full speed, sit down on the ground in front of you, and patiently await whatever you're about to say next 100 percent of the time.

Would you be satisfied if he responded to your call quickly 95 percent of the time but occasionally took his time (while coming back fast when it mattered most)?

This might seem like a subtle distinction, but it's anything but. If you're willing to not just tolerate, but expect behavior that's less than perfect—as long as it's enough to meet your needs—you will give your dog (or girlfriend, husband, child) the room to be himself, the room to surprise you with his brilliance!

You might be amazed by how quickly this can become a habit. The more you feel that people are grateful and appreciate your appreciation, the more you're going to want to give.

"OFF" LEVEL 2

When we started with "off," we held a treat right next to the dog's nose. Getting your dog to listen to you when you're not using a treat as a lure requires a few gradual steps.

In Level 1, your dog was listening to your verbal cue, but backed "off" because that was the only way he could retain eye contact with the treat. In Level 2, we're going to teach your dog the next step in focusing on the verbal cue instead of the treat.

Start with Level 1: Hold the treat next to his mouth and say, "Off." Next, move the treat from his mouth to your belly button, where he can see it but can't reach it. This will trigger an internal struggle for your dog: His wolf instincts are

---

telling him that he needs to move toward the treat which is now farther away in order to get it, but you're telling him that he'll get it if he moves farther away. He's going to have to trust you over his instincts, which he can only do if he's mastered Level 1.

"Off": Level two

If he chooses his instincts—moving toward the treat—go back to Level 1. It's not a failure—not everyone can be great at everything right off the bat, the same way that some students excel in math but struggle with history. Go back to the stage where your dog was successful and build from there.

The change from Level 1 to Level 2 may seem tiny to you, but

"Off": Level three

it's a big deal for a dog. You've changed the rules, and he'll need time to recalibrate his brain—this is a great time to practice your ability to be silent, giving him the space he needs to figure it out. Say his name, then "Off," and then wait. After ten to fifteen seconds, repeat—and if he doesn't get it, either go back to Level 1 or shuffle gently into him. Reward him with the treat as he backs off.

DAY 20

HOW TO TEACH YOUR DOG TO DO JUST ABOUT ANYTHING

I used to be an intelligence officer in the Israeli Air Force and got to team up with Israeli Special Forces. Talk about being part of a goal-oriented team! My job every day was to evaluate situations and create plans for dealing with them. When you're in the military, the success or failure of your plans can often mean life or death.

But "success" didn't always mean the plan went exactly as we hoped. If anything, it rarely did. It was important to have "drawer plans" to help us adjust to unexpected developments. What if the weather turned bad, a jeep or a helicopter broke down, or someone got sick or injured? We had to be ready to make constant adjustments to our plans.

Coaching your dog requires a similar strategy. Planning is

important, but you can't focus only on the outcome you're hoping for—you have to pay attention to what is really going on and always be willing to change your approach.

If you break the process down into these six steps, there are almost no limits to what you and your dog can accomplish!

1. DEFINE THE BEHAVIOR YOU'D LIKE YOUR DOG TO LEARN.

Okay, there may be *some* limits. If your daughter is six years old and weighs 150 pounds, she's probably not going to be a ballerina. Your dog isn't likely to learn how to speak fluent Spanish or drive a race car. Your goals need to be realistic.

That being said, I have clients who have taught their dogs to dance, fetch them beers from the refrigerator, and bring in the morning paper—and are even able to distinguish the *Wall Street Journal* from the *New York Times*.

It all begins with a clear definition of the behavior you want your dog to learn. You have to be specific—"cleaning up the house" is too vague a goal, as you can't expect your dog to have the same idea of neatness as you. But with a little effort, you can teach him to "pick up socks and put them in a laundry basket."

2. IT'S LESS IMPORTANT TO SEE WHAT YOUR DOG IS DOING WRONG THAN TO SEE WHAT HE'S DOING RIGHT.

Whether you're trying to teach your dog how to slam dunk a doggy basketball or lift up his paw and wave, every new behavior can be broken down into a series of steps. The most successful coaches remember to reward their dogs for every little bit of progress along the way. These little victories are the building blocks toward greater success.

By focusing on what your dog has achieved instead of what he hasn't, you'll also create an environment that is conducive to success. Most marketers will advise people starting new businesses to promote and publicize every achievement, no matter how tiny, in order to build an identity. Doing the same with your dog will help him to become more self-confident and less afraid of making mistakes. Your dog is going to want to take chances for you!

3. DEVELOP A PLAN.

I love how my friend Kyra Sundance tells Chalcy, her Weimaraner, to go "night-night"—her dog finds the nearest blanket and rolls himself up in it.

Kyra didn't spend hours repeating "night-night" while twisting Chalcy around in a blanket like an egg roll. Instead, she strung together a series of behaviors her dog already knew— "come," "down," "take it," "roll over," and "head down"—in order to create the new behavior.

When you're trying to teach a new behavior, start by breaking it down into behaviors your dog has already mastered. How can you use them to get from point A to B to C to D? (And don't forget how, on Day 9, I showed you that it's easier to start with D.)

4. TAKE ACTION!

It's not enough to have a plan—there also has to be *commitment* and consistent *follow-through*.

By commitment, I mean really making an effort. Dogs are like kids, in the sense that they both know when a parent or coach is "faking it." It's hard to teach your dog how to catch a ball if your focus is on the TV set or some unresolved problem from work. But when we commit to really being present with our dogs, to engaging them directly with enthusiasm, they'll respond with excitement, often giving us much more than we ask for.

The follow-through comes from consistency. A good plan is just the beginning. You've got to put it into practice, a few times each day. Otherwise, it's like trying to live more nutritiously by eating one healthy meal a week. If you're going to eat cheeseburgers the rest of the time, you're not going to get the results.

5. REVIEW THE RESULTS.

James Dyson got fed up with vacuum cleaners. Every model he tried wound up getting clogged up and spewing dust all over the area he was trying to clean. So he set out to build a better version.

His first attempt was a failure. His second attempt was a failure. His tenth, his hundredth, his *thousandth* attempt was a failure. But he stayed true to his dream, using each failure as an opportunity to learn from his mistakes. He made slight adjustments to his strategy, each time bringing him closer to the vacuum cleaner he had in mind. On the 5,127th try, he finally got it right. James Dyson—or *Sir* James Dyson, as he was called after being knighted by the queen of England—went on to make billions of dollars.

Failure is an inevitable part of any success. Many successful people learn to appreciate failure as an essential part of the process, a chance to learn from one's mistakes and create a better strategy. If it seems like your coaching isn't producing the behavior you want from your dog, don't blame the dog for being SDS (stupid, dominant, or stubborn)—take a step back and evaluate your coaching curriculum and style.

Maybe you're trying to teach your dog at a time of day when he's hungry or has low energy. Are you ending each coaching session on a high note, as we discussed way back on Day 9? Do you have unrealistic expectations about the progress you're making? Many dogs need to repeat a behavior many times in many different environments before they master it. Maybe you need to be more enthusiastic or clearer in your communication. As a foreigner, I occasionally have trouble understanding English. Once I've finished explaining to the speaker that they don't have to talk *louder*—my hearing is fine, thank you—he or she will usually figure out how to rephrase the comment or question in a way that I can understand.

6. BE FLEXIBLE, CREATIVE, AND MOST OF ALL, PLAYFUL AS YOU ADJUST YOUR STRATEGY.

Once you've identified a potential flaw in your approach, you can make adjustments to your plan. Flexibility may be the most important part of achieving success. Trees bend in the wind. Living creatures mutate and adapt in order to survive. There are many different ways to achieve a particular outcome. You just have to be creative enough to find them, open-minded enough to use them, and persistent enough to keep trying until you find one that works.

Jeffrey Katzenberg, whose Hollywood career has taken him from assistant to studio head, once said, "If they throw you out the front door, you go in the back door. And if they throw you out the back door, you go in the window. And if they throw you out the window, you go in the basement. And you don't ever take it personally." The key is to be flexible and never accept NO as an option! Sometimes along the way, we wind up changing our idea of success. As Garth Brooks sings in one of his songs, "Some of God's greatest gifts are unanswered prayers." You might not teach your dog to do exactly what you set out to do, but you may accidentally wind up with a new behavior that you hadn't anticipated. If your dog is having trouble distinguishing between the socks you want him to pick up and the remote control to the TV, then teach your dog how to fetch the remote! You can go back to the socks later. Great coaches try to keep their minds open to serendipity, the magical results they haven't anticipated, and are ready to reward those behaviors as well.

Finally, it's helpful to remember that real success is a journey, not a destination. As long as you're a loving and playful coach, the time you spend coaching your dog will never be wasted time. You'll always be learning new things about each other, developing mutual respect, and deepening your bonds of trust. That's what I call success!

By the way, these are the same strategies that are regularly used by all kinds of successful people to achieve the results they're looking for in virtually any area. In other words, you don't have to use them to change things about your dog—the same strategy can be used to change your home, your job, or anything else about your life.

"TARGET!"

Teaching your dog how to touch a target with his paw or nose isn't only a cool trick, it's a building block that will help you to teach your dog all kinds of more complicated behaviors, from answering the phone when it rings to ringing a bell to let you know when he has to go outside.

The easiest place to start is your hand. Rub a treat on your palm and hold it out to your dog. As soon as he touches your hand with his nose, say, "Touch!" or "Target!" and reward him with a treat from your storage hand. As he starts to get the hang of it, ask your dog to "Target" as you move your hand higher, lower, or away from him.

Once he's learned to target your hand, you can switch to objects. Choose an area that doesn't have too many distractions, like a room with a lot of open space or your backyard. Your "target" can be just about anything—a traffic cone, a stick in the ground, or a Post-it note stuck to a chair. Place a treat on top of the target, somewhere your dog will be able to see it, and stand with your dog about six feet away. Point toward the target and release him, announcing, "Target!" as you do. Your dog should run to the "target" and eat his reward.

Once you've done it a few times, try it without placing a treat on the target. Just say "Target!" and when your dog touches it with his paw or nose, reward him with a "Good target!" and a gold treat.

DAY 21

COOL DOG TRICKS

There are so many good reasons to teach your dog new behaviors. You'll deepen the bonds between you and learn how to communicate more effectively. It's great mental stimulation, which you'll remember is part of your dog's seven basic needs. Teaching new behaviors is a fun way to spend time with your friend, especially when he masters a complicated trick or surprises you with a completely unexpected behavior. You'll build each other's self-esteem—your dog will be happy to please you, and you can amaze yourself with what an excellent coach you've become.

Best of all, you'll totally impress your friends and family!

HOW MUCH COACHING DO I NEED TO DO?

Most of us don't have the time to spend several hours a day coaching our dogs so that they can star in Hollywood movies.

At the same time, tossing your dog a few treats while you're planted in front of the TV set isn't going to get you very far unless your goal is to fatten him up. So how much time should you spend coaching your dog?

Many "trainers" recommend about twenty minutes daily. I think that's the wrong way to think about coaching. You wouldn't limit your kid or spouse to twenty minutes a day of conversation and shoo them away the rest of the time they wanted attention or feedback, just as you can't build a great relationship with your dog by ignoring him for twenty-three hours and forty minutes every day.

Instead of separating "dog time" from the rest of your day, try to incorporate it wherever you can. Try to spend about five minutes coaching your dog whenever you have an opportunity. You probably won't have enough time to do as many sessions as I recommend to my clients—a million times a day—but ten per day can easily be done. Chances are you'll find the three to five minutes stretching into longer and longer sessions as your dog's progress and desire to learn make you feel great about your abilities as a coach.

Even when you're not engaged in an active coaching session, there are always opportunities for relevance coaching, passive coaching ("narration"), and socialization, which can take place whenever the two of you happen to be interacting. The narration, in particular, is really easy and very useful—just smile and tell a dog what he's doing, as in "Down, what a good down!" when he happens to be lying down, or

"Drink, drink!" when he's drinking water. Ask everyone in your household to do the same.

If you're introducing a brand-new behavior, you should set aside a block of time long enough for your dog to really understand what it is you're trying to teach. Just remember to end the session while your dog is still enjoying himself. If he's having trouble understanding a particular behavior and you're ready to wrap it up, switch to a behavior he already knows and finish on a high note.

Your coaching sessions should be all about fun and doing what you can to get your dog to succeed. At times, that means changing the way you act toward your dog. When you're teaching a behavior like "come," for example, it's best to be happy and enthusiastic—you want your dog to want to sprint toward you. "Stay" works better when you're calm and encouraging. On the flip side, if you're feeling tired or cranky, don't force yourself. Your dog's not going to give you a hard time for missing a session. Better yet, use your dog to cheer yourself up—science has shown that petting a dog reduces stress and lowers blood pressure. When "coaching" starts to feel like "training" or "drilling," you've probably spent too much time in the classroom. If your dog looks unhappy and tries to run or hide from you when it's time for a session, you may be pushing him too hard. The goal is a dog who *wants* to be coached, to be challenged, and to spend time with you. That's when you'll know you have a Loved Dog.

COMMON COACHING MISTAKES

Here are a few of the most common mistakes I see people make when they're trying to teach their dog a new behavior:

Sessions that are too long or too repetitive (when the dog gets bored). It's so important to end on a high note, with your dog feeling good about the results rather than feeling like a failure.

Progress that's too fast. Don't move on to the next step just because your dog has done something "right" once or twice—make sure that he's really mastered that particular step before raising the bar.

Reducing the number of treats (or stopping them altogether). Let's say you're earning a steady paycheck until one day you come into work and discover that your salary has been reduced or eliminated. Would you feel motivated to take on a new work-related challenge? Or would you feel stressed out and confused as to what you did to deserve the pay cut? It's okay to reduce rewards for behaviors that your dog has already mastered, but don't cut them out completely—you want your dog to always believe that there's a chance of receiving a reward for a behavior well done. The Las Vegas Method of winning random jackpots works very well for a reason—use it with your dog as well.

Testing the dog. Instead of coaching through small, gradual steps, some owners try to teach concepts that are way above their dogs' heads, creating a sense of failure for both the dogs and their coaches.

TAKE A BOW

The great thing about "taking a bow" is that you can teach it without any real effort, like when you're half awake in the morning, still too tired to get out of bed. As you've probably already noticed, most dogs "bow" naturally—it's the way they stretch when they get up after lying down for a while. Your dog does it every morning. When he does, narrate the behavior by saying, "Bowwwwwwww" in a drawn-out voice. Add a hand signal, that little flourish that theater actors do when bowing to an audience. If you're up and about, give your dog a treat; if you're still in bed, it's a great time to practice "catch" with a treat from your nightstand. Repeat this routine for a few mornings, and you'll soon have a dog who will bow on cue. I've found that it's a great way to break the ice with kids who might be a little skittish around dogs.

PLAY SOCCER

Your dog may not be able to "bend it like Beckham," but you can teach him to kick a soccer ball into a net.

Many dogs will instinctively understand the game—kick around a soccer ball for a few seconds and gently pass it to your dog. If he bats at it with his feet, enthusiastically say, "Soccer!" and reward him with a treat. As he begins to understand what you're asking him to do, slowly increase the distance he's got to roll the ball in order to get a reward.

If your dog doesn't take naturally to the game, you can try getting your dog a "treat ball" from your favorite pet store. They're hollow balls with holes that allow you to fill them with treats. When you roll one of these balls toward your dog, he'll knock the ball around with his feet in an effort to get at the treats inside. Say, "Soccer!" and reward him when he does. Once he's grasped the idea, you can replace the treat ball with a real soccer ball.

Once your dog is able to roll the ball a few feet, you can introduce a net into the game. Run with your dog toward the goal and say, "Soccer!" Reward him if he pushes the ball into the net. It helps a lot if there's a clearly defined line on the ground.

If soccer's not your thing, then teach your favorite sport. Many dogs make excellent hockey goalies (my dog Clyde is one), athletic wide receivers, or slam-dunking basketball stars. (You can find doggy basketball kits at many pet stores. I'm also a big fan of a product called the eGGe, a big plastic ball shaped unevenly so that a dog can't pick it up in his mouth. But he'll try, leading to hours of fun as he bats it around.)

THE SNEEZING GAME

Dogs became "man's best friend" for a reason—they've been helping people out for thousands of years, doing everything from tracking prey to herding sheep to protecting villages. Even if you don't have any prey to track, sheep to herd, or villages to protect, you can teach your dog to do other things that tap into his natural desire to help. The "sneezing game" is one of my favorites—and a huge crowd pleaser. You'll have to have first taught your dog how to "take it," "fetch," and "drop" to play it.

There are two versions of the game:

Bring me a tissue! Tape a box of tissues to the floor. Wiggle one of the tissues for your dog and tell him to "Take it." Reward him if he pulls the tissue out of the box. Once he starts to get the hang of it, take the box off the floor and hold it at different heights.

When he's got this part down, move a few feet away and point toward the tissues, pretending to sneeze ("Achoo!") and saying, "Fetch." When your dog brings the tissue to you, say, "Good achoo!" and ask him to "Drop it." Make a party with a silver reward. Once your dog begins to understand the game, you can start to eliminate the "fetch" and "drop it," until he's performing the behavior every time you say "Achoo!" If you're convincing enough with your fakery, you'll have a dog who will bring you a tissue every time you actually sneeze—a great friend to have when you're sick!

Bring me the box! If you're actually sick and need a tissue, you may not want one that your dog has slobbered all over. Instead of teaching him to bring you an individual tissue, you can teach him to fetch the entire box. Just pretend the tissue box is a toy, using "Achoo, fetch!" as your cue. After a while, you can start to hide the box in different places—ask him to "Stay," then release him so he can go treasure hunting to bring you the box. "Make a *big* party" for him when he does.

If you're ready for a bigger challenge, you can even teach your dog to throw the used tissue away (or at least a crumpled one that looks used). When you've finished using it, hand the tissue to your dog, say, "Take it" and "throw it away," and point toward the trash can. You can teach him how to use the trash can by holding a treat over the opening whenever he has a tissue in his mouth. When he sniffs the treat, ask your dog to "Drop it," then "make a party" if he drops the tissue in the can. Eventually, you'll be able to ditch the "take it" and the "drop it."

HIGH-FIVE/WAVE GOOD-BYE

High-five was one of my dog Duke's favorite behaviors. He did it naturally whenever I dared to stop petting him, pawing at me to let me know that he wanted more. I could have corrected him for being pushy, but instead I named the behavior he so kindly offered me: "High-five!" Try whenever you can to resist the natural urge to correct—it's much more fun to come up with a silly name for an undesired behavior. Once you've named it, you can always stop the behavior by saying, "No more."

Don't worry if your dog's not a natural high-fiver—the key to teaching almost any behavior is to reward your dog's progress in small increments. You can use this method to teach him how to wave good-bye every time you leave the house.

First, you'll have to teach him how to "shake." Hold a treat in your hand, low to the ground. When he raises his paw, even slightly, to investigate the treat, slide your hand under his, say, "Shake," and reward him with a treat from your storage hand. If your dog won't lift his paw off the ground, smile and gently shake his hand, just until he gets the hang of it. Easy, right?

Once your dog associates "shake" with lifting his paw, keep raising the bar—hold back the praise and rewards until he's raised the paw a little higher than he did the time before. Most dogs will use their paw to signal that they want something: when they were nursing and wanted a larger volume of milk, they used their paw to press on their mother's teat.

You'll gradually reach a point where your dog can "shake" with his paw up around his eye level, and you can teach him how to wave. Hold your hand out to your dog and say, "Shake" (which he knows) and "Bye-bye" (the new word). When he tries to shake your hand, pull it slowly away from him so he can't reach it—he'll look like he's waving. Just make sure that you praise and reward him so that he knows you're not punishing him; he's doing what you want him to do. Eventually you'll be able to stop saying "Shake," and every time you say "Bye-bye" to your dog, he'll wave to you.

RING TO GO OUTSIDE

Want your dog to tell you when it's time to go to the bathroom? All you have to do is teach him how to ring a bell when he has to go.

You can buy a specially made "doggy doorbell" from a pet store, but the bell can be anything your dog can ring with his paws—a cowbell on a rope, a string of jingle bells, or a wind chime will work just as well. Hang the bells next to the door, in a place where your dog can reach with his nose.

You don't have to wait until your dog really has to go to teach him how to ring the bell. If you've taught him how to "target" (as described on Day 20), have him target the bell. When he hits it, say, "Outside," and, as a reward, let him go outside!

The downside is that you're probably going to have a dog who wants to ring the bell every time he feels like going outside, so you're going to have to connect it to potty time. Put a leash on your dog, if that's what you ordinarily do when you take him for a walk, and take him outside. Keep him on the leash until he finishes, reinforcing the idea that this is potty time. You can release him and let him play once he's done, but if he doesn't go within a few minutes, bring him back into the house before taking him off the leash. You can try the same routine again a little later.

Eventually, your dog will associate ringing the bell with going outside to eliminate and will ring it on his own. You don't need to make a big deal when he does—going outside is its own reward. When you're sure he really understands the idea that the bell means potty time, you can stop using the leash. If he backslides, ringing the bell every fifteen minutes because he wants to go outside to play, you can reintroduce the leash until he figures it out again.

WEEK 3 REVIEW

Every time someone tells me that their dog needs more discipline, I have to disagree. Because I believe it's the coach who needs discipline. The discipline to have a plan, a map, a framework, a set of goals. The discipline to stick to the plan, and the discipline to change course when it's not working as well as you wanted it to, or at all.

But don't get caught up on the word "discipline" either. Coaching your dog isn't about following a rigid path—it's about creating a platform for exploration. A good coach is constantly looking for new ways to excite her students so that they will want to explore new ways of getting a better outcome—because they want to get better. It's about presenting learning as a game, one with rules that your dog (or child, or spouse, or employee) can't wait to figure out. It's about observing your dog and learning what he loves and what really drives him. Successful coaching feels great, but the real rewards come from learning about each other's inner worlds, developing a profound and meaningful relationship with another living creature.

WEEK 4

We must be the change we wish to see in the world.

—*Gandhi*

DAY 22

TAKING YOUR DOG
FOR A WALK

I was working with my client Michael and Charlie, his eleven-month-old chocolate Labrador. Charlie was a friendly dog, playfully engaging the other dogs he met in day care or at the park. But when they were out on a walk, Charlie's behavior suddenly turned aggressive.

I decided to start by accompanying Michael as he took his dog for a walk. It took only a few seconds to see that it was actually the other way around—Charlie, all of sixty-five pounds, was easily moving Michael, who weighed about two hundred pounds, wherever he wanted to go. Michael had begun using a retractable leash with the hope that it might discourage Charlie from pulling, but instead, the situation only seemed to get worse.

I love dealing with these kinds of issues. Not only are they easy to solve, but when you do solve them, the owner suddenly realizes, hey, walking the dog is actually enjoyable. Let the fun begin!

Before we got into the aggression, I started by addressing the pulling. A dog's instincts tell him that if he wants to get from point A to point B, he should just go. The idea of slowing down his pace to take an enjoyable stroll with his owner is something he's going to have to choose to do. By now, you'll probably guess that the best way to do that is to make it more pleasurable than following his instincts.

First, we got rid of the retractable leash and replaced it with a regular leash, four feet long (see "Retractable Leashes" below). If I wanted Charlie to know how close to me I wanted him to walk, I had to show him. I fastened the leash to my belt, which left my hands free for toys and treats. I fastened the other end to Charlie's collar. Although he was ready to take off on the walk, I remained in place, asking him to "Take it" as I fed him treat after treat. (It helped that he had skipped breakfast!) I wanted to let Charlie know that it was worth his time to pay attention to me.

RETRACTABLE LEASHES

I don't like to use retractable leashes when I am teaching a dog the proper way to walk. A dog's instincts tell him that the harder he pulls against the leash, the farther he'll go. Retractable leashes reinforce that instinct, making a dog believe he can pull farther and farther away, until the owner hits the brakes, creating a harsh correction.

The goal is to teach your dog to *choose* to stay near

you because you're the source of pleasure and fun. In order for him to make that choice, you have to show him how far away from you he's allowed to go. A regular four- to six-foot leash does exactly that. Later, once your dog has learned how to maintain the proper pace and distance, you can switch to a retractable leash . . . or no leash at all (if that's allowed in your neighborhood)!

Finally, I said, "Let's go!" I took one step forward, Charlie tugged at the leash, and I immediately stopped. I wanted to establish a rule with Charlie, letting him know that when the leash was pulled tight, my legs wouldn't work. I should point out here that I am a very little woman, five feet, one inch and all of ninety-two pounds. So I wasn't going to stop a young Labrador, full of piss and vinegar, by using brute force. Instead, I use what I call the "sumo stop," planting my legs on the ground and lowering my center of gravity the way a sumo wrestler does when he wants to keep his opponent from knocking him over. When I work with very large dogs, I'll usually make sure there is a fence nearby that I can grab for extra support.

Once Charlie pulled, I'd stopped. I asked Charlie to "Take it" and held out another treat. In order to accept the treat, he had to let the leash go slack. I gave him the treat and began walking again. Charlie lunged forward, and once again I came to a sumo stop, repeating the process.

It took us ten minutes to go fifty feet, but I noticed that

In between treats, smile and say, "Close," constantly.

Charlie was beginning to turn around when he sensed that the leash was tighter. I knew that, with practice, Charlie would learn how to adjust his pace so that he wouldn't have to stop the moment he felt the leash going tight.

I'd also noticed that Michael said very little to Charlie during their walks, other than corrections like "no" and "heel." I started using words like "walk" and "close" when Charlie was walking the right way or came close to me to check in—there could always be another "take it" or "close" waiting for him. After about twenty minutes, Charlie's pacing was about 50 percent better.

When I coached Sunny and Lauren Winfrey, I was on a very tight time frame, so I started them walking off leash, by my side, right off the bat. We had the luxury of a fenced-in property where they couldn't get hurt if they ran away. Instead of feeding them breakfast, I asked them to earn it. I started by calling them to me, and when they came, I said, "Come close." As long as they stayed by my right side—I'm right-handed, so it's easier for me to give treats that way—I repeated the word "Close" and rewarded them with their breakfast or dinner. At first, I rewarded them frequently, every few seconds, but gradually moved to thirty seconds, every minute, every few minutes. We reached a point where they stayed close for so long I had to say, "No more," and stopped rewarding the behavior because I wanted them to go and explore the property.

By saying "Close" the whole time, I taught them how to walk by my side without ever having to use the harsh methods involved in teaching a dog to "heel." It

"Close" with treats

was so cute to see Sunny and Lauren walking right by my side, their little faces looking up at me, showing me how connected we were. I had to count trees and other landmarks to keep myself from rewarding them too frequently; to say that I love these two dogs is an understatement—I'm crazy about them!

By starting with "close" while they were off leash, I also made it easier to teach them the proper way to walk on leash, which they'll have to do when they're in Chicago. I highly recommend teaching "close" off the

Note that the leash is attached to my belt

leash—you can do it around the perimeter of any fenced-in yard, or even inside your home (homeschooling).

TO HEEL, OR NOT TO HEEL

For years, a dog's "basic training" started with "heel," a command that grew out of World War II, where dogs played an important role, helping to do everything from watching over sleeping soldiers to carrying medical supplies. "Heel" meant the dog was expected to snap quickly to a soldier's left side in order to stay out of the way of the rifle on the right. Teaching "heel" usually meant hours of boring repetitions and harsh corrections done with a choke chain, preventing the dog from exploring, intent on breaking a dog's spirit and making him submissive. The idea remained popular among dog trainers after the war as a way of enforcing discipline during walks, keeping your dog from exercising his "dominance."

I don't believe in teaching a dog to "heel." Yes, it's important to keep your dog under control when you're on a walk. Having your dog wildly pull you around every time he smells something interesting is a great way to turn a walk into a chore. If you're trying to push a stroller at the same time, an out-of-control dog can be dangerous. That said, I don't believe in "heel" for three reasons.

1. Dogs need the exercise. For many dogs, the walk is their best chance to release a lot of energy. "Heel," however, causes the dog to bottle up his energy. Your dog might return home tired from the walk, but frustrated because his basic wolf needs—running, romping, and rolling with a big silly grin on his face—haven't been met.

2. We're not in the military! Walking the dog isn't a life-or-death situation. It's a chance for two friends to spend some quality time together, for you to recharge your batteries, and for your dog to sniff up all of the latest gossip.

3. It's a topsy-turvy approach. When dogs "misbehave" during their walks, it's not about dominance—they're reverting to their wolf instincts. All of the new sights, sounds, and smells are putting your dog on alert, triggering his natural prey drive, and tickling his brain with pheromones.

Forcing your dog to "heel"—commanding him to ignore his natural instincts or face the consequences—creates pain. Instead, I hope you've spent the first three weeks developing a phenomenal relationship with your dog, teaching him that making humanlike choices is more pleasurable than reverting to his wolf instincts.

Instead, you're going to coach your dog into choosing to stay close to you because it's more fun to stay close to you. At the same time, you're going to compromise, allowing your dog to read all of the "p-mail" he wants as long as he keeps the same pace you do and doesn't tug on the leash.

Let's return to Michael and Charlie: There was still the issue of the dog's "aggression" during walks. It's not uncommon for a normally mild-mannered, Don Juan of day care to turn suddenly into a fighter when he's attached to a leash. Why? As I said on Day 18, when a dog encounters a potentially stressful situation—in this case, another dog—his instincts tell him he has three options: freezing (hoping the other dog won't notice him), fleeing, or fighting. Thanks to the leash, fleeing is out of the question. In fact, many owners will *tighten* their grip on a leash when another dog approaches, exacerbating a dog's sense of feeling trapped. Big mistake. That leaves a dog with only one option—as they say, the best defense is a good offense!

This type of aggression can be treated with the kinds of socialization techniques we've talked about throughout the book, gradually helping your dog to attach the experience of meeting new dogs to feelings of pleasure instead of pain. However—and this is a big *however*—not all leash-based "aggression" is actually aggression.

I asked one of my employees at The Loved Dog Center to walk toward us with another dog, one that Charlie had been playing with earlier. I realized quickly that what Michael had described as "aggression" was actually out-of-control excitement—Charlie's crazy barks, lunges, and dancing on his back legs didn't mean that he wanted to kill the other dog, but that he wanted to play. It was completely natural behavior for a gregarious Labrador puppy. Imagine if we had tried to address this issue with a choke chain or a prong collar!

CHOKE CHAINS AND PRONG COLLARS

Let's say I'm trying to teach you a new language, and every time you seem distracted, I yank a cord that causes metal prongs to dig into your sensitive neck. Would that help you focus? Of course it would—it hurts! Which happens to be the reason choke chains and prong collars "work"—any trainer who tells you that they don't cause pain is an imbecile. By now you know that using pain and intimidation as "teaching tools" is an obvious no-no in The Loved Dog Method. We want our dogs to *want* to do things our way.

I asked my employee to stop in place with the dog he was walking. Without any display of emotion, I said, "Close," and "Take it" to Charlie, giving him a treat. Then we took a step closer to his doggy friend and asked Charlie to "Leave it!" And he did! He completely ignored the other dog as he passed by us, focusing instead on the jackpot he'd earned as a reward. After taking a break—allowing Charlie to romp unleashed with the other dogs in day care for a few hours—we took him for another walk, continuing to coach him through his two issues.

I suggested to Michael that instead of giving Charlie his meals "for free" in a bowl, that he receive his food as a reward for "close" and "leave it" during his walks, whenever they saw another dog. When they returned ten days later, Charlie was no longer a "sled dog," wildly pulling his owner around, and had learned that he didn't have to greet every dog he met. Michael proudly reported that when they did encounter a new dog, Charlie immediately turned toward him, as if to say, "Okay, here's a dog. Can I do 'leave it' and get my breakfast now?"

It will take a dog anywhere from one session to a few weeks to master this behavior. And using the dog's food as well as gold treats is an effective way to teach it to him.

THE OUTSIDE WORLD

I was walking with one of my clients, an elderly and very elegant woman, and Bella, her Italian greyhound. Bella met a new dog and, without hesitation, presented her butt, even lifting a leg for the dog to sniff.

"Oh no! What is she doing?" my client exclaimed, clearly very embarrassed.

"She was giving him her business card, letting him 'read' all of the information that is stored in the gland under her tail," I replied.

The idea of "walking the dog" sounds like a chore to some people, but for your dog, it's an amazing adventure. There are new friends to meet, potential threats to assess, new sounds to process, and hundreds of new smells to sniff as your dog reads his "p-mail," catching up on the latest neighborhood news. There are also plenty of things to trigger his wolf instincts: squirrels to chase, piles of poop to nose around, and strangers to investigate. It's unrealistic to expect that your dog won't occasionally succumb to the temptation to chase a rabbit or get scared by a kid on a skateboard. Many dogs are hardwired to chase prey. While it's helpful to give them the opportunity to make good choices instead of following their wolf instincts, we all act on our instincts from time to time, temporarily abandoning good manners when we're stressed, excited, or afraid. Your dog should have the same leeway.

It's your job, however, to make sure your dog understands that he's expected to observe the same manners in the outside world as he does at home. Whenever you can, practice the foundational behaviors— "sit," "come," and "leave it"— while you're walking your dog.

"GO BACK"

Watching a dog tangle his leash around a tree or a pole might seem cute, but having to constantly circle those trees and poles to untangle your dog can get tiring in a hurry. So why not teach your dog how to retrace his own steps?

It's easy to do by using a version of the "magnet" that you used to teach your dog how to sit. It's easiest to start when your dog is tangled up behind you. Instead of twirling to face him, hold a treat behind your back in the hand closest to him, then move it to the other hand, the one representing the direction you want him to go—i.e., if you

"Go back": step one

"Go back": step two

want your dog to move left, start with your right hand, then move it behind your back into your left hand. Your dog will follow the "magnet" in a circle around you,

"Go back": step three

learning how to untangle himself. When he does, say, "Go back!" and give him a jackpot.

You don't have to wait until you're tangled around a tree to practice this behavior. Try it at home, off the leash, teaching your dog how to maneuver from one side to the other.

TO THE MARKET

It's not only important to practice good behavior on the walk—don't forget about socialization! The outside world is a much different place from your living room. Be sure to bring along a lot of treats and to name the different sounds and objects your dog might encounter.

I like to take dogs to the supermarket. It's a great place to help your dog learn to trust all kinds of different people (and shopping carts!) while developing the proper respect toward cars.

One note of caution: PLEASE don't ever leave your dog tied to a pole outside the supermarket, or anywhere else for that matter. Dog fighters will sometimes steal companion animals to use as "bait" for the animals they're training—my dog Duke was one of those unlucky souls!—or to be sold into laboratory research. HBO did a great hidden-camera documentary called *Dealing Dogs* that I encourage every owner to see. Make sure that your dog has proper ID tags and is microchipped, and never let your dog outside without supervision.

MICROCHIPS

The idea of implanting your dog with a microchip may sound like something out of science fiction, but it's actually a reality that, over the years, has reunited many lost dogs with their families.

It's a painless process using a small needle to implant a microchip in the scruff of a dog's neck. Nearly every veterinarian and shelter has a scanner that can read these chips. There are a couple of competing formats, however, so before you implant your dog with a particular chip, you may want to check and see which version is used by the shelters in your neighborhood.

A dog who is microchipped can't be sold for laboratory research. If your dog gets lost, God forbid, the microchip gives you the best chance possible to be reunited with her.

OFF THE LEASH!

This can be a scary moment for a lot of dog owners, but there's an incredible feeling waiting for both you and your dog when you're ready to let him walk off the leash. Before you unsnap your dog, make sure he has proper identification and will respond quickly when you ask him to "Come" and "Leave it." Choose a place away from busy roads and free of too many distractions—your Labrador is going to have a hard time overriding his instincts if you take him to a pond used by hundreds of low-flying birds. I like to start on wide and well-marked trails whenever possible. Be prepared with super-gold treats. It helps if your dog is on the hungry side (meaning she missed a meal) the first few times you do it.

There's a game I like to play when I first take a dog off the leash. It's like hide-and-seek—I hide behind a bush or a tree and let the dog keep walking. When the dog notices I'm gone, there's usually a brief moment of panic as he thinks, *Oh no! Where is the rest of my family?* When he finds me—I make it very easy, and will call out if the dog starts really panicking—I "make a party."

That brief, flickering moment of emotional pain is usually enough to teach a dog to always keep an eye on me. It's a small price to pay for the chance to watch your dog sprint across a sandy beach or saunter along a wooded hiking trail, connecting with your friend in his most natural state, while he makes sure to keep you in sight.

I always like to test the dog's appreciation of his owners or coach. When I was coaching Sunny and Lauren, we became very close to each other. But after ten days together, I wanted to test how much they valued me. So I went on a hike with the other three dogs—Luke and Layla, the goldens, as well as with Sadie, the cocker spaniel.

We had fun—all of the dogs were having the best time chasing each other, chasing butterflies, and sniffing the smells left behind by the raccoons and ducks. I was looking for an opportunity to hide from them and see what they would do. The moment I saw a big tree with a thick trunk, I let them all keep walking while I hid behind the tree. About twenty feet into the walk, you could see Sunny and Lauren stop and look around, before running back as fast as they could to look for me.

They elected me as their leader and made it clear that although it was so much fun with the others, they felt complete when they were with me. Now, that's what I want you to have with your dogs.

WAIT

Seeing a dog running out the door or a gate into a busy street can give anyone a heart attack. It brings on a primal fear as we feel helpless and terrified that we'll see the dog get run over right in front of our eyes. Most people react in a very angry way, correcting the dog as soon as they get him to come back. It may be a way of releasing the huge anxiety they've just been through, but it doesn't teach the dog what he's supposed to do. A dog's instincts tell him

---

that it's a good thing to explore, looking for interesting "p-mail" or potential intruders, but it's our responsibility to coach them into resisting that instinct and making a conscious choice not to run out an open door or gate.

Oprah's front gate is very busy with people coming in and out, but we wanted it to be off-limits for her dogs. We made sure to keep them away from that gate, using a smaller gate in the back whenever we took them outside the property.

One day, someone walking the doggies made the mistake of taking them out through the front gate. Although it only happened once, it was enough for the dogs to think it was okay to run toward the gate, hoping that it might open and allow them to continue into the street. We needed to teach them to keep away from the gate and its vicinity.

I began by placing a strip of blue electrical tape on the ground about thirty feet from the gate. This was going to be the clear, easy-to-see boundary that I didn't want the dogs to cross. I also prepared three "shaker cans"—empty soda cans each filled with around twenty pennies and the top taped—that made a terrible racket whenever I shook them.

Normally when coaching a dog, I'll set him up to win. But in order to teach the dogs not to run into the street, I wanted at least one of them to screw up so I could show the others what *not* to do. If a dog doesn't "sit" or "lie down" right away, I will have other opportunities to show him how to get it right. With running out the door/gate into the street, I may not get a second opportunity. It is the one time in the whole coaching process that I want a dog to associate fear instead of pleasure with a particular behavior.

I began with Luke, the big golden retriever boy. While the other four dogs watched, leashed a short distance away, I walked Luke toward the blue line. He was already familiar with the concept of boundaries—we had created one a few years earlier at the back gate—and he knew to stay far away from the blue tape. I quickly rewarded him, "making a party" for doing such a great job.

I did the same thing with Lola the golden retriever, who did just as well. But Sadie, the cocker spaniel, didn't have a clue. The moment she placed a paw on the blue line, I pretended to go ballistic, saying "Waiiiit!" in a very intense tone of voice while stomping my foot on the ground. It was as if I'd transformed into a scary wolf, changing my facial expression and breathing, stomping my foot, and throwing the shaker cans on the ground in a way that made her move back from the blue tape, insisting that she "wait!" It's a technique I call Level 8 (which we'll come back to on Day 24). The instant Sadie stepped back from the line (and the scary wolf), I switched to a happy demeanor, "making a party," showering her with love, rewarding her with a jackpot, and saying "wait" in a singsongy tone of voice. After one more try, I saw she understood and I stopped there. I didn't have to do anything even close to Level 8—it was all about telling what a great "wait" she did and "making a party" for her. I wanted to leave her feeling successful. Later we did it again with distractions near the gate, like toys or other dogs. I used my dog Clyde, as he doesn't live there and has no need to know that gate as a boundary.

I coached the same behavior with the two springer spaniel puppies Sunny and Lauren. At first, like Sadie, they had no clue, but after a couple of times they realized that I didn't want them to cross the blue tape. Over the next few days, they learned that no matter what I'm doing around the gate—tossing their favorite toys or a huge treat, walking or running away from them toward the gate, or walking with Clyde—they were never to cross the blue electrical tape line that I taped to the ground. Because, at all other times, I was nothing but loving, encouraging, and sweet with them, because they never heard me barking a command at them, they were never desensitized—they were very surprised and unhappy about seeing me unhappy with them.

All the dogs did great and over a period of two weeks never fell for anything that I or any other people did in order to encourage them to venture toward the big front gate. That is, until walking for the first time with their mom, Oprah. While we were filming a segment for her show, I asked Oprah to walk toward the gate. Lauren, thinking that it was okay because she was with her "mom," crossed the blue line. The scary wolf came out again in a Level 8 and Lauren quickly ran back to the "safe" side of the tape. The lesson worked so well that, to this day, Lauren makes a huge circle just to avoid getting anywhere *near* that blue tape. The tape itself has mostly worn away, but the dogs now think of the area as a "no cross zone" and we don't need the clear marking on the ground.

But what if the boundary that you don't want your dog to cross is also the door that he must go through for his walks? There is a simple solution: Your dog must ask permission. You're going to teach him that the only time he can cross that threshold is when he hears you say, "No more, let's go." (Or some other phrase that makes sense. Just don't use "okay"—if you happen to say the word in some other context during the day, your dog might interpret it as permission to go explore the streets on his own.)

Start by teaching "wait" as I described earlier, but after two or three repetitions—and *before* you ever use the Level 8 technique—entice your dog to cross the boundary line by crouching down, smiling, and repeating, "No more, let's go." You might have to bribe him with a gold treat if he's too worried that you'll be upset when he crosses the line. If he knows that coming to you, when called, means pleasure, you can ask him to "come" and reward him while repeating, "No more, let's go."

Keep practicing this behavior, like all the other behaviors, for the rest of your dog's life. Don't be surprised if you have to use "no more, let's go" at times and in places that don't require permission. That what's so adorable about dogs: They really don't want to screw up. They're looking to do the right thing, to be loved, and to be appreciated.

DAY 23
DIET

Not long ago, I read a report about dog food written by the Animal Protection Institute that really terrified me. I was shocked, for example, to find out that some commercial dog foods had traces of pentobarbital, the drug that's used to euthanize animals in shelters. In other words, there is a strong possibility that euthanized shelter cats and dogs are being used to feed cattle, who are then being used to feed cats and dogs! Or that dog food manufacturers could legally use vegetables treated with pesticides and fertilizers that couldn't legally be used on human food. I couldn't believe that these products, far below any standard for human consumption, were being marketed to people—sometimes even through unsuspecting veterinarians or clinics—as a superior dog food. As John Stossel used to say on *20/20*, "Give me a break!" I was scared straight, committed to thinking about how to improve my dog's diet, which research has shown may also extend a dog's life.

My friend (and Oprah's veterinarian) Dr. Barbara Royal brilliantly combines the best of western medicine with a more holistic idea of doggy health (something we'll get into on Day 28). As Dr. Royal says, "When I see an animal with myriad troubling symptoms, I know eighty percent of the issue could be diet related."

Part of being a loving parent to your dog is making sure that he's eating right. Just because some dogs will eat anything doesn't mean that they should. There's also a lot of evidence to show that they benefit from a varied diet, not the same boring (and less nutritious) kibble that we've been led to believe is good for our dogs.

WHAT SHOULD DOGS EAT?

In the wild, dogs are carnivores and scavengers. Much of what they eat comes from animal carcasses, meaning mostly meat protein, some fat, and the occasional piece of bone. They get a little fiber from the parts of the carcass that are hard to digest, like fur, feathers, and cartilage. Occasionally, they eat some fresh grass, berries, or tree bark. Carbohydrates are nearly non-existent. Everything is raw, and nothing is processed.

A dog's body is designed to thrive on this kind of diet. Anything else, and you're opening him up to all kinds of potential problems. Protein deficiency will wreak havoc on a dog's immune system. The bones provide necessary calcium. Fiber is a must, and studies have found that dogs have absolutely no need for carbohydrates—in fact, too many can lead to medical issues ranging from painful arthritis to obesity. And as Dr. Royal points out, "Trying to train an animal that is eating a high-carb diet is like trying to teach a child on a candy diet."

HOME-COOKED MEALS

Let me start by saying that making your own dog food is not for everyone. It's time-consuming and can be more expensive than buying commercial dog food. You have to pay careful attention to what you are doing—making the same meal over and over again won't work (dogs, from a nutritional standpoint, need variety in their diet) and it's easy to overlook certain nutrients. There are plenty of great, healthy commercial products that you can feed to your dog. But if you have the time and inclination to prepare a meal for your dog, even if it's just from time to time, you'll be doing him a really big favor while potentially reducing vet bills and extending his life span!

There are a lot of different recipes out there, but every dog has different needs based on his weight, level of exercise, preferences, and particulars, like food allergies or specific nutritional needs. If you're going to be a full-time chef for your dog—a group that includes Oprah and Charlize Theron, among many others—you've also got to be a careful researcher and a nutritional scientist of sorts.

All recipes, however, should revolve around protein. You can use pretty much any kind of meat that your dog likes, but as a general rule, the better it is for people, the better it is for dogs. In other words, the human-quality meat at the supermarket is fine, but pasture-raised, organic beef is fantastic! You're also going to need a little fat, some kind of fiber, like vegetables (unsweetened pumpkin is great) or psyllium, and some source of calcium and phosphorous, like bonemeal. Yes, many of my clients tell me that their dogs eat better than they do.

RAW FOOD

When Duke was sick and fighting for his life (a story I'll come back to on Day 28), Dr. Royal advised me to put him on a raw-food diet to help Duke boost his immune system. I decided to try it with both of my dogs, gradually moving them from dry food to cooked food to food that was completely raw.

There are many local services that will deliver frozen raw food directly to your home. For about a hundred dollars per month, I get a variety of protein sources, like chicken, beef, salmon, venison, and buffalo. I add some roughage, using steamed vegetables like broccoli, cauliflower, cabbage, or pumpkin from a can. It's not that time consuming or expensive if you consider that it will save a fortune in veterinarian bills and buy you extra years with your dog. And it feels great to see Clyde, thirteen years old, running around with the energy of a four-year-old!

There are also several foods your dog shouldn't eat, so check out the list of doggy no-nos in the sidebar.

DOGGY NO-NOS

It's fun to let your dog try a lot of things to see what he likes best, but dogs aren't equipped to digest all the same things that we are. Some seemingly innocuous foods—like grapes and onions—can actually be dangerous for your dog! Here are a few foods and drinks to avoid:

Alcohol. Drunk dogs might seem funny on YouTube, but even slight intoxication can lead to coma or death. I've seen dogs fight for their lives because a few college kids thought it would be hilarious to let them drink beer.

Avocados. This one is a little controversial. According to the ASPCA, avocados and their leaves contain a toxin that can give a dog an upset stomach. But many nutritionists think they're incredibly healthy for dogs and there are even commercial foods made from them. Personally, I like avocados for dogs.

Bones. They're great for dogs as long as they're uncooked. Cooked bones will break into small, sharp fragments that can do serious damage to your dog's digestive system, tearing into everything along the digestive tract, sometimes resulting in a slow, painful death.

Caffeine/Chocolate. Many dogs love sweets, but the caffeine in chocolate gives dogs heart palpitations that can lead to tremors, bleeding, even death. Your dog will probably survive after ingesting a small amount by mistake, but keep him far away from the candy jar, loose tea, or coffee beans.

Citrus Fruits. Dogs are sensitive to citric acid—too much of it can actually kill them.

Grapes/Raisins. We still don't know exactly why, but there's something in grapes and raisins that causes many dogs to suffer severe kidney failure.

Onions. These have ingredients that can damage your dog's red blood cells, leading to anemia. Some processed foods, like crackers, may have onion or onion powder in them, as do some commercial dog foods. These should be avoided as well.

Peanut Butter. More controversy, as many owners—and even vets—swear that the nutrients in peanut butter do everything from boost a dog's immune system to giving him a shinier coat. But many dogs have allergic reactions to peanut butter, particularly the large, commercial brands, leading to ear and skin infections.

I hope I haven't totally intimidated you—cooking for your dog is actually a lot easier than it sounds! Below, I've included a recipe from Dr. Royal that's a great place to start. You can also buy a commercial "pre-mix"—most of them just require you to add the meat—that will ensure your dog is getting a healthy meal. And cooking doesn't have to be all about meals—some steamed broccoli and hummus, for example, is an easy-to-make treat that my dog loves!

DR. BARBARA ROYAL'S
EASY ULTIMATE CANINE FOOD RECIPE

This is a meal that's designed to feed a thirty- to forty-pound dog for one full day—if your dog is significantly larger or smaller, you'll have to adjust the quantities so that you don't over- or underfeed him.

1 pound raw organic chicken, deboned, with well-chopped heart and liver and some (not all) of the skin intact (You can include bones if you're willing to grind or chop them finely.)

½ cup (unsweetened) pumpkin

¼ cup cooked green beans

⅛ cup (about 2 tablespoons) blueberries

1 pet vitamin tablet

2,000 mg calcium from bonemeal (about 2 teaspoons)

About 400 to 500 mg fish oil

Cut chicken into pieces—it should make about 2 heaping cups—and put in a large bowl. You don't have to use chicken—it's a good idea to vary the protein sources if you're cooking regularly for your dog. You can include bones as long as you're willing to grind or chop them—you can use them instead of the bonemeal—but never cook the meat with the bones! They become too brittle and are dangerous when cooked. Add the pumpkin, green beans, blueberries, and the vitamin. Dogs need their vitamins too! Just avoid brands that add sugar.

Add bonemeal and mix. Many dog chefs forget to put

enough calcium and phosphorous into their meals. For every pound of meat-based food, you'll want to add between 800 and 1,000 mg of calcium and 400 to 500 mg of phosphorus. Bonemeal makes life much easier, as it's a good source for both and it's usually in the correct ratio (between 1.4 to 2 parts calcium to 1 part phosphorus). Add fish oil and mix well.

You can feed it raw or cooked, as you prefer, but add the bonemeal and the fish oil after you cook it.

Advise your dog that dinner is served!

WET FOODS

If you're not going to cook for your dog or give him a raw diet, canned wet foods are the next best thing. They have a high moisture content that's good for your dog's kidneys and helps him to feel full faster.

That being said, not all wet foods are created equal. Many of America's biggest pet food companies are actually subsidiaries of huge, multinational corporations that also own human food or agriculture businesses. It's a profitable arrangement. About 50 percent of every slaughtered animal is considered "waste" that can't be served to humans, stuff like animal brains, organs, hooves, bones, and even unborn babies. Pet food manufacturers, however, are happy to use these leftovers as "meat by-products." That in and of itself is not bad, because wolves will eat those things in the wild, so it is natural for dogs to consume them, but they're also allowed, in many cases, to use diseased animals or vegetables grown with pesticides and fertilizers considered unfit for human consumption. And that is a problem!

When you're choosing a wet food for your dog, pay careful attention to the ingredients. Try to use the same guidelines that you would use to cook for your dog, choosing a product that's high in protein (preferably one that tells you exactly which animals are being used) and low in carbohydrates. Avoid foods with meat by-products, "meal" (which refers to foods that have been "rendered," a process we'll get back to in a minute), added sweeteners, partially hydrogenated anything, and artificial colors, flavors, and/or preservatives like BHA or BHT.

DRY FOOD

Dry food may be the easiest and least expensive way to feed your dog, but it's also potentially the least nutritious. Protein—the most important part of your dog's diet—can become damaged when it's cooked, and dry foods are cooked twice. The first cooking, called "rendering," involves melting whatever animal by-products happen to be on hand in a huge vat, creating "meal." Then the meal is cooked in a machine called an "extruder," which uses steam to mold it into the shape of the kibble. The protein in the food gets damaged by this process, so it's not only less nutritious, but may also play a part in allergies, food intolerances, or bowel disease.

Many commercial products are the equivalent of white

bread, creating a momentary feeling of fullness that goes away a short time later. Many products are artificially sweetened or colored, which isn't good for your dog. A lot of products go heavy on the carbohydrates, also a no-no. It's harder for your dog to digest, requiring more water and a longer time to work its way through the digestive system. Dry kibble actually decreases the amount of digestive enzymes your dog's body produces, making it harder for the intestines to properly process and absorb essential nutrients. And despite what certain companies would have you believe, it's *not* better for a dog's teeth—in fact, a high-carb kibble will stick to a dog's teeth in a way that makes it harder for him to lick them clean. You wouldn't brush your teeth with crackers, would you?

Dry foods are also more vulnerable to bacterial growth, a risk that, according to many experts, may increase if you mix the food with any kind of liquid. In other words, it's a bad idea to blend kibble with water, milk, or even wet food.

Not all dry foods are terrible, as long as you choose one using the same guidelines that I gave you for home-cooked and wet meals—lots of protein, no artificial ingredients, preservatives, "meals," or meat by-products. Make sure your dog is also drinking plenty of water after he eats, as he's not getting any moisture from the food.

OVERWEIGHT DOGS

If you think Americans have a problem with obesity, try this one on for size—veterinarians estimate that as many as *half* of all the dogs in the United States are overweight.

Like people, the number of health issues goes up with the number of extra pounds. Overweight dogs have less energy and more problems like arthritis and diabetes. Studies have shown that dogs who eat 25 percent less than their littermates have fewer age-related problems and live up to two years longer.

Fortunately, dogs have a unique ability to gain and lose weight quickly and safely. They're natural scavengers with bodies that are very efficient at burning up fat during the lean times between meals.

I find that the issue, more often than not, isn't the dog, but an owner who gets joy from feeding her dog. (I'm one of them, by the way, which is why I let my dogs snack on veggies, organic yogurt, and the occasional serving of organic cottage cheese.) Some people are "emotional feeders," trying to squelch their guilt over not exercising their dog with extra food and treats. You can help your dog keep a healthy weight by not overfeeding him (the "suggested" amounts on many commercial foods are often more than your dog needs) and not letting him overdo it on the table scraps (see "Table Scraps" below). Many dogs (like people) are more prone to weight gain as they get older and require fewer calories to get by.

If your dog is overweight, the easiest way to help him drop a few pounds is simply to feed him a healthier diet and exercise him more—what a novel concept! His body will do the rest. There's no reason to mess around with "diet" dog foods, which may skimp on fat or other ingredients that are vital to your dog's health.

TABLE SCRAPS

There's nothing wrong with treating your dog to scraps from the table—assuming that what you ate was healthy and dog appropriate (nothing spicy or saucy and no carbs)—as long as you aren't feeding him *right from the table*. You'll be teaching your dog that it's all right to beg, since you'll be rewarding his behavior. Allowing your dog to prewash your plate once you've finished eating is a nice treat you can use to reward your dog for staying away from the table during the meal. I like to save the plate for a few minutes, then ask my dog to "Come" once he's forgotten about it, making it a reward instead of something I'm giving away for free.

Table scraps can have a lot of calories, which you should take into consideration while calculating how much your dog has eaten that day. Instead of always feeding him scraps around mealtime, save the leftovers to use as yummy gold treats you can use during walks, "come" games, or other coaching sessions.

WATER

During waking hours, your dog should always have access to fresh water. It only takes a few hours for a dog to become seriously dehydrated on a hot day, creating severe health issues. Most dogs need to drink two or three times as much water as the food they eat, even more when temperatures are high or they're getting a lot of exercise. And dogs who eat dry food need more water than those who eat canned food, which has a much higher water content.

Many dogs prefer to drink water that's cooler in the summer and warmer (room temperature) in the winter, but your dog's tastes may vary. If he seems thirsty but hesitant about drinking the water in his bowl, you may want to experiment.

It's also important to keep your dog's water bowl clean to keep it free of bacteria and viruses. Be sure you wash the bowl daily, disinfect it from time to time, and replace it if it starts to look too scratched or worn. A good rule of thumb is to look at your dog's bowl and ask yourself if you would drink from it. If it doesn't look like something you should drink from, your dog probably shouldn't either.

EATING DISORDERS

While it's unlikely that your dog will ever become bulimic or anorexic, many dogs do suffer from eating disorders. *Pica* is a condition that causes your dog to eat things that are ordinarily indigestible, like rocks, glass, coins, rubber bands, or even upholstery.

Pica is very often a behavioral problem caused by separation anxiety, the need for attention, or boredom. But in some cases it can actually be a medical condition arising from digestion difficulties or missing nutrients. If your dog's seven basic needs are being met and he's still chewing the curtains, you may need a veterinarian to prescribe medicine and/or supplements. You can also try adding a small amount (no more than a teaspoon for every ten pounds your dog weighs) of a vegetable oil to your dog's diet—coconut oil is best—which helps in the assimilation of nutrients.

One particularly disgusting form of pica is called *coprophagia,* or excrement eating. Disgusting to us, anyway—in the wild, some wolves will eat anything they can find, even poop, as long as it has some nutritional value. Coprophagia can be a sign that your dog isn't getting enough mental stimulation, causing him to scavenge. Some dogs eat poop as a way of resource guarding from other dogs. Your dog may enjoy cat poop for its undigested protein.

If your dog is engaging in coprophagia, the first step is to make sure he's on a good, complete diet. Add supplements if necessary, particularly the digestive enzymes (sold for people) in the refrigerated section of many health food stores. You also can make a dog's stool taste (even) less appealing by reducing its nutritional content. Avoiding grain-based foods— which are harder than proteins and fats for your dog to fully digest—will help. But remember that the cause may not just be physical, but behavioral—you don't want to focus only on stopping the problem, missing a possible cry for help.

For more information about what goes into commercial dog foods, please go to http://www.bornfreeusa.org/downloads.pdf/PetFoodReport_BFUSA.pdf.

DAY 24

IN THE COMPANY
OF DOGS

As I've said many times, dogs are social creatures, animals who enjoy the company of a pack. They want and need a healthy social life with other dogs, in the same way a kid needs to be around other kids.

Keep in mind, however, that wolf packs are actually families—dogs are instinctively wired to see dogs from other packs as intruders or potential threats. Good socialization through creating pleasurable association to other dogs is a must. Not every dog loves the dog park (we'll get into that later in the chapter), but if your dog is into it, it's a great place to develop these relationships.

Like a kids' playground, the dog park can be an exciting place—and a little bit intimidating. Dogs can get bullied—or become bullies—and there are occasional fights. Running with a pack is both an opportunity for fun and a chance for your dog to mirror the behavior of other dogs, which is great for learning social skills, but can reinforce or amplify his wolf instincts. (The same, by the way, is true of doggy day care—make sure you choose one where they not only love the dogs but understand their behavior well enough to screen for bad apples as well as manage the group dynamics.)

All in all, the dog park is a fantastic experience for many dogs, as long as you go prepared.

BEFORE YOU GO

The first impression a lot of people have of the dog park is complete anarchy. There are, however, rules and etiquette to be followed and safety issues to be considered.

First of all, you should never consider taking your dog to a dog park before he's fully vaccinated. You should also be sure that he'll respond quickly when you ask him to sit, come, and leave it before you let him off the leash.

Every dog park has its own set of rules and customs. Many require dogs to have a license or to be spayed or neutered. Most don't allow small children.

Although it's fun, it can be touchy to bring toys or even treats, which can create a situation where dogs are fighting over them. See what the other people in the park are doing. In the park I go to, we're allowed to bring toys, but no treats.

It's a good idea to scout out a park before taking your dog there. Do the dogs generally run in wild packs or pair off in groups of two or three? Are there separate areas for big dogs and little dogs? Do the dogs chase each other in a friendly way, or does it seem more violent, with body slams or cornering? Do you see any obvious bullies?

Finally, ask yourself if your dog is ready for a dog park. Like I said earlier, socializing with strangers isn't a natural behavior for many dogs (or many people!), especially if your dog has had any trauma in the past. Before you go, you may first want to see how your dog does with strangers in a controlled setting—invite a dog or two over to your house for a small get-together or visit a friend who has dogs. Like any form of socialization, it's best to coach your dog through it in gradual increments as opposed to throwing him into the deep end of the pool. Sometimes it's easier to go the first few times with a doggy friend. Some dogs who do not like the dog park do very well on hikes with other dogs.

THE FIRST TRIP

Even if your dog is a social butterfly, you should still plan your first visit for a time of day when the park isn't too crowded. When dogs come into contact with one another, they tend to amplify one another's wolf instincts. You want to give your dog the best chance possible to make good choices.

Don't just let your dog go and then start chatting with the other "parents." You have to keep a watchful eye on your dog, at least at the beginning. Here are some of the things you'll want to pay attention to:

Your dog's body language. Is your dog smiling and behaving playfully? Or does he seem stressed and scared? Remember the *Fear Factor* analogy—you're not going to cure anyone of a fear of spiders by dropping her in a room full of them. If your dog seems like he's not having fun, get him out of there!

The other dogs. If your dog is old, don't expect him to run with a pack of youngsters. The opposite is also true—it's not much fun for a young, energetic dog to be dropped into a group of geezers. If the park allows big dogs and little dogs to mix freely, make sure your small dog isn't being viewed as prey (and that your large dog isn't picking on the little guys!).

At The Loved Dog Center, we separate dogs by their personality and energy level, not by their size. Downstairs is the indoor dog park (we are in the middle of Los Angeles, after all!) where we encourage high-energy play; upstairs is the doggy lounge, a place to play at a slower pace. Some clients request that their dogs be moved from one floor to the other, but we always check with the dog to see which option he or she finds more comfortable. A tiny Jack Russell terrier might scare the dogs in the lounge half to death (or at least drive them crazy), while thriving in the high-energy environment of the indoor dog park. Many Chihuahuas prefer the indoor park to the lounge.

Signs of overarousal or violence. Like wolves, dogs have unspoken hierarchies and rules. For example, it's natural for an older dog to growl at a young upstart, expecting him to show some sign of submission, particularly if the youngster is overbearing. You can even help the process by encouraging your dog to sit or lie down—if his energy level is too much for the other dogs to take, you don't want him to cross a line and then get bitten.

But if a situation looks like it might be getting violent, it's okay to separate two dogs. Letting them work it out is one thing; putting your dog in harm's way is another. If you get a bad vibe from a particular dog (or owner!), leave immediately. You can plan your future visits for a time when that dog isn't likely to be around. How can you tell if your dog is getting abused by an overbearing player or if he actually likes it? Remove or restrain the other dog and see if your dog is disappointed or relieved.

NASCAR pit stops. Call your dog over to you every few minutes or so to give him a super-gold treat and water. Make sure that he doesn't seem dehydrated, overtired, or overaroused, then send him back for some more wolf-style fun. You don't want your dog, when you call him, to worry that the fun is going to end. A few of these NASCAR pit stops will teach him that he can have his cake (praise for coming and a jackpot of gold treats) and eat it too (more playtime with his friends). You want to do everything you can to give your dog the best chance to create pleasurable associations with the dog park and with coming back to you.

MY DOG HATES THE DOG PARK . . . WHAT DO I DO?

The beautiful actress Eva Mendes and her boyfriend called me to see if I could help them with their dog, Hugo. He was a Malinois, a type of Belgian shepherd often used as a police dog, who had, in fact, been trained to provide protection. Hugo didn't like going to dog parks, and his "parents" worried that he wasn't experiencing the joy of running around with other dogs in that kind of setting.

I told them there wasn't much I could do—or should do! Some dogs, I explained, just don't like the dog park. It didn't necessarily mean anything was wrong with Hugo. Maybe it was Hugo's training, but he actually preferred "human" companions and games to connecting with his "wolf" instincts. He'd rather be babied and treated like a member of their family than a member of the pack.

I have a friend who loves to get massages. Her husband does not. My friend thinks that he's weird—who doesn't like massages?—and teases him every time the subject comes up. She doesn't understand how he couldn't like something that she considers an amazing treat. He can't understand how someone could relax with a stranger touching his skin.

My point is that we're not always very good at accepting individual choices and preferences among our own species, so it isn't surprising that we can have the same problem with our dogs, a different species altogether. Your dog may be like Hugo. Some people are social butterflies who feel at home at large parties. Others prefer quiet dinners and intimate circles of friends or staying home alone. Remember that it's not about doing the things you think will be fun for your dog in the hope of molding him, but about observing your dog and his preferences and creating activities and experiences that will make *him* happy.

If your dog hates the dog park, try to find other playmates he can interact with in a less overwhelming setting. Seek out other dog owners, preferably with attitudes similar to yours toward coaching, and schedule a playdate. But don't forget to take hikes that aren't overrun by other dogs, long walks on secluded beaches, or any of the activities that your dog loves.

"OFF" (LEVEL 3)

Once your dog has mastered the first two levels of "off," he'll be ready for the third and final level—practice for when you're out in the real world with your dog, without treats.

Start with Level 2, then go to Level 3: Hold a treat behind your back and ask him to "Off." He might be confused at first, as there's no visible treat to back off from, so repeat the request: "Max (or your dog's name), off!" If he still doesn't understand, gently shuffle your feet into him to remind him of what "off" means.

"Off": Level three

When he moves backward, bring your hands to the front, "make a party," and give him love and treats. Soon you'll be able to ask him to back "off" without any treats at all. Once he's mastered it, be sure to practice it often with relevance coaching.

LEVEL 8

I've spent a lot of time criticizing "conventional" dog trainers, so I feel it's only fair to point out that Level 8 feels controversial to some trainers who believe that you can achieve absolutely everything by being nice and loving. I agree with them 99.9 percent of the time, but I also feel it's important to have a menu option to convey urgency.

Level 1 is simply turning my back on a dog. Level 10 is an *imaginary* nuclear option, where I "kill" the dog on the spot. The highest I will ever go is Level 8.

Level 8 is a performance, a show that will grab a dog's attention without physical contact. I act like an angry wolf who is holding herself back from attacking. Use Level 8 with your dog even once, and you'll have an equivalent of "the look" you get from a parent, spouse, or friend when you're about to say something inappropriate at the dinner table. "I'm warning you," it says. "Don't go there."

Again, it's an acting job—there's no real anger behind it. But it does look very scary, particularly because I won't use it until after a dog has already established me in her mind as the sweetest and most pleasurable thing in her life.

Here we go . . . I take a deep breath, hold it, and stiffen my body—a wolf signal that means I'm ready to pounce. I take another deep breath and hold it in, make the angriest face that I can imagine, lift my shoulders, and stick my face out. My voice becomes low-pitched and assertive. If you've seen the movie *New Moon* and remember the werewolf who held himself back from attacking the heroine, then you know what it looks like.

Level 8 is so scary, I'll usually warn people in advance before I use it. I once did a demonstration during an appearance on *Oprah*—it was cute to watch the audience snap to attention when my facial expression changed from human to wolf. But Level 8 isn't for people, it's for dogs. Since I'm so loving with dogs, on the very rare occasion that I have to use Level 8, it never fails to get them to jump to attention or stop in their tracks.

Which is exactly the way I want it. Level 8 can save a dog's life. It's the voice I'll use in emergency situations to keep a dog from running blindly into traffic (when teaching the "waits") or chasing a coyote into the wilderness, where he'll be killed by the coyote pack. I'll pull it out to break up a serious dog fight or any other time when I urgently need a dog's attention, to startle him into stopping something that he's doing, or something he's about to do. It's my version of the prong collar, only it's not physically painful, and I don't use it unless it's necessary. I don't want a dog to ever get used to hearing it. Gandhi once said that "in order to maximize power, you have to use it sparingly."

In reality, Level 8 is only a level or two above the voice used by some Spanish Inquisition–type trainers to bark commands on a regular basis. But in my case, because I haven't desensitized a dog to hearing a very upset tone of voice, it's very effective on the rare occasions when I have to use it.

HOUSEBREAKING CHART REVIEW, PART II

Time to take another look at the chart. Have you uncovered any more clues to your dog's bathroom habits? Can you see the times when your dog needs to be more supervised? Are there times when she has too much access to water without an adequate opportunity to go to the bathroom?

I often hear from clients that their dogs went to the bathroom outside, only to go again inside a few minutes after returning to the house. Some dogs don't eliminate everything at one time. Sunny Winfrey was a perfect example: I had to make sure she'd peed twice and pooped twice before I could trust her with thirty minutes of free time in the house while her sister Lauren was "empty" after one of each.

The chart exists to help you understand your dog's physical habits and needs. Keep using it to get as many clues as possible so you can continue to make adjustments to your action plan. Also, don't think that your dog will never be housebroken because he's still not getting it at this point. Just like learning to ride a bike, surf, or rollerblade, all of a sudden things will start going the right way and making "mistakes" will be a thing of the past.

DAY 25

FLYBALL, AGILITY TRAINING, AND NOSEWORK

What do you think of when you hear the words "dog competition"? Most people pull up an image of purebred dogs, noses raised high in the air, trotting gracefully around an arena while the audience politely applauds.

I'm not trying to sound dismissive toward these types of competitions. It takes an incredible amount of training to teach those beautiful dogs such impeccable manners (which I hope they're doing without resorting to methods from the Dark Ages). But there's something a little weird about dog shows, the way there is something a little weird about beauty pageants for little girls. Like those pageant contestants—who don't exactly seem like real, natural young girls—show dogs seem to be cut off from the instincts that make them dogs.

Over the last twenty or thirty years, a few new dog "sports" have started to become popular. Instead of squashing wolflike instincts, they celebrate them. If traditional dog shows are like beauty pageants, these new games are like triathlons or gymnastics. Your dog doesn't have to be a purebred with a perfect coat of fur in order to participate. These dog athletes have the chance to get into top mental and physical shape, develop self-confidence, and have an entertaining outlet for exercising their natural wolflike desires.

These games are a gift from the gods for the hyperactive or destructive dog. I mean, *poof!* No more behavior problems. I can't recommend them strongly enough, if you want a dog who is so full of joy and gratitude that he will die for you. Some of these sports are really intense, requiring months of coaching on specialized equipment, and they're definitely not for everybody. But if you want to take the time to explore your dog's amazing talent and potential, while giving yourself the gift of an immensely good time with your dog and other dog lovers, give one of these sports a try.

FLYBALL

I saw flyball for the first time about eighteen years ago, in Houston, Texas, when a friend invited me to watch her and her border collie try it out. I was blown away by the unbelievable energy, the order, and the chaos. I felt like I was watching world-class athletes in an Olympic village, half of them getting ready to give it their all, the other half coming down from the amazing adrenaline rush of competition. There were so many happy dogs of all shapes and sizes (although border collies always seem to dominate any kind of athletic competition) having a blast with their happy owners. My friend's border collie couldn't wait to start playing—it was a thrill watching her learn the rules of the game.

According to legend, flyball began in Southern California in the late 1960s. A group of trainers were teaching their dogs how to jump over a series of boxes—an old hunting game called "scent hurdling"—when someone threw a tennis ball into the air.

Forty years later, more than four hundred clubs with nearly seven thousand dogs belong to the North American Flyball Association. There are detailed rule books, sophisticated electronic judging systems, and official "flyball boxes" to launch the tennis balls into the air.

So what is flyball? It's structured like a relay race, with two teams of four dogs competing against each other. When the game starts, the first dog on each team races down a fifty-one-foot track, leaping over four hurdles to reach the flyball box. At the box, the dog pushes (or, more likely, pounces on) a button with his paw, launching a tennis ball into the air. He has to catch the ball and race back over the four hurdles and across the starting line before the next dog can begin. The fastest flyball dogs can run a "lap" in under four seconds; the world record for an entire four-dog team is under fifteen seconds!

But those are just the facts. In practice, it's an explosion of energy—dogs practicing and running, with their teammates barking their support, while the parents/coaches scream at the top of their lungs. So much fun!

These competitions are great social gatherings for people and dogs. Any dog can participate, regardless of size or breed, as long as he's healthy. They're a great way for dogs to get a lot of exercise in a really fun way.

FLYBALL COACHING

Even if you don't want to participate in an official flyball competition, you can still practice some of the coaching with your dog. You already know how to teach your dog to catch a tennis ball—now you're going to coach him into jumping over a hurdle.

Set up a bar for your dog to jump over—a broomstick stuck between two chairs will work. It's better to start low, maybe three to six inches (depending on your dog's height), so your dog will succeed quickly and want to do more. (Official flyball hurdles are between seven and fourteen inches high, depending on the size of the dog.) Show your dog what you want him to do by saying "Jump!" as you jump over the bar. Some dogs will get the idea faster if you run toward the bar with him (on a very loose leash) as you show him the jump. Make sure to say "Good jump!" and to reward your dog with a gold treat when he follows your lead.

If your dog seems reluctant or scared, get a friend to help you. Set up the jump in a way that your dog can't go around it, but has to jump over it if he wants to get to the other side. Have the friend hold your dog on a leash while you move to the other side of the jump. Since you've already established an amazing relationship with your dog based on love and fun, your dog will want to come to you when you call. Tell your friend not to release your dog from the leash until the second or third time you've called him, which should get him revved up and eager to clear any hurdle to get to you. "Make a *huge* party" when he does!

If your dog is still too scared, lower the bar to the floor and begin by stepping over it. As his confidence grows, you can raise the bar.

AGILITY TRAINING

Think about what a wolf goes through when he's chasing prey—running along and jumping over rocks and fallen trees, scrambling up hills, squeezing through tight spaces, holding tight while quietly planning his next move—and you'll have an idea of what "agility training" is all about. These competitions are the ironman triathlons of the dog world!

A handler (you, the coach!) directs a dog, using only verbal cues, as quickly as possible through an obstacle course. The types of obstacles are different for every course—some of the more common ones are tunnels for the dog to run through, planks to run along, seesaws and A-frame slopes to run up and over, hurdles and tires to jump over and through, rows of vertical poles to weave in and out of, and "pause boxes" where the dog has to stop and rest for a few seconds. Because the course is different every time, the dog can't just learn a routine—it's up to his coach to run alongside him (assuming you can keep up), directing each move. These big-time competitions certainly aren't for every dog. Many dogs need six to nine months of daily coaching before they're ready to run an official course. Puppies and dogs older than eight years old are excluded from most competitions. Short-nosed dogs, like boxers or bulldogs, may have a tough time with the intensity of the exercise, while short-legged dogs like dachshunds may not be able to clear the jumps. You should never even think about participating without first getting the okay from your dog's veterinarian.

You don't have to be a type-A competitor to enjoy this great way to let your dog release some of his bottled-up energy. You also don't need to compete on a professional level—do it for fun! Agility trainers are crazy about their sport, pointing out that dogs get to exercise so many of their natural instincts while strengthening their bonds with their human trainers. It's hard to imagine a more physically and mentally stimulating set of activities for your dog.

Nor does your dog have to be a world-class athlete to incorporate elements of agility training into his regular routine. It's a great way to channel his wolf instincts, build his confidence, get a lot of exercise, and develop an amazing sense of teamwork between you and your dog.

You can set up a series of poles and teach your dog to weave in and out of them, using a treat as a "magnet." Or show him how to jump through a tire by holding a treat next to a hula hoop, gradually raising the hoop as your dog gains confidence.

NOSEWORK

Not all sports have to be physically grueling to be enjoyable—plenty of people prefer golf to running. Nosework gives your dog a chance to use one of his most powerful wolf assets—his amazing sense of smell—to play a game that helps establish you as the most wonderful coach in the world. After all, he's always going to win. You'll also be teaching your dog a "marketable" skill—spray a little scent on your keys and you'll never lose them again!

A few years ago, a couple of trainers in Southern California became interested in teaching dogs how to do narcotics and explosives detection. They set out to develop a program and wound up inventing a new sport!

All you have to do to play is arrange three or more boxes in an open area. You're going to hide a yummy piece of food in one of them, so try to use boxes that will hide the prize but not the smell, like shoe boxes or Tupperware containers with holes punched in the lid. Let your dog smell the food, then "sneak" it into one of the boxes without letting your dog see which one you've chosen. (Ask your dog to "Stay," or ask a friend to hold your dog on a leash while you hide the food.)

Then release your dog and let him find the box with the

food. Be sure to "make a party" when he finds it and, of course, let him enjoy the food.

Keep practicing, making sure to switch boxes (or just change the location of the food box) every time. As your dog gets better at finding it, you can start hiding the food *outside* the box, teaching your dog to look for scents in unexpected places. And when your dog grasps that concept, you don't even have to hide the food itself—you can swab it with a Q-tip, then hide the Q-tip anywhere in your house. When he finds it, "make a *huge* party" and give him a gold treat or a toy.

When your dog becomes an expert noseworker, you can switch from food to essential oils, like anise, birch, or clove. There are a growing number of competitions. Whether you're doing it for sport or fun, your dog will have a great chance to get in touch with his inner search-and-rescue dog!

DAY 26

SO NICE TO
BE TOUCHED

Many studies have shown the benefits that humans get from petting dogs, everything from lower blood pressure to stress reduction and comfort from grief. There has been a lot of recent evidence to suggest that petting is just as beneficial for the dog. The human touch can cause a dog's brain to release good hormones, lowering blood pressure, relieving stress, and improving the cardiovascular system. Dogs who do not get good physical contact from their owners may be more prone to depression.

Not just any touch will work. Rubbing, fast scratching, or petting against the grain of the hair can actually arouse a dog. Most dogs respond better to slow, firm (but not heavy-handed) petting. But the truth is that every dog likes to be touched in different ways. Some of it is based on natural preferences, the way that people like to be touched in certain spots that others find uncomfortable or ticklish. Some of it is based on a dog's history—abuse, neglect, or a lack of socialization can have a huge impact on if and how a dog likes to be touched. A lot depends on the situation—some dogs who normally love a pat on the head may hate it if they're playing a game, in the middle of eating, or trying to go to the bathroom.

When you touch your dog, look for signs that you're doing it right, paying close attention to his body language. If he's showing any signs of stress, he probably doesn't want to be touched in the way you're touching him at that particular moment. Some signs to look for include freezing (when it seems like the dog has stopped breathing), flattened ears, licking the lips, panting, yawning, twitching eyebrows, avoiding eye contact, holding his breath, flinching, growling, snarling, nipping, or just trying to get away.

When you're doing it right, your dog should seem happy and relaxed. If a dog sneezes or stretches his limbs when you touch him, it usually means he's enjoying himself—generally speaking, a sneeze means a dog is happy, excited, or pleased. (Many dogs sneeze when their "parents" first come home or when asked to go on a walk.) An offer to touch a particular part of his body, like rolling over onto his back to show you his belly, is also a good sign. My dog Clyde, like many others, offers me his butt the moment I start to pet him—a lot of dogs love to be scratched on their lower backs, right by their tails. (Which, by the way, is the best spot to touch first when meeting a new dog—not their heads.)

Over time, you'll develop a sense of how and when your dog likes to be touched. If your dog growls or snarls at any contact, don't correct him! These kinds of corrections can be disastrous for a dog, and for other people as well. You will have to teach him, slowly, to associate being touched with immense pleasure. Use the socialization techniques described on Day 10, rewarding your dog with raisin-size bits of gold treat for allowing you to rest your hand on that special spot by his tail for a split second, working your way up from there.

If you don't trust your dog to allow you even this kind of contact and following any of the socialization advice in this book seems too scary for you, get professional help from a behaviorist. And if you're touching him in a way that he usually enjoys, but he starts showing symptoms of pain and nervousness, there may be something else wrong. Consider a trip to the veterinarian.

TTOUCH

There have been conventional trainers, over the years, who have advised owners that petting should be used only to reward good behavior. Fortunately, today there are newer, less caveman-like trainers who argue that petting and being affectionate are essential for any social creature and a must for creating good behavior. It's cruel to withhold affection from dogs (or any social creature, like those monkeys I mentioned at the beginning of the book).

I got a call about Annie, a four-year-old black Lab mix, who'd just tried to attack a TV repairman. Annie showed aggression toward almost every new visitor, making her owner, seven months pregnant, very nervous about how the dog would respond to a new baby. As soon as I met Annie, I knew we'd have some work to do—she wasn't interested in me, she wasn't interested in treats or toys, and she definitely wasn't interested in being touched. She seemed like she was living her life while holding her breath, or what you might call "Waiting to Exhale."

According to the owner, she'd been that way from the day they'd brought her home from the pet store. (Yes, they do sell mutts at pet stores, often giving them cute names like "Labradoodles" or "puggles" and selling them for thousands of dollars.) Since going outside and interacting with the world seemed to stress her out even more, they'd stopped taking her out. In other words, Annie had received zero socialization with other people or dogs.

I began with a week of pheromone collars and Rescue Remedy to calm Annie down. Then I taught her owners to touch proof her (see Day 10), tying the process into her feeding so that touch became not only pleasurable, but a necessity.

A week later, Annie was much better at accepting touch, but I needed her to look forward to it. That meant I had to loosen up the tension she'd been carrying in her body for her entire life. I so wanted to see her exhale. I placed a soft hand on her, smiled, made sure that I exhaled, and began to do TTouch on her.

The T in TTouch is short for Tellington. The method was invented around forty years ago by Linda Tellington-Jones, a horse trainer who realized that through proper physical contact—based on mutual respect rather than force, fear, or pain—humans and animals could create a deeper rapport, one that connected their minds and spirits. This may sound a little New Agey to you, but it's rooted in the Feldenkrais Method, which is used by the Israeli army. The horses Linda was working with were thoroughbreds worth millions of dollars, and she was the only one who, at the time, was able to get them to overcome some seriously debilitating mental blocks—clearly she was doing something right.

Consider the practical side: In the years since, TTouch has been used on dogs to relieve all kinds of behavioral issues, including aggression, barking, chewing, jumping, anxiety, and shyness. It's been just as powerful in treating physical ailments, from car sickness to age-related conditions. Dogs who receive TTouch have been shown to recover more quickly from injuries.

A TTouch practitioner uses her fingers and hands to make circular movements all over a dog's body, including his face and mouth. The size of the circles, speed, and pressure of the touch all depend on the dog. But the results don't—when TTouch is properly applied (and you don't need to be a professional to do it), it stimulates a dog's senses and nourishes him on a cellular level in a way that actually changes the patterns in his brain waves. The feeling has been compared to turning on the body's electrical lights.

When I used TTouch on Annie, the change was immediate. She actually leaned into me, wanting more! When I stopped the session, she clearly looked disappointed—in fact, she moved her body closer to me, asking for more. So I started again. And then it happened: Annie exhaled! In one big breath, she finally let her body relax. I was so excited that my eyes welled up with tears. I had to concentrate on staying calm, taking big breaths and exhaling to match Annie's rhythm. What a wonderful moment!

After another week of daily TTouch sessions, we brought back the TV guy. We placed a baby gate between him and Annie—the poor man was rightly worried about being attacked again—but not only was she excited to take treats from him, he was also able to sneak in a couple of soft pats on her head. Annie's owners continued to socialize her to a few strangers on a daily basis. A few months later, they sent me an email with a picture of Annie and the baby. Not only had Annie begun allowing people to come and go without acting aloof or aggressive, she'd also been beyond loving and sweet with the newborn.

TTouch is one of the most powerful tools you can use to love your dog. Whether you're trying to treat a behavioral problem, heal an injury, or just want to give your dog an amazing experience, it's worth trying a local TTouch practitioner—or checking out their website!

A SIMPLE TTOUCH

Instead of just petting your dog, try rubbing his ears. A ten-minute ear rub, using your thumb to gently rub the inside and outside, working all the way to the tip of the ear, will not only help your dog to "chillax," but will foster a deeper bond between you and your dog.

OTHER FORMS OF MASSAGE

You don't need to be an expert to give your dog a massage. There are plenty of books, DVDs, and Internet videos that will show you different techniques. (I personally like Nickie Jan Scott's DVD, *Therapeutic Holistic Dog Massage*.) You can also experiment with your own methods, as long as you're paying close attention to any of the signs of stress listed earlier in the chapter.

Dog massage isn't that different from human massage. You can use long, slow strokes or rapid, drumlike pressure with the fingers and hands. You can knead his muscles or pet him gently in a way that doesn't move his skin. Most important, remember to breathe—the more relaxed you are, the more relaxed your dog will be.

Choose a place where your dog is comfortable lying down. Start by settling down and allowing yourself to relax. When you're ready to touch your dog, take a deep breath and exhale, then use long, gentle strokes from his head to his tail. Many dogs love to be stroked or gently rubbed on their ears and the area between their eyes that starts on the bridge of their noses. They'll often respond to acupressure if you know what you're doing.

Not all dogs want to be massaged, but if your dog does, you'll have a powerful way to connect with him that goes beyond just touching.

DAY 27
DOG SAFETY

As much as we want to protect our four-legged (and two-legged) children, we can't always control everything. But I do believe that every dog "parent" can make better choices that will help prevent tragedies, when possible, and deal with them when they occur.

GENERAL PREPAREDNESS

First of all, every dog owner should have a doggy first-aid kit, which you can get from most pet stores. You should also keep, on the fridge or in some other visible location (you might not always be the one who is there when an emergency occurs), the telephone numbers for your veterinarian, local emergency clinic, and poison control, as well as a folder with your dog's medical history and vaccination schedule.

Many human foods and household items can be dangerous for your pets. I listed a few of the foods to avoid on Day 23, but it's worth visiting the ASPCA website (www.aspca.org) to see a comprehensive list of medications, plants, cleaners, and other toxins that will poison your dog. Some of them may surprise you!

If you live in a place where there's a potential for catastrophe—earthquakes, floods, tornados, hurricanes, etc.—and you already have a disaster or evacuation preparedness kit, make sure you have one for your dog. Make sure you have a crate, enough food, bottled water, and treats for a couple of weeks, an extra leash, feeding bowl, toys, and any tool you can use to calm your dog, like a pheromone collar or Rescue Remedy. You may also want to keep a list of friends, relatives, or pet-friendly hotels and motels where you and your pets can stay in the event of an evacuation. Make sure to have a photo of you with your dog on hand, so you can prove that she's yours in case you are separated. Your dog should always have his ID on his collar and, if possible, a microchip, but it's a good idea to keep write-on, temporary tags on hand as well, so you can add a new phone number if your service gets interrupted.

I highly recommend getting pet insurance for your dog so that the cost of emergency care will not be as big an issue.

Finally, if you have a living trust or will (and you should), don't forget your dog! Make it clear who you want taking care of him in the event that something happens to you, and be sure to allocate some money to your dog's new family to cover his food and medical expenses.

SUMMER

Dogs are great summer companions. They love to go on hikes. Some dogs seem like they were born to spend the day at the beach, sprinting across sand dunes, digging holes, and jumping through the surf. While the beach may seem like a natural environment, there are a few summer risks to keep in mind.

HEAT RISK

Sweating, as annoying as it may be, is critical to cooling our bodies. Dogs don't have the ability to sweat like we do. While they have a couple of sweat glands in their feet—that's why a dog leaves wet footprints on a hot day—they can't use sweat alone to regulate their body temperatures.

Instead, they pant. When you see a hot dog with his tongue hanging out of his mouth, he's not just acting cute, he's trying to regulate his body temperature. Panting is an effective way to cool down, but it has limitations. When human body temperature rises, we sweat more. If a dog's body temperature rises faster than he can cool off, he goes into heatstroke.

If you're using any kind of muzzle on your dog in the summer (aside from a Halti or a Gentle Leader, which do not restrict the mouth's opening) make sure you don't leave it on for more than a few minutes at a time, taking it off for long periods to let your dog drink, pant, and cool himself. I recently saw a tragic event on the Venice boardwalk, on a warm spring day, when a dog with a Mickey Muzzle couldn't pant properly and suffered heatstroke. It wasn't a particularly hot day and the dog wasn't doing anything more rigorous than walking, but the physician who happened to be nearby was unable to revive the dog.

Even a mild case of heatstroke can kill a dog. It takes only twenty minutes for a dog to suffer organ failure and die.

The best way to deal with heatstroke is to prevent it:

- Make sure your dog isn't playing or working too hard on days that are very hot or humid.
- If you're out with your dog on a hot day, make sure that he's getting plenty of shade and cool water. (Water that has been standing in the heat won't help him cool down.)
- Never use a muzzle—especially a Mickey Muzzle—on a hot day, not even for five minutes, as your dog won't be able to pant.
- Never leave your dog in a car. Ten minutes in the car, even if the windows are rolled down, creates a greenhouse effect that can kill a dog. (There's a great resource at www.mydogiscool.com/x_car_study.php if you want to learn more.) When I have to leave my dog in the car, even for five minutes, I park it in the shade and leave it running (using another key to lock it) with the air-conditioning on. I check my Freon levels regularly to make sure that the car will stay cool.
- Never leave your dog in his crate on a hot day.
- Some breeds, especially those with thick coats or smushed noses—like pugs, boxers, and bulldogs—are more susceptible to heatstroke. Take special care with them.

Some of the symptoms to watch out for include:

- Constant panting or difficulty breathing
- Sluggishness or unusual clumsiness
- A faster-than-normal heart rate
- Pale gums
- Excessive thirst (or no thirst at all)
- More salivation than normal
- Discolored urine (dark yellow or even red)
- Collapse

You can also take your dog's temperature. It's usually between 101 and 102 degrees. If it reaches 106 degrees, he's in severe danger—107 will kill most dogs.

If you think your dog may be suffering heatstroke, try to cool him down by moving him to a cooler place or spraying/soaking him with cool water. You can also place cool rags on his belly or inner thigh. (Never use ice-cold water—it can dangerously stress your dog's internal organs.) Then get your dog to the vet as quickly as you can.

Some vets recommend using dog pads soaked in alcohol to cool a dog down, but many (including the brilliant Dr. Barbara Royal) consider this a dangerous practice. When a dog is overheating, his pores are open, making it easier for him to absorb the alcohol, which is poisonous to dogs, into his body—the last thing he needs when he's already fighting for his life!

RIDING IN CARS

There are more risks than just heatstroke when you take your dog on a car trip. It may seem cute to let a small dog ride on your lap, but you'll be interfering with your physical and mental ability to drive. In the event that you do get into an accident, the force of the crash will hurl your dog into the windshield. A passenger-side air bag, if deployed, can kill him.

I would strongly recommend against it, but if you must have your dog ride in the front seat with you (and don't have a passenger-side air bag), let him sit shotgun, using a specially designed seat-belt harness to buckle him in. You can find ones that most dogs don't mind wearing, and if he does, use treats to help him associate it with pleasure.

Even if your dog likes to ride in the backseat, you should encourage him to "sit" or "lie down" during the trip to prevent him from distracting you.

FLEAS AND TICKS

Fleas and ticks can be a year-round problem, but they're much more prevalent and active during the summer. Fleas don't actually live on your pets; they live in your rugs, your carpets, and your furniture, hopping onto your animals for mealtime. Once your dog has a flea problem, your house has a flea problem, so it's best to start with prevention and treat your house and your dog simultaneously.

Fleas are parasites, and parasites tend to go after the weakest creatures. When I was backpacking in Nepal, I was the only one in my group who didn't get devoured by fleas and lice. I was also the only one who took vitamin B complex religiously. I've had success giving vitamin B to dogs as a flea preventive—I buy the children's version in liquid form and add it directly to their meals.

Make sure your dog is getting plenty of exercise and eating right—a raw diet in particular can help boost a dog's immune system, making him less appealing to pests.

Proper bathing and grooming can help. You can use shampoos that have natural flea-repelling scents in them, like eucalyptus and cedar. I've found that Avon Skin So Soft, poured into a spray bottle and applied lightly, can also help. It's sold in many sporting goods stores, as outdoorsmen swear by it.

Another natural way to get rid of insects is diatomaceous earth, which you can find in many places, including pool supply stores. To us, it feels as soft as flour, but on a microscopic level, its particles are lined with sharp edges that will tear insects to death without resorting to pesticides. You can sprinkle it on your rugs, carpets, and floors in the areas where your dog likes to hang out.

Keep your home clean, and wash your dog's bed and favorite blankets frequently.

> ## GETTING YOUR DOG CLEAN, TOE TO HEAD
>
> Like just about everything else in this book, baths are much easier when you get your dog to associate them with pleasure instead of pain. One of the simplest ways to do that is to start with the tail instead of the head.
>
> Think about it from a dog's perspective: Would you rather have water sprayed in your face, or have someone start with your feet or hands? Wetting your dog in the face with water or a washcloth is a good way to make your dog hate the bath. Starting tail-first allows your dog to get used to the water and the sensation of being washed.

There are a lot of commercial products that are supposed to prevent fleas, but some dogs are allergic to them and suffer skin reactions—make sure you research them before you use them on your dog. Many of the most popular ones warn pregnant women not to touch them, as they can cause miscarriages. With a warning like that, I have a lot of trouble believing that they're somehow safe for dogs—even though you're applying them topically, they're designed to enter a dog's bloodstream, aren't they? I don't like the idea of putting pesticides on or in my dogs.

I prefer the natural route. There are many interesting holistic products. Adding garlic to a dog's diet is supposed to help; so are products that have a flea hormone that is supposed to stop baby fleas from maturing into adults. I also like to use brewer's yeast, which I buy in tablet form—many dogs think they're a treat!

As for ticks, they're also parasites, so your dog's good health is the best defense. A friend of mine who hikes often with her dog also swears by this natural remedy:

> 2 tablespoons vegetable or nut oil (almond oil has sulfur, which is a repellent in its own right)
> 10 to 25 drops rose geranium essential oil

Shake the two ingredients to blend them well, and apply a few drops to your dog's collar every time you're out.

SWIMMING

Many people assume that all dogs love to swim. But not all dogs are natural swimmers, not even "water" dogs like Labradors and golden retrievers, especially when they fall into the water by accident. I was once on a client's yacht when everyone started screaming that "Sam fell overboard!" Sam, a ten-month-old Lab mix puppy, was happily exploring the ship until he took an unplanned three-story leap into the ocean. Needless to say, the poor dog was terrified, and was very lucky that someone noticed him and had the courage to leap into the water to rescue him. Losing contact with solid ground for the first time can cause stress and panic, meaning that throwing any dog into the water is an absolute no-no—it's not only cruel, but will teach a dog to dislike swimming and distrust you. When you're introducing your dog to the water, you should do it in a gradual way.

If you have a swimming pool, make sure that the first

thing your dog learns is how to get in and out of it, whether by using the ladder or a doggy ramp, and that he can do it without too much difficulty. Even the best swimmers get exhausted—if your dog doesn't know how or otherwise isn't able to get out of the water when he's tired, he may drown. Play the "come" game, in and out of the water, as a way to condition your dog to always find the exit. There are also products that you can put in your pool that will trigger an alarm if someone (dog or child) falls in.

While it might sound weird, if you take your dog canoeing, rafting, or on any other kind of boat, or are spending a lot of time next to the water, strongly consider a life jacket specifically designed for dogs.

SUNBURN

Some dogs, especially light-colored and short-haired breeds, can actually get burns—and even skin cancer—from overexposure to the sun. Consider picking up a doggy sunscreen at your local pet store. And if you shave your dog for the summer, as some owners do, make sure you leave enough fur to keep his skin protected from direct exposure to the sun.

DOGGY CPR

You will hopefully never have to use it, but you'll be grateful to know it if you do. I highly recommend that every "parent" take a doggy CPR class or purchase a dog safety book and/or video from the American Red Cross (www .redcrossstore.org). It's a low-risk, high-return investment.

WINTER

Dogs love the snow, and many of them have been bred for it. But once again, this isn't true for all dogs. Greyhounds, dachshunds, and other lean, short-haired dogs are particularly susceptible to cold.

Many people have reservations about putting a sweater on their dogs. As strange as it may sound, however, *not* dressing up a cold dog can lead to bad behavior, including aggression.

Vicki, a client of mine, insisted that she'd never "dress up" Max, her miniature dachshund—she didn't want to be one of *those* people, "who treat their dog like an accessory." But even the relatively mild Los Angeles winter was enough to make little Max shiver. Any time Vicki saw that her dog was cold, she picked him up and carried him against her warm sweater or jacket. This quickly became a nuisance, as Max began jumping on her, expecting to be carried.

So we taught him to "ask" to be picked up by sitting instead of jumping, but soon noticed a new issue: When encountering new people, Max became aggressive. It was easy to see what was causing it: Whenever Vicki wanted to talk to someone, she put Max down. He began associating new people with the pain of losing that warmth and began barking aggressively, even nipping at anyone who came close.

I finally bought Max a sweater and told Vicki that he must wear it. We eventually undid all of the bad habits, but it took a while—it would have been much easier and less time-consuming to have helped him stay warm in the first place.

I use "dressing up" as a game in all of my puppy classes at The Loved Dog center. It's simple, fun, and gets the dogs used to being dressed by different people. I even did a "Dress for Success" competition at Nickelodeon's Fido Awards, where three "moms" had fifteen seconds to put as many clothes as they could on their dogs. The champion turned out to be a dachshund in a wheelchair, which allowed me to announce, "The weiner has won!" to a cheering audience. We played the game again on the *Today* show, where Al Roker chose as the winner a dog dressed in a bikini top.

In addition to clothing, make sure your dog's bed isn't damp or drafty.

Don't forget to wipe your dog's paws whenever you come in from a wintertime walk. Salt and other ice-melting agents can irritate and burn them. Also, keep an eye out for cracking in the skin on a dog's feet and red or gray skin, especially around your dog's ears, tail, and feet—it could be frostbite. Musher's wax or booties, available at most pet stores, can help protect your dog's paws.

ANTIFREEZE

A good thing for cars, a silent killer for dogs: For some strange reason, antifreeze has a smell and a sweet taste that many dogs find irresistible. Unfortunately, even a small amount can kill a dog. Make sure that any bottles of antifreeze are properly sealed and well stored, and quickly clean up any spills in your garage.

> Many states have passed or are considering legislation requiring antifreeze manufacturers to add a bittering agent to their product in order to make it less appealing to animals.

THE HOLIDAY SEASON

The winter holidays can present a few new risks for dogs. If your dog likes to try new "foods," keep him away from tinsel and ribbons. They can clog his intestines, potentially threatening his life.

Take care with Christmas lights, especially if your dog is a chewer. Once, while at the vet, Duke and I saw a dog who had eaten a string of glass lights: A border collie, already bored out of her mind after a series of rainy days limited her outdoor playtime, was driven nearly insane by the endless flickering of the Christmas lights. So she tried to eat them. Even the tech on duty gaped with horror when she saw the glass sticking out of the dog's bleeding mouth. They had to operate on the poor dog, who, luckily, survived.

Make sure you're using pet-proof extension cords that won't allow a dog to chew through them and electrocute himself, and discourage him from drinking water from the Christmas tree stand, which can upset his stomach. You can put a ScatMat around the tree that will give your dog a slight static shock if he gets too close. I know it's not the most "Loved Dog" thing in the world, but I believe it's way more humane to get a little static shock when getting too close to danger than potentially to die from electrocution or eating glass.

Finally, as appetizing as it may look to your dog, keep him away from the holiday turkeys. Turkey bones can kill a dog—make sure he's eating only boneless meat. And make sure you throw them away in a place where he won't be able to reach them. Many dogs know to stay away from the table, but hover around the trash can.

DAY 28

GOOD MEDICINE

During the process of writing this book, I noticed that my "son" Duke seemed low on energy. My first thought was that he'd overdone it while running and playing on the beach during a recent vacation together. When he seemed slow to recover, I thought it might be because we had a friend's dog staying with us—he and Duke played nonstop. But when our four-legged guest departed and Duke's energy didn't get better, a few days after Christmas I took him to the vet.

The doctor diagnosed him with anemia, but thought there might be something else going on. He referred us to another veterinarian, a top specialist in L.A. whom I trusted completely, as he'd helped my other "son," Clyde, through a tough situation ten years earlier. After a few nonconclusive tests, the new doctor suggested that we take a bone marrow sample.

With my "sons" Clyde and Duke and their friend Oscar

Duke has two deformed back legs, thanks to his previous owners, who used him as target practice for pit bulls fighting, and I had expected them to take the sample from his pelvis. Instead, they took a sample from one of his two good front legs, damaging a shoulder nerve in the process.

I got a casual call a couple of days later. The vet was departing for vacation, but wanted to first let me know that he thought Duke had leukemia, although the test hadn't conclusively said so, and that my dog had one or two weeks left to live. Happy holidays.

I was heartbroken. Duke's lethargy seemed to get worse and, despite a prescription for Tramadol, the pain from the botched bone marrow sample had him barely hobbling lifelessly around the house. His original vet recommended a blood transfusion, hoping to buy us more time to figure out what was really wrong with him and perhaps making Duke feel a little better. It helped some, but my baby was noticeably depressed and had difficulty breathing. I made plans to have the vet come over to put Duke down—why would I force him to live out the rest of his few remaining days in such depression and pain?

During this ordeal, I was given the name of a holistic veterinarian in Chicago, Dr. Barbara Royal (whose advice on diet is on Day 23). I was immediately struck by a difference in her approach—each of the other vets I'd contacted had asked for the other doctors' diagnoses. Dr. Barbara wanted to see his actual tests, not to mention Duke himself—we spent three hours on Skype that afternoon. In other words, before she latched on to some preconceived notion about Duke's condition based on what other doctors had determined, she wanted to examine the big picture for herself. I immediately related to her approach. In my line of work, I constantly encounter dogs who have been diagnosed as "aggressive" by trainers who haven't taken the time to study the complete picture.

Dr. Barbara immediately took Duke off Tramadol, a narcotic that, as it turned out, didn't agree with Duke and was sapping my sweet dog's will to live. She asked me to get him to stand up, helping to clear his lungs, and to take him out to the backyard to get his sense of smell going. She showed me how to massage him, and prescribed a diet and supplements that allowed him, within hours, to catch the ball a few times, run to greet guests, and even enjoy a little stroll on the beach. She called each and every day, even on weekends, to see how my dog was doing—and how I was doing. Words cannot describe my gratitude. My wish is that every dog owner is lucky enough to have someone like Dr. Barbara as her dog's veterinarian.

Ultimately, my sweet Dukie died, but he enjoyed a few more weeks of life. His human friends gathered at my home, late one night, and his vet came over and released him from his beautiful and suffering body. Even as I write it now, I can't stop the tears from rolling down. I so miss him!

I still don't know what caused his death, other than it not being leukemia, and can't help but feel like he might have had a better chance had his shoulder not been damaged or had antibiotics been prescribed earlier. I wish I had insisted that the bone marrow sample be taken from his pelvis and that I'd known earlier about the potential side effects of the Tramadol. I've learned that I need to question even more than I normally do and demand answers from my dogs' doctors, even those who aren't used to having to explain their decisions.

All I can do now is hope that some element of my experience helps you to someday help your dog. When it comes to your dog's health, you are his best advocate. That means doing your homework, asking lots of questions, not being afraid to challenge the answers when something feels wrong or incomplete, and getting second and third opinions. I can't recommend enough that you find a veterinarian who shares the same values about animal care that you do. You may not find everything in just one person—some doctors excel at diagnosing problems, have an exceptional manner with dogs, or are well versed in the latest holistic theories, but come up short in other areas. It's okay to use more than one veterinarian—after all, what you're looking for is the big picture—so make sure that everyone you are working with can function as a "team player."

Finally, the best time to find a veterinarian is *before* you really need his or her help. Start building those relationships today and you'll be asking yourself a lot fewer questions when a crisis actually arises.

THE FIRST TRIP TO THE VET

The first visit to the doctor can be terrifying to a dog. Here are a few tips to help ease his anxiety:

Take plenty of treats. Hand them out throughout the visit (saying "Take it" each time), especially as the doctor is examining your dog. You can also ask the doctor and any other strangers to give your dog treats as well, helping your dog to associate them with pleasure.

Let your dog explore. If it's okay with the other patients, allow your dog to sniff around the waiting room, getting comfortable with his surroundings.

Leave the examination room door open, even if it's only a crack, which helps the dog stay busy, focusing on what is going on in the office and waiting room. Closed doors make a lot of dogs anxious.

VACCINATIONS

Earlier I mentioned how important a healthy diet is in extending dogs' lives. The other important factor, of course, is medical progress. Today dogs have access to an incredible wealth of medical options, from specialized medicines to MRIs. It is important to have a veterinarian who knows how to take advantage of all of the tools that are out there. Most of them do. One of the first questions (and a potential source of disagreement) to work out with a new doctor is the issue of vaccines.

Research has shown that it's incredibly important to vaccinate any puppy. The schedule is generally broken up into a series of four shots, spaced out by three or four weeks. Spacing them out this way helps a dog's immune system accept all of the vaccinations. There are also a few herbal formulas on the market that are supposed to help boost their natural immunities.

Many veterinarians will recommend that your dog return every year for the "core" vaccine. The problem is that most dogs don't need to be vaccinated every year—many vaccinations will be effective for three years or even a lifetime!

Just as there is a growing discussion over the role of vaccines and how to space them out in human children, there is evidence that overvaccinating a dog can leave him more vulnerable to illness, allergies, anemia, arthritis, digestive disorders, even cancer. About ten years ago, my dog Clyde developed a case of hemophiliac anemia from being overvaccinated that almost killed him!

In fact, the evidence in the case of dogs is much less controversial—and much more convincing—than it is with humans. Several scientific studies in the 1990s demonstrated that cancerous tumors were more likely to form in the spots on an animal's skin where rabies and leukemia vaccines had been injected. The findings caused many veterinarians to rethink the "standard" ideas about vaccination, most of which had been provided by the manufacturers of the vaccines themselves. Further studies revealed that many vaccines, once given, keep a dog immune for much longer than a year. Plus, some dogs develop a natural immunity to certain diseases when they contract it in small doses and fight it off. Adding additional vaccines to an already immune dog leads to all kind of problems, including immune- and nervous-system disorders.

So what should you do? Luckily, there's a great solution. After the initial vaccinations, switch to the titer test, an annual blood test that checks a dog's immune defenses. Your dog's blood is chemically tested to see how immune the dog is to individual viral diseases. If the dog's immune response to a particular disease is low, you can get the vaccine again. But if it's adequate, no vaccine is necessary. These tests, which have been developed after many years of intense scientific research, are gaining more and more popular acceptance among veterinarians and cities that require mandatory vaccinations for dog licenses. If you're rescuing a dog, start with the titer test instead of subjecting him to a full slate of vaccinations that might not be necessary.

DON'T FORGET THE TEETH!

A dog's jaw is designed to pull raw meat off of bones. For a dog in the wild, that constant gnawing naturally helps to keep their teeth and gums clean.

But many of today's dogs live on commercial food. Despite the claims by some manufacturers that their products will clean a dog's teeth, many foods—especially kibble—will create buildup and plaque the same way they would in a human. If you don't want your dog to suffer from cavities, gum disease (which, in a dog, can actually lead to an infection that can spread through his bloodstream, damaging internal organs), or any of the other problems that keep dentists busy, you're going to have to brush his teeth.

Many dogs won't take to it naturally, especially if you try to jam a toothbrush into his mouth. You can start by rubbing your finger over his gums and teeth, making sure to wet your finger first so it won't stick. Make it short and fun, offering lots of praise and treats when you're done.

Once he's used to your finger, you can try using doggy toothpaste—it make take a few tries before you find one with a flavor your dog will tolerate. You can also buy specially designed toothbrushes at most pet stores. (The best ones, in my opinion, slide over your finger like a sleeve.) There is also some evidence that the coenzyme Q10, an antioxidant, helps with gingivitis and other oral problems.

You can also, instead of brushing, take your dog for regular cleaning sessions with a doggy oral hygienist—look for one who doesn't require your dog to be placed under anesthesia.

If you notice a change in your dog's eating, chewing, or playing habits, excessive sneezing, nasal discharge, or crankiness, they may be signs of tooth troubles. Your vet may recommend a doggy dentist. Not that it happens often, but dogs are occasionally prescribed everything from braces to root canals.

HOLISTIC CARE

In this book, I've tried to give you a more holistic way of understanding your dog's behavior. I believe that the same approach is important when examining your dog's health.

Take hot spots, for example. They are painful, itchy skin lesions caused by excessive biting, licking, or scratching. Your dog will usually try to alleviate them through more biting, licking, and scratching, which only makes the hot spot worse.

There are creams that will help with the itching or pain, but the only real, long-term way to get rid of a hot spot is to break the cycle of biting, itching, and scratching. That means figuring out what is causing your dog to create the hot spot in the first place.

The cause could be an insect bite or a food allergy, so you'll have to examine his environment and diet. Upgrading to higher-quality food, eliminating some of the usual suspects like corn, wheat, soy, meat by-products, and artificial flavors, can often solve the problem. There are also nutritional supplements that can help with the healing process.

Many times, however, a dog will bite, lick, and scratch his way into a hot spot out of boredom or stress; in other words, because his seven basic needs aren't being met. It's always a good idea to look at the big picture.

When something does go wrong with your dog, make sure that you examine all of the psychological and environmental issues in his life. Are his needs being met? Is he eating a balanced and healthy diet? Has he been exposed to any potential allergens? Are there toxins in your home that could be causing the problem? In your yard?

The same thinking applies to treatment. There are more options than there have ever been before. Vitamins and herbs can be used to treat everything from pain to digestive problems. Massage, as I talked about on Day 26, can do wonders for a dog. Some cutting-edge veterinarians use acupuncture to address everything from allergies to kidney disease, or "cold laser" light therapy to help dogs cope with pain and inflammation.

The important thing is to keep doing your research and asking questions. Be open to both old and new ideas, but don't be afraid to challenge them either.

WEEK 4 REVIEW

By now you've seen that The Loved Dog method isn't just a bunch of techniques you'll use during coaching sessions—the principles apply to virtually every aspect of your dog's life.

Children aren't raised solely in the classroom or through "parenting sessions." Much if not most of their upbringing depends on the hundreds of tiny actions, interactions, and decisions their parents and caretakers perform every day. The same goes for your dog, whether it's the way you speak to her, the things you pay attention to (and those you ignore), how you interact on a walk or at the park, or the actions you take to help keep her healthy and safe. Being a loving owner isn't just about getting your dog to behave the way you want her to, but being committed to helping the dog be all that she can be, patiently coaching her from acting instinctively to making humanlike conscious choices. You'll discover, in return, that you will become a happier person while developing an amazing, enduring, and profound relationship that will fill both of your lives with love and joy.

WEEK 4½

If you want to change the world, you must change the metaphors.

—*Joseph Campbell*

ALL YOU NEED IS LOVE

A friend of mine told me a story that took place at a school for animal trainers. A seal, whose trainer was a novice, was having trouble learning new behaviors. The trainer really wanted to show off his skills, but while he used positive reinforcement, he wasn't always clear in his requests and was pushing through the seal's lessons way too quickly.

The seal became more and more frustrated with the training. *I can't get it right,* he seemed to be thinking, *so why bother? It's not like I'm going to get any treats.* He began to associate the training sessions with pain, eventually refusing to try any new behaviors or even repeat the ones he already knew.

The seal was eventually teamed with a new, more experienced trainer. The first thing she did was give him treats, without asking him to do a thing in return. Some of the other trainers grumbled, "She's rewarding him for bad behavior. He's never going to start working now."

But the treats had an entirely different effect on the seal—he perked up and started paying attention again. The treats made him feel good, so the seal quickly became intrigued by this person who seemed to want to give him unconditional love and wanted to hear what he had to "say." His interest in learning reappeared and, this time, he felt safe enough to experience hope. That hope eventually led to success.

It's easy to see how that story, even though it's about a seal, can apply to dogs. I want you to take it one step further: So much of what we've been saying about dogs can also be applied to people.

Dogs aren't the only creatures governed by instincts—people do things out of instinct all the time. We tend to do our best when we are feeling resourceful and loved, and usually don't do so well when we are hungry, understimulated, stressed, or afraid of messing up. Each day, we choose not to act on instinct alone and instead make conscious choices. At times, I have to remind myself that what I want to say comes from the part of my brain that is instinctual and I must consciously choose to alter my response to better fit the situation. We all do.

We may want the people in our lives to behave in a certain way, according to our set of rules. Sometimes you can scare people into doing what you want them to do, guiding their behavior through intimidation and harsh corrections. But if you want something that lasts—a shared connection that will have your boyfriend, your wife, your kids, your friends responding to you because they are your raving fans—then you could do worse than try some of the principles in this book.

Help the loved ones in your life to fill their basic needs. Try, wherever possible, to associate change and growth with pleasure instead of pain. Accept them for who they are—their instinctive selves—but give them the knowledge they need and the opportunity to make better choices.

Most of all, they all need to know that they can feel safe with us, that we love them even when they are not abiding by our rules. That we're not going to set the bar so high, and be so stingy with our praise and rewards, that they're going to give up on us, on themselves, or on the relationship.

Whether it's your dog, your family, or your friends, "shower the people you love with love, show them the way that you feel."

FOR THE LADIES:
ELEVEN REASONS MEN ARE LIKE DOGS

A producer for Telemundo asked me to do a segment for them on how men are like dogs. "Great!" I said. "But you might be surprised by my take on the topic." I would never compare a "bad boy" or a "playa" to a dog. That would be insulting to dogs! Fortunately, the producer was in a great relationship with her boyfriend and was excited to hear a different spin.

1. Both men and dogs are hunters who love to provide for and protect the pack. It's in their programming.

2. Both need clear instructions when it comes to understanding us. But they don't want us always hovering over them, giving advice: They need time and space to figure it out on their own.

3. Both need to be loved, touched, and appreciated. They love the feeling that comes from impressing us and will do almost anything to get it.

4. More than anything else, they want to please us.

5. Both are relatively uncomplicated, with very basic needs.

6. Neither dogs nor men like being criticized. When they are, they'll often shut down and won't "come" when you call them.

7. Both are single focused—you can't hunt and talk on the phone at the same time. They do one thing at a time.

8. They both love to be on your bed.

9. Both love to play competitive sports with their friends.

10. They seem more courageous when they're in a pack.

11. Give them the chance, and they'll surprise you and steal your heart.

DAY 30

Congratulations . . . You've made it!

Well, almost, anyway. Before we wrap up this course, I'm going to ask you take a final exam. Don't worry—it's short, you won't be graded, and there aren't any right or wrong answers.

1. What do you feel have been your three biggest accomplishments with your dog over the last thirty days?
2. What are three things that you could be doing better?
3. What has been the biggest surprise? The biggest disappointment?
4. What are the three qualities you love most about your dog?
5. Name one new thing about your dog that you have noticed or discovered in the last week.

While this brings an end to the thirty days, I hope that it's just the beginning of an amazing relationship for you and your dog, where he is your willing partner. Success isn't a result, it's a process. Try to notice something new about your dog every week and don't hold back in sharing your love, and your relationship will continue to grow.

CELEBRATE!

You already know how to "make a party" for your dog. Today, we're going to Make a Party!

Bake your dog a cake. Give him a gift Baggie. You can even invite a few of his friends over to play musical chairs or tic-tac-toe.

MUSICAL CHAIRS

Play it with your friends (and their dogs) the same way you normally would—one chair less than the number of players, walking in a circle until the music stops, when each of the humans in the game has to find a chair. The twist is that the players aren't allowed to look for an open chair until their dogs are seated. No chair hovering allowed!

The next level of the game requires the dogs to sit *and* stay. Draw a line a few feet from each chair, where the dogs have to wait patiently for their owners to find an open chair. If any dog gets up or crosses the line, the owner has to go back to coaching him on how to "sit" and "stay."

TIC-TAC-TOE

Play this one outside, in a wide-open space. Use chalk or electrical tape to create a large (ten feet by ten feet) tic-tac-toe board. Instead of Xs and Os, use dogs wearing blue and red bandannas. Every time a dog is "placed" in one of the squares, he has to "stay." If he gets up before the game is over, the space becomes available. First team to get three in a row wins! You can start by rewarding the dogs who stay with treats, but once the second round begins, it's game on: The dogs have to remain in their designated squares with no rewards. (Verbal praise is always allowed!)

DRESS FOR SUCCESS

This game's the most fun when you've got at least two dogs and two people to dress each dog. Put together a big basket full of fun clothes, including bikinis, silly hats, T-shirts, boys' shorts, or anything else you can find in your closet. Make a separate pile of just socks. The winning team is the one that can put the most clothes on its dog—including at least three socks—in thirty seconds. Have fun!

CONCLUDING THOUGHTS

I know it may sound a little ambitious, but I really hope this book has changed the way you think about dogs. I want you to join me when I say that the days of dog training are over—now it's about dog coaching. As with children, it's no longer about being obedient, but about good manners. No more submission, but empowerment!

It's a new era in the dog world. It's taken a while to get here, but it also took women a long time to get the right to vote. Now that we're here, it's our job as loving owners/parents/coaches to build our moral muscle and to focus on knowledge, wisdom, and progressive thinking when it comes to the way we live and interact with our dogs. Together we can throw out the macho, ignorant ideas based on fear and dominance, replacing them with the idea of dogs and people working together as a team, in harmony, respecting our differences while helping each other to grow.

Our beliefs are a reflection of who we are. Some may believe that dogs are here to be subservient and to serve us. I choose to believe that our connection with dogs allows us to tap into something much more profound.

I believe that we were put on this Earth for bigger reasons than to merely control and use nature. I believe that we are alive in order to grow, not only as people, but also as souls, learning patience, kindness, gratitude, and to be in awe of all that we cannot understand.

It's an unbelievable opportunity to build a bridge to another species, where the bridge goes both ways.

There is no easier way to connect with nature than through dogs. Sharing our lives with them is an opportunity to learn humility, how to listen to and understand those who are different from us. It's a daily invitation to be kind and to realize that maybe, just maybe, whoever created dogs knew what He was doing.

Dogs see us in a way that we often cannot see ourselves. They love us in the way that we wish we could love ourselves—steadfast, with unwavering consistency. At times they are more in tune than we are with the deepest parts of our souls, the parts that we so yearn to be in touch with. It is a miraculous love that, in my mind, is God's gift to us (whatever you perceive God to be). The disregard toward or domination of a dog is a vexation to the human spirit and to nature.

Let's look at dogs with new eyes and take the steps toward

loving ourselves by treating our dogs as the gift that they are. Together we can coach our dogs to rise above making decisions based solely on instinct to make decisions based on conscious choice. We can practice the same idea with ourselves every day, strengthening gratitude muscles, thanking God for dogs, and taking the time to notice all the little things that make life so juicy and beautiful. What a world that would be!

But we have to back our ideals with action. Shower your dog with love, shower the people in your life with love, and don't forget to love yourself. Happiness comes from progress, not perfection!

Smiles,
Tamar

APPENDIX A
PUPPY FACTORIES (PUPPY MILLS)

It's an image so strange and horrifying it's hard to believe that it could be real: Justin Scally, wearing a gas mask to allow him to breathe through the horrific stench of urine, running out of a building with as many miniature poodles as he can carry. Outside, volunteers check on and comfort the poor dogs before transporting them to an animal shelter, where a medical staff and many dog lovers are waiting for them. For Justin, these kinds of scenes are routine—just another successful raid on a "puppy factory," saving several hundred more dogs from unbelievable abuse.

As an Israeli whose family members were murdered in the Holocaust, I grew up hearing about the horrors that American soldiers encountered when they liberated Jews from the camps in Poland and Germany. Unfortunately, a version of these camps still exists today, in America of all places, not for people, but dogs. It's very frequent that Justin, who works for The Humane Society of the United States (HSUS), goes into one of these horrible places to free the captives inside.

There are hundreds, sometimes thousands, of dogs in each of these puppy factories. The wire cages are stacked on top of each other, often five high, ensuring that any dog who isn't on the top row will get peed and pooped on for years. There's no professional veterinary care. Many of the dogs have missing teeth, tongues that hang from the sides of their mouths, untreated infections, and broken limbs. They're kept from barking by painful muzzles that limit their movement, or by amateur surgeons (often the breeders themselves) who snip their vocal chords without anesthesia. These dogs live lives devoid of love, affection, and healthy socialization. It's not uncommon for them to remain in these cages for ten years or more.

The dogs have only one purpose: to breed. They are kept in a near-constant state of pregnancy, producing litter after litter of pups, usually delivered by C-section, often without anesthesia. The "products" of these factories are sold to pet stores for an average of $200 to $300 per pup. The pet stores sell them to an unsuspecting public for thousands of dollars more. It's a very lucrative business.

Pennsylvania, home to many of these puppy factories, recently passed a state law prohibiting breeders who aren't veterinarians from snipping vocal chords and surgically removing litters from birthing mothers. In many more places, however, these practices continue. The USDA, who is supposed to oversee the puppy industry—yes, puppies are considered agriculture—don't have enough inspectors to monitor every facility. These poor creatures rely on the HSUS and Justin Scally's long list of dogs to be rescued.

No one likes to see sad videos, but I recommend that everyone watch just one of these raids to get a real sense of what is going on in the puppy factories. It's tough to watch, but also heartwarming to see dozens of volunteers carrying frightened dogs out of their cages and into the arms of loving people, promising them that, from this day on, they will be loved and cared for. That they can relax. That people are good and can be trusted.

I admire Justin Scally for saving these animals. He doesn't sleep much anymore, plagued by nightmares created by what he's seen. He spends his time speaking up on behalf of these poor animals, testifying on cruelty cases as well as teaching law enforcement and animal care professionals all over the country. But his work is not enough. These practices will never stop until people stop buying what these factories are selling: the cute puppies that play so sweetly and innocently in the windows of pet stores around the country, unable to speak about the conditions and abuse their parents have had to endure.

The first step is to never, under any circumstances, buy a dog from a pet store that isn't selling rescued dogs, as some now do. The stores that don't are just a pretty front to an abomination. I can't believe society can accept it. It's barbaric, and we need to talk about it, to shout about it from the mountaintops.

You also need to take great care when dealing with "breeders," especially those who sell animals over the Internet. There are a few good breeders out there, people who spend a lot of time and money raising the puppies like family. Both mothers and puppies receive tons of love and attention, proper diet and nutrition, pregnancy care, and ongoing veterinary care. The mothers aren't kept in cages or bred every time they're in heat. Both parents and pups are properly socialized to people, sounds, and touch. But these kinds of breeders are often the exception, not the rule.

If you must get a puppy from a breeder (instead of rescuing an amazing orphan dog from the shelter), it's important that you get to see the pups *with* their mother. If someone tells you that the mother will act aggressively toward anyone who looks at her pups, that mother hasn't been raised by a good breeder, one who has taught his dogs to trust that humans are safe. Don't put a lot of stock in a puppy whose parents were "champions"—all that means is that they won a beauty contest. Who cares about beauty if the dog was neglected or abused (like Cheri, whom I told you about on Day 18)? Isn't it more important to have a healthy and smart dog than a pretty one?

One of my clients bought a Newfoundland puppy girl from a "breeder" in Northern California. In the puppy's first six months, she had to go through thirteen (!) surgeries just so she could walk. She's suffering from a genetic condition that will keep her forever handicapped. The "breeder" couldn't care less—she'll keep breeding that puppy's parents, raking in the profits.

Or another client who paid a lot of money for their Cavalier King Charles spaniel only to have a huge list of health issues including deafness. After some research they found out that they're not alone and other dogs from that breeder suffer from the same issues.

I'll leave you with some good news if you are looking for a particular breed: almost every breed has its own rescue club. With a little patience and flexibility, just like when you're looking for a human partner, you may find your perfect doggy mate.

You can follow "Stop Puppy Mills" on Facebook. There's also plenty more information and videos at the Humane Society, http://www.humanesociety.org/issues/puppy_mills/qa/puppy_mill_FAQs.html, or through the Best Friends' "Puppies Aren't Products" campaign: http://network.bestfriends.org/campaigns/puppymills.

ONE FINAL CASE FOR SHELTERED ANIMALS

Whether you're choosing a new dog or adding a second or a third, I hope that you will strongly consider adopting one from a shelter (or, as I like to call them, animal centers). I want to leave you with this letter from a shelter manager that, even for me, was a huge eye-opener.

A Letter from a Shelter Manager

I think our society needs a huge wake-up call. As a shelter manager, I am going to share a little insight with you all . . . a view from the inside, if you will.

First off, all of you breeders/sellers should be made to work in the "back" of an animal shelter for just one day.

Maybe if you saw the life drain from a few sad, lost, confused eyes, you would change your mind about breeding and selling to people you don't even know. That puppy you just sold will most likely end up in my shelter when it's not a cute little puppy anymore.

So how would you feel if you knew there's about a 90 percent chance that that dog will never walk out of the shelter it is going to be dumped at? Purebred or not! About 50 percent of all of the dogs that are "owner surrenders" or "strays" that come into my shelter are purebred dogs.

The most common excuses I hear are:

"We are moving and we can't take our dog (or cat)." Really? Where are you moving to that doesn't allow pets and why did you choose that place instead of a pet-friendly home?

Or they say, *"The dog got bigger than we thought it would."* How big did you think a German shepherd would get?

"We don't have time for her." Really? I work a ten- to twelve-hour day and still have time for my six dogs!

"She's tearing up our yard." How about making her a part of your family?

They always tell me: *"We just don't want to have to stress about finding a place for her,"* *"We know he'll get adopted,"* or *"She's a good dog."*

Odds are that your pet won't get adopted. Do you know how stressful it is to be in a shelter? Well, let me tell you, your pet has seventy-two hours to find a new family from the moment you drop it off. Sometimes a little longer if the shelter isn't full and your dog manages to stay completely healthy. If it sniffles, it dies.

Your pet will be confined to a small run/kennel in a room with about twenty-five other barking or crying animals. It will have to relieve itself where it eats and sleeps.

It will be depressed and it will cry constantly for the family that abandoned it.

If your pet is lucky, I will have enough volunteers on that day to take him/her for a walk. If I don't, your pet won't get any attention besides having a bowl of food slid under the kennel door and the waste sprayed out of its pen with a high-powered hose.

If your dog is big, black, or any of the "bully" breeds (pit bull, rottweiler, mastiff, etc.), it was pretty much dead when you walked it through the front door. Those dogs just don't get adopted.

It doesn't matter how "sweet" or "well-behaved" they are. If your dog doesn't get adopted within its seventy-two hours and the shelter is full, it will be destroyed.

If the shelter isn't full, and your dog is good enough and of a desirable breed, it may get a stay of execution. But not for long.

Most dogs get very kennel protective after about a week and are destroyed for showing aggression. Even the sweetest dogs will turn in this environment.

If your pet makes it over all of those hurdles, chances are it will get kennel cough or an upper respiratory infection and will be destroyed, because shelters just don't have the funds to pay for even a $100 treatment.

Here's a little Euthanasia 101 for those of you who have never witnessed a perfectly healthy, scared animal being "put down":

First, your pet will be taken from its kennel on a leash. They always look like they think they are going for a walk—happy, wagging their tails.

Until they get to "the Room." Every one of them freaks out and puts on the brakes when we get to the door. It must smell like death, or they can feel the sad souls left in there. It's strange, but it happens with every one of them.

Your dog or cat will be restrained, held down by one or two vet techs depending on the size and how freaked out they are.

Then a euthanasia tech or a vet will start the process. They will find a vein in the front leg and inject a lethal dose of the "pink stuff."

Hopefully, your pet doesn't panic from being restrained and jerk. I've seen the needles tear out of a leg and been covered with the resulting blood and been deafened by the yelps and screams.

They all don't just "go to sleep"—sometimes they spasm for a while, gasp for air, and defecate on themselves.

When it all ends, your pet's corpse will be stacked like firewood in a large freezer in the back with all of the other animals that were killed, waiting to be picked up like garbage.

What happens next? Cremated? Taken to the dump? Rendered into pet food? You'll never know and it probably won't even cross your mind. It was just an animal and you can always buy another one, right?

I hope that those of you who have read this are bawling your eyes out and can't get the pictures out of your head that I deal with every day on the way home from work.

I hate my job, I hate that it exists, and I hate that it will always be there unless you people make some changes and realize that the lives you are affecting go much further than the pets you dump at a shelter.

Between four and five MILLION animals die every year in shelters and only you can stop it. I do my best to save every life I can but rescues are always full, and there are more animals coming in every day than there are homes.

My point to all of this: DON'T BREED OR BUY WHILE SHELTER PETS DIE!

Hate me if you want to. The truth hurts and reality is what it is.

I just hope I maybe changed one person's mind about breeding their dog, taking their loving pet to a shelter, or buying a dog.

I hope that someone will walk into my shelter and say, "I saw this and it made me want to adopt." THAT WOULD MAKE IT WORTH IT!

Please don't breed or buy while shelter animals DIE. Please spay/neuter to SAVE LIVES and ADOPT from a rescue or animal shelter.

THANK YOU!

INDEX

empowerment, and coaching, 3, 7, 207, 217, 375

endorphins, and barking, 184

environment, 236–37, 238, 239

euthanasia, process of, 388–89

exaggeration, 67–68

excitement and surprises, 24–25, 76, 79, 201

expectations, 7, 253–54

facial expressions, 68, 108, 109, 176

favorite activities of dogs, *218,* 219–20

fear:
  and aggression, 39, 103, 105, 206
  and barking, 185
  and emotional complexity of dogs, 126
  and growling, 189, 190
  and housebreaking, 62
  list of dog's fears, 221
  and security, 20–21
  and shelter dogs, 39
  and socialization, 104, 105, 106, 151, 152, 154, 157, 158, 160, 162, 237, 243
  and tone of voice, 70
  and training methods, 17, 21, 29, 70, 103, 157, 167, 206, 207, 240, 375–76
  and TTouch, 335
  and "wait," 295

feeding:
  foods to avoid, 78, 303–4, 340
  and health, 299–300
  and housebreaking, 61, 233
  preparations for dog's arrival, 48
  as reward, 287
  and social hierarchy, 23

and socialization, 156–60
  see also diet

fetch, 209–12, 215, 271

final exam, 371

Fisher, Derek, 207

fleas, 344–47

flyball, 324–27

front door, and "sit," 82

games:
  agility training, 327–29
  catch, 212–13, 215, 326
  and "come," 96, 97
  dress for success, 350, 373
  fetch, 209–12, 215, 271
  flyball, 324–27
  and mental stimulation, 26
  musical chairs, 372
  nosework, 329–30
  power of play, 84–85, 86, 170
  sneezing, 270–72
  soccer, 269–70
  and social hierarchy, 24
  and "stay," 172–74
  tic-tac-toe, 373
  toys for, 92
  treasure hunt, 90
  and trust, 119, 121, 124, 227
  tug-of-war, 118–25, 209, 211, 215

Gandhi, Mohandas, 72, 207, 321

"gentle," 94, 95

"go back," 289–90, *289, 290*

"Good dog!," as generic, 58, 60–61, 69, 162, 220

grapes, 78, 304

gratitude, 250–51, 377

growling, 188–89, 190

hand signals:
  and body language, 68, 115
  "no more," *96*